Special Commemorative Edition
50th Anniversary of the Anacostia Community Museum 1967-2017

THE MAN
THE MOVEMENT
THE MUSEUM

*The Journey of John R. Kinard
as the First African American Director
of a Smithsonian Institution Museum*

JOY G. KINARD, Ph.D.

A. P. Foundation Press | Washington and London

© 2017
A.P. Foundation Press
Washington and London

Copy Editor: Dorothy Colding
Production Editor: Jenelle Walthour
Creative Direction and Graphic Design: Angela Dyson

Library of Congress Cataloging-in Publication Data

Kinard, Joy G.

The Man, The Movement, The Museum: The Journey of John R. Kinard as the First African American Director of a Smithsonian Institution Museum

p. cm.

Includes bibliographical references.

ISBN: 978-1-892236-03-6

British Library Cataloguing-in Publication Data is available

Manufactured in the United States of America

01 00 99 98 97 96 95 94 5 4 3 2 1

The paper used in this publication meets the minimum requirements of the American National Standard for Permanence of Paper for Printed Library Materials.

Contents

Dedication

This book is dedicated to my mother Marjorie Anne Williams Kinard. Thank you for supporting John R. Kinard's destiny of leadership in addition to your children's dreams by giving up your own.

Acknowledgments

I would like to acknowledge the following people, institutions, and organizations for their support of this research: The Anacostia Community Museum, Archives, Library and staff. The Amistad Research Center Archives, Andrew Salinas, staff archivist, and to those of you who graciously shared your stories through oral history, I appreciated your transparency and time. Thank you to Gail Lowe and Zora Martin-Felton for creating the book, *A Different Drummer: John Kinard and the Anacostia Museum 1967–1989*. I can't tell you how many times I have read it along with my sisters. It continues to be a source of inspiration and pride to the Kinard Family. To Dr. Elizabeth Clark-Lewis, my dissertation advisor, you have been a source of support, understanding, and inspiration throughout this process. Thank you for dedicating your career to ensure that this dream comes to fruition. You assist students in fulfilling the legacy of Dr. Carter G. Woodson through Howard University's History Department. I also thank you for your intellectual contribution, *Living In, Living Out: African American Domestics in Washington, DC 1910–1940*, which also helped inspire this work. I want to thank Caryl Marsh, Leonard Jeffries, Dr. Frasier, staff of the Moorland Spingarn Research Center, Charles Sumner School DCPS Archives, Smithsonian Institution Archives, Harry Robinson, Bob Stanton, Vernon Shannon, John Wesley Church family, members of the Anacostia Historical Society, the Livingstone College Alumni Association, Omega Psi Phi Fraternity, Inc., and Delta Sigma Theta Sorority, Inc. I want to thank members of my National Park Service family: Patty Trap, Cam Sholly, Gayle Hazelwood, Alex Romero, Robert Parker, George McDonald, Fred Cunningham, Major Horsey, my God parents, Barbara and Clennie Murphy, my Aunt Dorothy Colding, Aunt Alberta Kinard, Aunt Virginia Garcia, Uncle Richard Williams, and Cousin/Lawyer D. Michael Lyles.

To Sarah Kinard, Hope, Christopher, Kameron, Kareem, Courtney, and Caitlyn Wilson much appreciation is shown. And last, but not least, I would like to express my heartfelt gratitude for the support, love, guidance and encouragement of my mother Marjorie Kinard.

Foreword

The Lasting Presence of John Robert Edward Kinard
Elizabeth Clark-Lewis

At an early age, John Kinard worked hard to become a valued son and positive role model for all of his family members. He was a community and youth leader in the schools he attended in Washington, DC. As a student he was always willing to foster new ideas for himself and other students. This was a young man who willingly worked to reshape new educational contours in the public schools of the nation's capital.

As a college student he helped to formulate local and regional civil rights protests. The protests he led helped to end segregation in several North Carolina cities. Standing firm against racial discrimination and malice were distinguishing features of John Kinard while he was an undergraduate and graduate student member of the academy.

In African communities the work of John Kinard included constructing homes and encouraging links between Africans and African Americans. His projects involved extensive teamwork and grueling physical labor; however, each project created new resources that improved the lives of people living in rural areas of East Africa. The process of forging group-oriented solutions, which always incorporated new cultural paths, would remain a distinguishing feature of his life.

As a minister, John Kinard instituted Christ-led service projects that encouraged the daily life of worshipers. Compassion and care for the less fortunate rather than concern for established rules led to him having a spiritual life shaped by empathy for others. In out-of-control situations he was called to build unity by donning the garments of gentleness, humility and patience.

John Kinard built a community-based museum with an astonishing conviction. The institution would be far more than a building where objects of historical, artistic, or scientific interest were exhibited, preserved, and studied. The museum he created was intentionally located in an African American community with the goal of saturating the minds of visitors in new ways. Every visitor from every age group left that museum with a new understanding of the ways the world's landscape was shaped by people from Africa. This museum would focus on how the African Diaspora's myriad contributions and luminous cultural legacy, passed down from generation to generation, reframed the world.

This is how I knew John Kinard. He was an exemplar as a museum leader with exceptional skills and an energy level that was unrivaled by other museum directors. The Anacostia Museum and its innovative curatorial platform were recognized all over the United States – and at many international conferences – for their compelling ingenuity and educational initiatives. John Kinard for me, while I was a graduate student, Smithsonian post-doctoral fellow and Humanities Council grant recipient, was an educated, knowledgeable, and expert museum specialist who was most of all always approachable.

I admired him as a husband who showed love, compassion, kindness and an enthusiastic interest in every segment of the life and wide-ranging activities of his wife, Marjorie Willliams Kinard. I saw him proudly encourage his three daughters to have concern for others, exemplary personal principles and an unwavering set of community-service values. I was in awe of his ability to stress how, with faith in God, activists could rise above any adversary while always engendering community accountability.

This book is an exuberant testimony to a man who led an exhilarating life. He was, first and foremost, a devoted family man; a minister with a tireless drive to create an institution to equip and encourage his community; and a person who reminded everyone who knew him of the infinite power of faith. Nearly three decades after his death, his family life, community activism, and institutional leadership encourage Public Historians to always have a genuine sense of mission, an eager desire to serve others, and a sincere motivation to transform the world in which we live.

Why do we need real history? Why do we cherish culture?

In one section of the book, *The Long Walk To Freedom*, Nelson Mandela describes a crucial fact he learned as a young man. Early in his life as an activist, he, like John Kinard, learned how a shared history and culture can stir,

"Something
deep
inside all of us.
Something
strong
and
intimate
that binds us
to one another.
And...
links us all
together."

—Elizabeth Clark-Lewis

Preface

The Voice of the Anacostia Community Museum

A half century has come motioning the Anacostia Community Museum, formally known as the Anacostia Neighborhood Museum, into the pantheon of greatness. This museum has thrusted itself into a position of being; the beacon, the benchmark, and an enduring example of how to celebrate the global contributions of African Americans, the struggles and triumphs of our great leaders, the impacts of the African Slave trade on all continents, and the rights won through the Civil Rights Movements. The "voice" of this museum has been like a mirror to America, sharing the good and bad that will never die because the voice and its origins are eternal. The museum has told many stories that had never been articulated with intent, authenticity, and sincerity on a national scale for 50 years. On September 15, 1967 in Washington, DC, the founding director and trailblazing civil rights leader John R. Kinard made history when he opened the Anacostia Neighborhood Museum, becoming then, the first African American appointed to direct a museum under the management of the Smithsonian Institution; thus, paving the way for many other minorities to become leaders in one of the most prestigious cultural organizations in the world. The decision to create this museum came with the observation that many people visiting the Smithsonian Institution were non-native Washingtonians. The creators of the Anacostia Neighborhood Museum concluded, "If the people don't go to the Smithsonian, then the Smithsonian must be brought to the people." It was with this view, that Kinard took an abandoned theater, restored it, and established a museum of the Smithsonian Institution under the support of the Secretary of the Smithsonian Institution, Dr. S. Dillon Ripley. With Ripley's support and Kinard's vision, the Smithsonian fulfilled the dream of Carter G. Woodson, W.E.B. DuBois, Booker T. Washington, Anna Julia Cooper, Mary McLeod Bethune, Mary Church Terrell, and others who fought for a place to tell our history among all the other great American heroes whose stories the Smithsonian Institution told since its creation. Through its innovative and fresh approach, this museum inspired its broad constituency to embrace positive images by showcasing local African American visual and performing artists during the Black Studies and Black Arts Movements of the 1960's and 1970's.

Considered the epicenter of African American history and culture in the "Chocolate City," the museum supported grassroots activism and collaborated with national and local institutions such as Howard University, DC Public Schools, the NAACP, and the Drum and Spear Bookstore owned and operated by the Student Nonviolent Coordinating Committee. The museum taught and exposed the public to lesser known bold and new cultural practices and traditions of the time, such as the celebration of Kwanzaa, Black History Week and Month that encouraged many African Americans during this period to ask the questions: "Who am I?" and "Do African Americans really have a place in the American legacy?" The exhibits developed at this institution served as a mechanism to reach and teach. Under formidable circumstances, with finite resources and organizational constraints, John R. Kinard and his staff aimed high in creating an identity for this space within the Smithsonian Institution, making it honored, respected, and an exceptional example of what an African American museum could offer to the public as a vehicle to enlighten.

Introduction
JOY KINARD

Jack and the Beanstalk is a fable about a young boy who hesitated to listen to his mother, and traded a cow for some magic beans instead of selling the cow as his mother asked. After telling his mother what he did with the cow and showing her the beans he bought, she threw the beans out of the window in anger. From the seeds, this huge beanstalk grew from the ground to the heavens and led to the castle where a giant lived. Jack, eager to climb this stalk, proceeded to steal from the giant three times before the giant caught him to reclaim his possessions.

Throughout history there have been amazingly selfish people who put their own agendas at the forefront to capitalize on their missions, until those brave persons affected by this behavior stood up to reclaim their dignity, possessions and personhood. This can be found in American history from enslavement to the modern Civil Rights Movement. Apart from the negative aspect of this story, in the African American community many people, consciously and unconsciously, have sown seeds and nurtured the lives of people, institutions, organizations and communities that have grown into bean stalks—huge, purposeful entities representing strength and perseverance.

Contrary to Jack's story, in the story of John Kinard's life developed a legacy just as tall as Jack's beanstalk. This rich legacy, built in community activism, cultural advocacy, spirituality, the preservation of African American history, and the understanding of multiculturalism, is exemplified as a beanstalk that is still growing. It has been manifested in hard work, sacrifice and stick-to-itiveness that Kinard learned from his mother, the daughter of South Carolina sharecroppers.

This story of John Kinard can only fully be told by first acknowledging his strong foundation found in his family and the promise of his mother, Jessie Beulah Covington-Kinard of Greenwood, SC, who was subjected to, at an early age, the daunting tasks of hard work in the fields and domestic service. After growing tired of getting "dogged," like many African American women of the Progressive Era in the rural South, she fled to become part of the Great Migration, and moved to Washington, DC. By taking this bold and courageous move, Jessie Beulah Kinard was determined to reclaim her life and create a different one finding opportunity and the best possible resources for herself and her future offspring. She represented men and women all over the rural South, who were tired of the generational acceptance of oppression and who wanted to be part of the change. According to a book on migration to Washington, DC, women like Jessie Beulah Kinard who migrated thought of their suitcases as symbols of emancipation.

> *These women from all over the South (rural and urban areas) brought to Washington, DC parcels of the South, both literal and figurative, in their "freedom bags" — the small suitcases they brought from the South. In time, however, their urban experiences caused them to modify many of their southern ideas and values.*[1]

In these "freedom bags" were the women's dreams of success, social acceptance and ambition. Some of them, possessing beaten spirits like that of Covington-Kinard, kept their dreams silent and trained their children to be stronger than they were and prayed their children could one day walk through the doors and on the floors they cleaned. The homespun wisdom and southern hospitality that the friends and acquaintances of these women encountered on the trails they blazed with other budding dynamic leaders will be revealed in this book.

The story outlined in this book will explore the peerless life of John Kinard, an offspring of Jessie Beulah Kinard, a woman who left South Carolina to create a new life for herself in Washington, DC. The life of her son John Kinard is rooted in southern values, character, ingenuity, spirituality, and multicultural understanding. Kinard worked his whole life to bridge cultural gaps in America and abroad like many leaders that came before him. The voice of Kinard, and others throughout the history of the world, such as, Mahatma Gandhi, Howard Thurman, Mary McLeod Bethune, and Martin Luther King Jr., uniquely combated injustice. They used their voices and special talents to inspire a cause, which invigorated people to be uplifted. Kinard molded his distinct leadership abilities and was encouraged by the re-emerging problems around the world that he faced; by growing up in segregated Washington, DC; by fighting for injustice as a student at Livingstone College; and by serving as a participant and later a field representative with Operation Crossroads Africa.

In 1967, John R. Kinard made history when he became the first African American appointed to direct a Smithsonian Museum; thus, paving the way for many other minorities to become leaders in one of the most prestigious cultural organizations in the world. The Anacostia Neighborhood Museum was a place where residents from the District of Columbia's Anacostia community were welcomed as visitors, volunteers, and employees.

The idea for a small satellite museum located in a low-income urban setting grew out of a conference on museums and education held in August 1966. Jointly sponsored by the Smithsonian and the Department of Education, the conference sought to begin to discover ways of taking more effective educational use of the more than 5,000 museums that exist in the United States.[2]

THE MAN, THE MOVEMENT, THE MUSEUM

Through its innovative and fresh approach, the museum inspired its broad constituency to embrace positive images showcasing local African American visual and performing artists. It taught lesser known cultural practices such as the celebration of Kwanza, Black History Week and Month that encouraged many African Americans during this period to ask the questions: "Who am I?" and "Do African Americans really have a place in the American legacy?"

The exhibits developed at this institution served as a mechanism to reach and teach. For example, Doodles in Dimension (1967); The Rat Man's Affliction (1969); The Frederick Douglass Years (1970); Black Patriots In the American Revolution (1970); Toward Freedom (1971); The Evolution of A Community: Part II (1972); The Message Makers (1974); Blacks In the Westward Movement (1975); Black Women: Achievements Against the Odds (1976-1984); The Anacostia Story: 1608-1930 (1977); Out of Africa: From West African Kingdoms to Colonization (1979); Anna J. Cooper: A Voice from the South (1981); The Renaissance: Black Art of the Twenties (1985); Climbing Jacob's Ladder (1987); and The Real McCoy (1989) were recognized by people from all over the world for their balanced approach to educating the public about the contributions of African Americans in society. Through cutting-edge research, the questions of Blacks and their role in American history were validated through the Smithsonian Institution, a mainstream institution. The life of John Kinard, his efforts in community development and the impact of this research will be a core component in my historical analysis.

Observing that many people visiting the Smithsonian were non-native Washingtonians, the creators of the Anacostia Neighborhood Museum concluded that if the people don't go to the Smithsonian, then the Smithsonian must be brought to the people. It was with this view that Kinard took an abandoned theater, restored it, and established a satellite location of the Smithsonian Institution under the support of the Secretary of the Smithsonian Institution, Dr. S. Dillon Ripley. With this effort and Kinard's vision, the Smithsonian fulfilled a dream of Dr. Carter G. Woodson and others.

It is obvious in the case of a museum in a rundown neighborhood that the bookmobile museum in a slum implies something for nothing from rich folks somewhere else, a kind of charity, a handout, largesse in white gloves. Involvement can only be created if it is their museum. It must be on the spot, participated in by the people who live there....By June 1967 we had selected a director, Mr. John Kinard, a thirty year old Washington born youth worker who had worked in the neighborhood Youth Corps and the Office of Economic Opportunity. Under Kinard, who is vigorous and decisive, the exhibit plans were finally completed and the work was begun...The exhibits resulted from a vast number of suggestions, primarily from the advisory council, but also from the Smithsonian staff curators.[3]

This concept brought art, issues, and cultural events to people right where they lived, worked, and played. Through the directorship of John Kinard, the staff of the Anacostia Neighborhood Museum represented an era of African Americans professionally controlling their images. The Anacostia Neighborhood Museum represented hope for a poor, disenfranchised community. At the head of the museum, as Director and senior level manager, he was an activist who became a historian, art historian, and museum studies expert.

From some in the white community, along with interest, enthusiasm, and promises of foundation funds, there came expressions of skepticism and predictions of failure. The board members of one local foundation initially told us that while they agreed that Anacostia needed a museum [now was not the time]. A newspaper editor assured me the place would be vandalized and destroyed within the first week. It is worth noting that from the opening date to the time of this writing [12 months] there has been neither theft nor vandalism of any Museum object. During the turbulent time following the murder of Dr. Martin Luther King Jr., while there was destruction in the neighborhood, the Museum was untouched.[4]

John R. Kinard aimed high in creating an identity for this space among the Smithsonian Institution, making it honored, respected, and an exceptional example of what an African American museum could offer to the public as a vehicle to teach. This book will primarily examine the life of John Kinard and his impact professionally, as well as the legacy of multicultural advocacy and acceptance he left behind.

THE MAN, THE MOVEMENT, THE MUSEUM

Museums can no longer serve only the intellectually elite, the art connoisseur, and the scholar. Our visitors can no longer be limited to the enlightened, and the educated and the well to do. Any institutions that call themselves museums and do not note with great care the overwhelming possibilities for service to the community should rethink their position so that there can be no undue criticism of these respected institutions and their traditions. Museums must be sensitive to the cries of modern man for a more perfect way to live and to know the truth.[5]

Kinard's vision is currently being manifested and realized daily within every segment of the Smithsonian Institution, the Anacostia Community Museum, the National Museum of African American History and Culture, the National Museum of the American Indian, the National Museum of African Art, as well as colleges and universities that teach museum education and public history. He labored together with other museum directors, staff of repositories, and historical societies to gain support through meetings, conferences, and workshops. Kinard's efforts helped to establish the Association of African American Museums (AAAM) in 1978, as well as an ethnic part of the American Association of Museums (AAM).

In the United States, more than a hundred museums exist that celebrate black and African life. The range of their subject matter is astonishingly broad: from the Studio Museum in Harlem, the largest art museum run by blacks, to the Texas Institute of Culture, the home of the history of black cowboys; from the Black Fashion Museum in New York to the Banneker-Douglass Museum in Annapolis. Three farmhouses in Weeksville (in yes Brooklyn) preserved as an experience lost to today's urbanites. The Museum of African-American Art in Los Angeles is the first black art museum of its kind in the West. The University Museum at Hampton, with its collection of American Indian, African and Pacific artifacts, represents a long tradition at black colleges. Black museums and historical collections have existed for more than a hundred years, but in the last few years there has been a boomlet in their numbers and budgets, and in public interest as well. One of the most important forces fueling the mini-explosion is a growing sophistication in fund-raising and public financing skills tied in part to the growth of minority political power.[6]

Although omitted from the history of the AAAM, Kinard helped to secure many resources for it and other organizations. In fact, the first grant the organization received was from the Smithsonian Institution after the passing of the Museum Act. Through this and other partnerships, coalitions, and boards, Kinard continued to be inspired and uplifted and spread "The Kinard Philosophy." He persevered in insisting that his voice be heard in his attempts to persuade the Smithsonian Institution to re-examine its missions to hire capable minorities, diversify exhibitions within the museums on the National Mall and Smithsonian Institution affiliate sites, and properly deliver ethnic images in exhibits and other cultural education programming. As Kinard's life unfolds in this research, you will see him walk into his destiny incorporating a life full of ups and downs, all taking shape and growing upward like a mighty beanstalk.

Chapter 1

THE KINARD ROOTS
Living Beyond Jim Crow in Washington, DC

Jessie's Freedom Bags

Living in the world of Jim Crow segregation was one of terror and humiliation for many African Americans. Not only were you mistreated as an insignificant contributor to the American aesthetic, your rights were restricted in every sense of the word. All over the nation, more importantly in the South, few of the contributions enslaved Africans gave to this nation are acknowledged. As builders of the great plantations, shrines and temples of this land, these people of African descent, whose hands cared and nurtured the country, brought from Africa their methods of agricultural influence. Ultimately, their efforts supported the global market aiding in the United States becoming one of the most powerful economic forces in the world from its creation to present day. Slavery, this viciously devastating and brutal system, existed all over the colonies. But in South Carolina, unlike any other state carried such commitment to this peculiar institution of slavery.

The skeletons whose bones rattle most loudly in South Carolina's historical closet are those of slavery, and its attendants: secession and civil war.[1]

South Carolina represents the roots of the Kinard family. Not much research has been completed on the original Kinard slaveholders; however, there are strong suspicions that the Kinard name derived from the Kinnairds of English descent taking root in South Carolina much like the early founding fathers and merchants during the creation of American society. Throughout American history up to Reconstruction, many Blacks living in South Carolina carved out lives and endured the confines of racism, classism and sexism.

Jessie Beulah Covington, John Kinard's mother, at age 20 in 1926.
Kinard Collection.

Jessie Beulah Covington was born in Greenwood, SC on April 16, 1905, during a time in America when the country was in turmoil. As far as African Americans were concerned, forty years after the Civil War, the country repeatedly inflicted white supremacists' views and enforced the laws of Jim Crow throughout the country, although more in the southern states. The rights gained under the Thirteenth, Fourteenth and Fifteenth Amendments and freedom fought through world wars were met with promise by Blacks who earned these rights, but by opposition from whites who refused to see

Blacks having more than subservient roles. Contrary to the inconsistencies within the interpretation of the American belief system, for African Americans, citizenship, freedom of speech and rights were earned and used as a symbol of inclusion to equality. These rights were mocked in the harsh realities of Black life during the "Nadir" period, or lowest point in history that African Americans endured. African Americans were being barred from the ballot box, segregated in practically all areas of public life and lynched in record numbers.

> At the slightest sign of black political initiative or at no sign at all armed white men called "bulldozers" burned homes and even entire towns, raped women, and lynched both men and women. According to Ida B. Wells-Barnett, between 1878 and 1898, about ten thousand people were lynched in America, primarily in the South. A statement issued by white supremacist General M.W. Gray of South Carolina stated, "Every Democrat must feel honor bound to control the vote of at least one Negro, by intimidation, purchase, keeping him away or as each individual may determine how he may best accomplish it. Never threaten a man individually. If he deserves to be threatened, the necessities of the time required that he should die." [2]

The actual conditions of Black life in this period, in contrast with slave life, were a continuation of racial domination. Forty years after the Civil War, the country repeatedly inflicted white supremacist views and developed laws to separate resources based on race, which was a tactic used to control Blacks all over the country. In 1896, nine years prior to the birth of Jessie Beulah Covington, mother of John Kinard, the *Plessey vs. Ferguson* "separate but equal policy" became official, and Jim Crow policies were expanded. The *Plessey* ruling regulated policies and rules that were southern reactions to political exclusion causing more racial tensions and disenfranchisement among the Black race.

> In the post-Civil War South, nothing threatened whites more than the loss of control over African Americans. The federal government failed to institute a comprehensive land confiscation and redistribution program, and southern whites refused to sell property or extend credit to former slaves. As a result, African Americans largely

remained yoked economically to the people (if not the individual owners) whom they had served as slaves.[3]

In the early twentieth century, Black America faced dejected times. The effects of the *Plessey* ruling brought great misery to African Americans governed by Jim Crow policies, which continued to overlook their needs for adequate resources, such as schools, hospitals and jobs outside of agriculture.

Despite the obstacles of the *Plessey* ruling and the limitations of segregation, great strides were realized throughout the growth of African American communities nationwide. Through the founding of Black churches and Historically Black Colleges and Universities (HBCUs), the organizing of national groups and coalitions of influence, the development of black newspapers, and the attempts by Blacks to positively influence state officials, mass progress became contagious. Unfortunately, these strides were rendered insignificant due to the uneasiness of the larger white American population, ill-equipped to let go of destructive customs and embrace the progressive era of Black America.

By the twentieth century, the place for blacks in the political, social, and economic spheres of South Carolina was clearly defined. The new century needed only to refine those roles. Where no laws served to limit the role of blacks, prevailing customs had the same effects. The role that Afro-Americans should play in South Carolina was not a question which was addressed in a vacuum. It became the all-encompassing question on the southern mind. A southerner maintained that "the Negro in the South is the labor problem and the servant question; he is preeminently the political issue, and his place socially is of daily and hourly discussion." The large proportion of Afro-Americans in the population of South Carolina was an important reason why that race received so much attention. While blacks relieved white Carolinians of the pains of hard work, their presence was also a problem for them.[4]

However, progressive-thinking whites did embrace the Black community, helping to bridge the gap of multicultural understanding. For example,

THE MAN, THE MOVEMENT, THE MUSEUM

President Theodore Roosevelt appointed Dr. William Crum to a major office of influence.

Although they were not in the forefront in the campaign, racial feelings were deeply entrenched in the state. On January 5, 1903, President Theodore Roosevelt troubled the political waters of South Carolina by appointing Dr. William D. Crum, a black, as collector of the port of Charleston. D. D. Wallace stated that Crum was appointed because he was black and that white Carolinians objected for the same reasons. Roosevelt held his ground and refused to rescind the appointment of Crum unless "some valid reason other than color could be found." [5]

Remarkably, African Americans responded to these harsh conditions by rising above adversity and pressing forward in breaking barriers. In this era of progressivism, there were few Blacks as influential as Dr. Crum. He represented the "talented tenth" of Black leadership who would inspire and allure more working-class blacks to aim high and change the cycle of oppression through entrepreneurship and education. However, some African Americans could only see the past and present conditions, and refrained from mixing hopeless efforts of higher education for themselves and their offspring. Covington was raised in a working-class family of sharecroppers. The Covingtons ran a family farm (small productive workforces) in Greenwood, SC. Growing and harvesting cotton, as most sharecroppers in the community did during the early 1900s, with clarity she remembers:

I was the oldest one... Later on, Sarah come along, but she was my mother's cousin. Her mother and my mother were first cousins. Her mother took sick and died... My mother brought Sarah home and claimed her, so we raised Sarah. She said, "Beulah, we gonna raise this baby. Now you be the oldest sister, and she be the baby sister..." And then there was Cap [Edward]. Of course, me and Cap was full. Well, we grew and we worked in the country. Went to field every day. In the summer time, went to field, and never worked after September 'cause it was nothing to do. September, that was the gathering of the stuff done planted from the first of the year. We plant that and we would gather it. That's gathering time. We lived apart from each other, but it was a community you know... [6]

The sharecropping system led to abject southern poverty and underdevelopment at drastic rates in many southern areas of the United States. Sharecropping and its stunning close characteristics shared with slavery were an imposed system former slaves used to provide a living for their families. Impossible to make profitable strides in this profession, it was common among Blacks in the South to find themselves as sharecroppers, hinging the whole family together to aid each other in harvesting, rather than paying wage labor. Young Black women represented the foundation of families in the rural South. Covington, as the oldest sibling, was looked upon to serve and fulfill major responsibilities at an awfully young age, which was common during this era.

The post emancipation period was a time of economic crisis for African American families in the South. The adverse economic, political, and social-climate naturally drove kin groups closer and made them more interdependent. At the turn of the century, African American sharecropping families became even more impoverished as landlords began to insist on a fixed amount of cash rather than a share of the crop as payment for rent in the faltering staple-crop economy.[7]

This experience, similar to slavery, made families cleave closer together and urge financially feeble communities to seek support from area churches and other Black organizations. In a low but strong voice, she recalled how

...we worked, farmed, planted cotton, corn and stuff in the spring of the year... Where they would go buy food and stuff was nothing but two stores on the side of the railroad the train run up and down that road from Greenwood to Augusta, GA. I think the 7 o'clock train would come up from Augusta to Greenwood and then one would go down from Greenwood to Augusta. That was around 7 o'clock in the morning and 10 o'clock in the morning.[8]

Growing up, Covington became a functional leader in the home, raising her younger brother and cousin as her sister. She served as the lady of the house when her mother went away for months to work in Philadelphia, PA. Depending on her mother for guidance and mentorship was common and was practiced in this home until her untimely death. In a disconsolate tone, she explained a personally revealing part of her life:

> *My mother she passed away.... It was out that she was poisoned and some woman poisoned her, so they say... Well, we buried the poor thing...*[9]

This sudden death impacted Covington and the family incredibly, both economically and emotionally. Mary Murany's death was the first heartbreak Covington would experience. This lovely woman, well liked and of "mixed race" (Cherokee and Black), was a preacher's daughter and an example of how to be a hardworking woman with moral standards and strength in God.

This untimely death caused the Covington family to turn to family cooperation for survival. Although her father, James Covington, was present and provided for the family, he was left out of the responsibilities of child-rearing after returning daily from the cotton fields. Her tasks were regulated to supervising the home, washing clothes and finishing chores. Covington's tender years of adolescence and her right to enjoy life were interrupted and usurped to fully step in to help her family. The unending demands of family made her caretaker responsibilities stressful and often challenging.

> *She could be depended upon to clean the yard, to decorate the front with flowers, and to give things the aspect of a civilized life. In fact, this working woman was often the central figure of the family and the actual representative of the home.*[10]

Although African Americans faced huge burdens, Black women like Covington growing up in this era faced the double burdens of race and gender struggles captured in the philosophy of African American activist, feminist and civil rights leader Mary Church Terrell. She contends the following:

> *A white woman has only one handicap to overcome that of sex. I have two both sex and race. I belong to the only group in this country which has two such huge obstacles to surmount. Colored men only have one that of race.*[11]

Terrell, as the first president of the National Association of Colored Women's Clubs, the first national organization established to support the problems of African American women, and Covington represented the new generation of Black feminism that was submissive to the needs of the family. But, at the same time, detested it (the family) for standing in their way of opportunity. Covington was fortunate enough to be educated in the community of Greenwood, SC. She grew up with limitations, allowing her only to advance her opportunities of education later in life. She smiled and described her early education and community:

> *I went to a little school... The house was on one side and a little branch ran between the school and our house, and then it was a bottom that stayed wet in there practically all the time. It never ran dry. One month before Christmas and three months after Christmas, we would go to school, November to March. A white family lived down the road. And a little country school was on the side of the road going to Bradley. Bradley was a little shopping center. It was nothing but two stores. People would go there on Saturday and hang around there. And they had a cotton gin. My dad would take our cotton there, and a lot of people in the neighborhood would take the cotton there and gin it, sell it...*[12]

Quite commonly young women, like Covington, were prohibited from progressing further with their education. Mary McLeod Bethune, a native of South Carolina, was the one chosen in her family to further her education, a rare occurrence for girls in the Black community. Her thirst for knowledge began at an early age, and passing it on was a pattern that she and other women often employed. With this hunger and thirst as an impetus, Bethune created Bethune-Cookman College in 1904.

> *The establishment and uninterrupted operation of her college altered the public perception of black women's limited prospects in higher education. Bethune's emphasis on educating black girls reflected her years at Scotia and the popular notion of a "female burden" for racial uplift espoused by her role models such as Scotia graduate Emma J. Wilson and Atlanta University graduate Lucy Craft Laney. Wilson was Bethune's first teacher at Trinity Mission School near Mayesville, South*

Carolina, and Laney founded Haines Institute in Augusta, Georgia where Bethune apprenticed in 1896-1897.[13]

The fight for Black women to combat racism and sexism in order to progress in American society was a challenge some found hard to endure. Naturally, Black women made successful attempts to deflect the double burden they faced in history. Hearing about men being supported to progress, excel and achieve during this period was obviously met with no opposition and was greatly supported by both men and women. A native of Greenwood, S.C., Elijah Mayes managed to use his education to advance and become a leader at Howard University. He led Morehouse College for years as its president. If more women like Covington were provided the same support and motivation to succeed in these rural areas, then, like men, African American women would be further ahead than they were during the Progressive Era. This lack of support and dependency for Black women to be bled dry of their possibilities and tied to the confines of a home or farm, was criminal. For Covington, who endured the stagnant conditions of progression, and the burdening role as the woman of the house, a sense of emotional irritation began to fester within her. The family homestead became a prison. She planned a getaway in 1925, at the age of 20, that would change her life and the lives of others who were affected by it and who depended on her: the Covington family. With solicitude, she describes the multiple family demands that made stronger her decision to leave:

> *I left because my mother had worked in Philadelphia backwards and forwards to share money with daddy to work the farm. And, so she would send him money, you know, to put the cotton and all that kinda stuff corn and sharecrop. And then we raised cotton... After Momma died, she left me in charge of her brother's children. She left the children with my father and my father would depend on me to stir the hip so "I got tired of being dogged..." I just got tired of it. I wrote my Aunt Sarah in Alabama, I told her to send me some money and I would come out there... After I left they had to do the best they could... Pa got so mad. He wrote Aunt Sarah a hot letter "You took my child away from me blah blah blah..."*[14]

Covington, having family who migrated away from this small town, was eager to create a daring and adventurous destiny for herself, one that her family never imagined would happen so soon and abruptly. So, conveniently overlooking her dreams and aspirations for a better life, Covington represented many African Americans inspired by the Progressive Era and the Harlem Renaissance. They craved to be a part of this movement and culturally defining era and major exodus from rural southern living called the Great Migration. Covington's getaway plan was brilliant, leaving by train for a different life. With one brow raised, she never took a breath as she related her personal journey from the rural South:

Cap left the car that morning, and I took the car and I went to Bradley, got on that 10 o'clock train going to Augusta, GA. I was 20. I got that train and went to Augusta, Ga. to change the train. And, so I went there and I changed trains in Augusta to go to Aunt Sarah's to Heflin, AL. Finally, the train came and I got on that train, rode all night going to Heflin, Alabama, and Jessie Aunt Sarah's son he met me, I knew him because Aunt Sarah would send him to Grandpa's to stay a while and then he would go back home. I stayed there for two years [1925–27]. Then my first cousin lived in Washington; we used to write to one another. She said you come here and stay with me and you can share an apartment with me, and she lived with her brother. He was married, they had one child but the child died and, well I stayed with her until I got a job here in Washington, out in Chevy Chase, MD. Mattie Spearman, my roommate, got me a job out in Chevy Chase, not too far from her, and we used to go to work together and I worked two years with that lady. I cooked, cleaned up, for ten dollars a week. When I was still working for Mrs. Johnson, Mrs. Johnson died later on... I went back home to Pa, and went with this cousin that lived here, and they brought me here with them and I have been here ever since.[15]

Covington was much like the many working-class women who sought a better life and more opportunities of progression than in the rural South of her home in Greenwood.

The largest number of Negroes who have gone North during this period, however, belong to the intelligent laboring class. Some of them have become discontented for the very same reasons that the higher classes were tired of oppression in the South, but the larger number of them have gone north to improve their economic condition.[16]

Many migrants were strong, intelligent, and willing to withstand the Upper South, which still enforced racism through Jim Crow. Although cities like Washington, DC offered more abundant resources that hardly existed in the rural South–such as Black banks, clothing stores, clubs, schools, etc.–separate was never equal even in the nation's capital. In addition to the life of independence Covington gained by migrating to Washington, DC, she met like-minded people who were in search of self-realization. According to Alaine Locke, the "New Negro" cultural definitions found through the arts were reaching a level of consciousness in urban America all over the country. From the hub of Harlem, which birthed the great Harlem Renaissance and electrified many urban African American cities, there was an awakening or rebirth, which emerged through the dust of the years of the Great Depression, through World War II. From New York to Chicago, Blacks came in droves to escape from the lynching and discontent of rural southern life, to migrate to the big cities which some referred to as the "Black Metropolis." These Black artists gave birth to a new image paradigm based in cultural ideologies they defined and cultivated through the arts. This very movement, alone, changed the world's image of how African Americans would be defined. Using the creative gift of expression, this movement reclaimed control of self-respect, self-esteem and self-worth among the African American community. In addition, the cultural and Civil Rights Movements in urban America gained more political support from the 1932 presidential election of Franklin D. Roosevelt, who had a "Black Cabinet" of advisors in which a native South Carolinian was at the helm of leadership, Mary McLeod Bethune. She was instrumental in soliciting the able and willing aid of Eleanor Roosevelt, First Lady, who exhibited the utmost leadership and fairness among the Black community. Mrs. Bethune was regularly involved in aggressively addressing unequal accommodations under the Jim Crow policies, which ultimately affected DC residents. As Covington moved to the nation's capital, she became a new woman, independent and aware of the true struggles the Negro faced nation-wide. Now living in an urban environment, as opposed to the rural setting of her birth, she became conscious and involved in building a better world that included a multitude of civic-minded African Americans.

Living Beyond Jim Crow in Washington, DC

Prior to falling in love with independence and Washington, DC in the early thirties, Covington fell in love, and on June 26, 1933, Jessie Beulah Covington married Robert Francis Kinard. Surviving the Great Depression working in the common jobs found by the working class (she as a domestic worker, and he as a factory worker in a liquor distribution company), they managed to carve out a life filled with dreams and happiness. Speaking in a distinctive voice, that was never nonchalant, she related an archetypal episode for migrants dating in Washington, DC.

John Kinard at age 10 months with mother Jessie B. Kinard. Kinard Collection.

She wistfully recalled:

My husband he lived around the Greenwood area and he had a sister here that married my first cousin Sadie. She married Willie Spearman, and that is who I stayed with, and Mattie was Willie's sister. My husband was Sadie's brother. Well, I was living with Sadie here in Southwest D.C. And I was living with Mattie. Mattie was Sadie's sister in-law. She married her brother, and I stayed with them a while. And then later on as time went on, Sadie's brother Robert came here, and that is how we got together. I didn't know him before, so that's how I got a hold of him. We started courting, and courted about a year. And then we got married. We moved from Columbia Street to Ninth Street.[17]

While residing on Ninth Street, the newlyweds were able to enjoy living near the "Black Broadway of Washington" or U Street. This is the same neighborhood the Howard Theater served, which hosted the King of Jazz, Duke Ellington. Not allowed to attend the all-white shows at Constitution Hall or the National Theater, many Blacks during this era (and some whites), including the Kinards, enjoyed the segregated nightlife found in the heart of one of the most vibrant Black communities in the country.

Duke Ellington headlined many shows at Washington's Howard Theater; Duke Ellington and his famous Orchestra featuring Ivie Anderson in his revue "Harlem Speaks" with Bobby Caston, Four Blazers, Jerry and Turk, Snake Hips Tucker and the Duke's own moving stage.[18]

Kinard's parents dating in Washington, DC in the 1930s at Logan Circle.
Kinard Collection.

On November 13, 1936, most of the enjoyment of honeymooning ceased in order to plan a family and enjoy the birth of John Robert Edward Kinard, the second child born to Robert Francis Kinard.

Robert and Jessie Kinard's sons, John (age 4) and William (10 months), in 1941. Kinard Collection.

The first was Isaiah Benson, who belonged to Robert Francis Kinard from an earlier relationship before his marriage to Jessie Beulah Covington. After experiencing the loss of her first child, she desired another, and was blessed with John Kinard. Following his birth, William Douglass and later George Ellis Kinard were born.

Raising children in Washington, DC provided for more opportunity than in Greenwood, SC. Although, Washington, DC was segregated during the 1930s and 1940s, clearly the offspring of these migrants dealt with similar discrimination which existed in Washington, DC. The Kinards tried very hard to shield their children from the ills of racism and classism. As the New Deal administration prevailed and changed the course of the country, Blacks became more involved in national politics and federal policies. These efforts demonstrated and reflected the ultimate opportunity to later destroy Jim Crow by affecting change in the interpretation of federal policies and laws. Political aftermaths of Nazism were key factors in the success of the Civil

Rights Movement, which would bring about adequate changes to America for Kinard's generation.

While striving to make a living, Covington was a house servant working in the homes of white middle-class families in Washington, DC and Chevy Chase, MD. These were jobs that most African American women were forced to take when they had little to none of a long-term formal education or skilled trade. Foreign immigrant women migrating to America during this time took most of the abundant factory jobs. Many educated Blacks faced exclusion even from working in their own communities as department store employees. In order to overturn these disadvantages faced by the African American community, civil rights leaders led protests.

Although Bethune preferred the conference table to the picket line, she joined the protest against Peoples' Drugstore in Washington, DC in 1939 for its failure to hire black clerks in black neighborhoods.[19]

Unlike the southern hubs of the great migration, the midwestern destinations, which consisted of Chicago, Detroit and St. Louis, were vastly different in the 1940s.

In most of the stores, too, there are colored salespeople, although a white proprietor or manager usually looms in the offing. In the offices around you, colored doctors, dentists, and lawyers go about their duties. And a brown-skinned policeman saunters along swinging his club and glaring sternly at the urchins who dodge in and out among the shoppers.[20]

Covington later became a practical nurse and worked in the health care profession, which increased her earning power to save money for the future college education she wanted her children to earn.

As the oldest son from this union, John Kinard was taught hard work, responsibility, the ability to think critically, and to explore. The organic southern values of hard work were an essential part in raising the Kinard children to be men. These same men, who reaped the benefits through the sacrifice of their parents, were instilled with the multifaceted dimensions of courage and values found in the Covington/Kinard DNA. This upbringing, which hinged on the belief that "it takes a village to raise a child," was central to their development in defining their own destiny rooted in respect for family, God, your neighbor and life. Like Covington, Kinard as the oldest, fulfilled these high expectations and was propelled into a position of leadership and responsibility in helping to raise his brothers. With pride, his brother William recalled his brother never missing "a glorious opportunity" to encourage his family members to develop their abilities:

> He [John] was always my big brother and when we were young my mother never had to get a babysitter. John took care of us. When I got older and went to college, he was always the dynamic force telling me to go on and go further... "Do the best that you can do." He was an inspirational figure to me.[21]

Growing up in Washington, DC was unique during this era. The family enjoyed listening to the radio and watching television shows. Most Black families tried hard to provide their children more of the finer elements of life than what was afforded to the previous generation in order to ease deprived feelings which echoed from the segregation doctrine that was alive and well and being practiced in the nation's capital. This country, which had such a problem with rights and liberties concerning African Americans during this era, found itself under attack in 1941 as a result of the same violation of rights perpetrated abroad. On December 7, 1941, the Japanese attack on Pearl Harbor affected Washingtonians, both Black and white, who served in World War II.

> Some 27,000 Washingtonians were watching a football game at Griffith Stadium. Over and over, the stadium loudspeaker boomed out the name of some high-ranking army or navy officer being ordered to report to his command. The huge crowd began to murmur suspiciously. The football fans knew something was wrong... Later people found out about the Japanese surprise attack...[22]

Across the country after the Second World War, the struggle for equality among Blacks throughout the nation was tested, especially in Washington, DC. Segregation continued to exist in churches, the hotel industry and the workforce as African Americans continued to be denied equal rights. This was especially apparent in the segregation of neighborhoods. The Kinards lived at 1425 C Street, Southeast on Capitol Hill, at that time, a large Black segregated community.

> *Negroes, first from country to towns in the South following reconstruction, then from the South northward to the Border states and to Northern urban centers. The white population reacted with hostility to the great migrations... Segregation by city ordinance merely legalized the established practice of keeping Negroes within residential boundaries.*[23]

All over the nation, separate but equal laws had separated the races, and in several cases, were used to humiliate Blacks. However, segregation strengthened the economic power of the Black community all over the country through the patronage of Black businesses and living in Black neighborhoods, which were safe, carefree and supportive. In the 1940s, desegregation cases led by Charles Hamilton Houston were slowly breaking down the restrictive covenants of segregation, and in 1949, Mary Church Terrell formed the Coordinating Committee for the Enforcement of the D.C. Anti-Discrimination Laws. As the chair, Terrell (at 86 years old) led the successful integration of Hecht Company in 1951 and Thompson's restaurant in 1953.

> *In 1950, when the four visited the restaurant, they were denied service of the then general policy whereby white restaurants denied service to Negroes. Four persons who initiated the case which ended Monday with the Supreme Court outlawing racial discrimination in restaurants here yesterday revisited Thompson's Restaurant at 715 14th St., N.W. They reported later they received courteous service. They are Dr. Mary Church Terrell, Mrs. Geneva Brown, the Rev. W.H. Jernagin, and David H. Scull. Of the group, Scull is white and the others are Negroes.*[24]

These deeds of activism and steadfast persistence gave hope to Blacks in

Washington, DC, especially the Kinard family. This movement altered the makeup of Washington, DC and helped the youth get engaged in the democratic process, proving to Blacks that citizenship and rights are practiced and earned, not given. These planned activities of protest would later flood the South in the effort to obtain full integration under the law.

Some highlights of living in African American neighborhoods in Washington, DC during the thirties, forties and fifties were witnessing the spawning of youth activities. For example, Juanita Jefferson, who grew up in the Barry Farm community housing for retired Black World War II veterans, experienced a richly entertaining and cultural environment. She recalled dolefully:

> The young boys, they played their football...they would play a lot of horseshoes. That was a big game for us, for the boys in the community. And the boys were always singing. They were always singing and harmonizing on the corner, including my brother, and that was something they did every night under the lamppost, just singing until your mom would call you in. We had to go in at certain times. We weren't allowed to go out all hours of the night...[25]

Consequently, juvenile delinquency did exist. It was an issue that the Black and white community faced.

> Gradually horrified adults discovered that juvenile delinquency was by no means solely a product of the Negro slums. It invaded the white suburbs as well as the city and infected children of well-to-do white families as well as the underprivileged. Car stealing for joy rides went on everywhere.[26]

Living on Capitol Hill, the Kinard children attended both Payne Elementary School and Browne Junior High School. Although segregation was intended to be separate but equal, the conditions Blacks faced nationwide were far from equal. The Kinard children, as well as other Blacks, faced sad realities that affected children at play.

> Although the citizens' committee that year won the fight to open to colored members of the Amateur Athletic Union the boys' boxing matches and track meets held at

the privately owned Uline Arena, every plea for biracial use of playgrounds failed, even when a careful tally counted in an entire week only ten white children using the spacious New York Avenue playground while across the street a thousand Negro girls and five hundred Negro boys at the Dunbar High School had no play space at all. The sight of dark-skinned children peering wistfully through the fence at a well-equipped white playground in their neighborhood disturbed the equanimity of white parents as nothing else could.[27]

To avoid living under the separate but equal Jim Crow laws, some Blacks registered protest by leaving the country to live in Europe. Many entertainers like Josephine Baker, James Baldwin and others created better lives and homes for themselves by living abroad on a long-term basis.

As my two daughters grew up, the question of their education was often discussed. Several of my white friends urged me to send them to Europe. It was a revelation to me to see how clearly some of them saw the difficulties and disadvantages under which colored women labor in the United States. I was surprised also to see how keenly some of them felt about it. [28]

Although Terrell was of the elite class and had the financial means to educate her children in America or Europe, she wanted her children to be educated in the United States amongst the realities that African Americans faced. Unlike Terrell, many other African American women were unable to choose international or private institutional environments to ensure that their children were educated. The Kinards, like many other Black working-class residents of Washington, DC, depended on the exceptional skills and teaching staff of the segregated African American public schools.

A product of the District of Columbia segregated public schools, Kinard attended Dunbar Senior High School, the first college preparatory school for African Americans in the city, and then transferred to the new Spingarn High School closer to his home, from which he later graduated.

In 1949 Congress had appropriated $1,187,399 towards the new Spingarn Senior High School planned for 24th and Benning Rd., N.E. to relieve the *intolerable congestion at Armstrong, Cardozo, and Dunbar High Schools. The Spingarn building contract however, could not be let because Congress had never appropriated the full authorized cost of the school $2,505,000.*[29]

John Kinard at age 16. Kinard Collection.

A national trend was seen in Washington, DC. According to historian Keith Medler, a major shift in District of Columbia history took place. The Archdiocese of Washington ordered the system of Catholic parochial schools to desegregate, giving Black families the option to enroll their children in Catholic schools.

Attending African American schools afforded students the opportunity be nurtured by the best and brightest of the nation. Many scholars who trained at Howard, Harvard and other top universities were employed as schoolteachers in the segregated schools of Washington, DC. The best and brightest Blacks were often overlooked and never considered to be worthy in American society, but were praised within their own community. To be hired as a government or scientific specialist seldom occurred, but they were welcomed as teachers in the Black schools, which, ironically, was one of the positive effects of segregation. Washington, DC served as one of the nucleuses for the Black intelligentsia who settled here and taught in the segregated (Division II) Black schools. Members of this elite group were leaders such as Dr. Anna J. Cooper, Dr. Carter G. Woodson, Mary Church Terrell and Alma Thomas. These great instructors of influence were trained at the Sorbonne in Paris, France; Harvard University; Oberlin College; and countless other colleges and universities. These instructors were leaders in the New Negro era and the national Civil Rights Movement. An activist explained reality for many District of Columbia residents:

> When I came along in the segregated school system, I do remember there was a Division I and a Division II, which was two different systems. But I lived in a predominantly black community. I didn't deal with whites. I went to a black church, so I didn't deal with whites. So, my world wasn't so much revolved around the segregated system...[30]

While still at Dunbar High School, Kinard was able to learn from the cleverest and brightest of the race. According to Leona Gabel in *From Slavery to the Sorbonne and Beyond: The Life & Writings of Anna J. Cooper* (1982), ...the faculty of Dunbar prepared special tutorials to assist students for college entrance examinations, and Brown, Harvard, Yale and Oberlin agreed to admit students on the basis of the test results without requiring further preparation.

> During its heyday from 1900 to 1950, Dunbar sent a large number of students to Ivy League and Seven Sister colleges. Among its graduates were attorneys William Henry Hastie and Charles Hamilton Houston, who went on to Amherst; Robert Terrell, who graduated from Harvard; and historians Rayford Logan and Carter G. Woodson. Moreover, because of Dunbar's prestige and the inability to get job offers from white universities in the North, many of Dunbar's teachers were black scholars who had received advanced degrees at northeastern universities and used Dunbar as a training ground or waiting spot before they went on to college teaching positions at universities like Howard, Fisk, Atlanta, Morehouse, or Spelman.[31]

According to Constance M. Green in *Washington: A History of the Capital, 1800-1950* (1962), no other single colored school in the country had turned out so many promising graduates. Ambitious Negro families occasionally moved to Washington, DC solely to enable their children to attend Dunbar.

As a college-bound Dunbar student, faculty also groomed Kinard for greatness. However, in 1953, with a new Black school being built closer to the Kinard residence, he later enrolled in Spingarn. There, he also gained a superior education in academics. Involved in the Spingarn High School Hi-Y Club and track team, Kinard developed leadership and social skills, in addition to learning about the world and finding his place. In the Division II schools, students were encouraged to become leaders and be active in extracurricular activities. The face of a long-time friend energetically reflected meeting:

John Kinard in 1953 at Spingarn High School... I met him on the track team. We both ran long distances. I ran the three and one half mile in cross country and the eight eighty, John ran the same thing... He stuck out in my mind, [because] John was the kind of guy who would stick with it... I would run a mile and I had to be first or second ... John could run and not be first or second but stay with it all the time. I can visualize him now all sweaty... still running.[32]

Living in the same community helped to strengthen the race as opposed to becoming a basis for its demise. Some leaders thought the fight for civil rights was more about options than just integration. Civil rights organizations worked diligently to persuade society to look into the mirror of inequality and change its actions through the powerful and influential leadership of the National Urban League and the National Association for the Advancement of Colored People's legal division.

Arthur Spingarn became a member of the vigilance committee... The purpose of this committee was to seek out, publicize, and prosecute cases of injustice to Negroes in the metropolitan area. The national body carried on its legal work by engaging counsel as the need arose and when funds permitted. At this time Arthur Spingarn and Charles Studin volunteered responsibility for this phase of the Association's work. After Studin's death, Arthur Spingarn continued to carry on the legal activities alone until, in 1935, William T. Andrews was engaged to assist him. In 1936, Andrews was succeeded by Charles Houston as special counsel and Spingarn became chairman of the Legal Committee.[33]

It would later be due to the brilliance and courage of Charles Hamilton Houston, another Washington native, and his legal team that provided enough evidence to support the *Bolling v. Sharpe* legal case against segregated schools in Washington, DC. This was one of the many lawsuits that laid the foundation for the case of *Brown v. the Board of Education of Topeka, Kansas* that was presented to the Supreme Court. This is an example of what African Americans in cities all over the country were experiencing in their efforts to substantiate and amass facts to contradict the "equal" in the concept of "separate but equal." One interviewee shook her head and said:

> *I remember when I was at Langley Junior High, McKinley Technical High School was right next to Langley Junior High and at that time integration was just getting started; and I remember how the white students at McKinley did not want the black students to go there and so there was a lot of rebel rousing.*[34]

This frustration was fuel in the engine of integration. Right in the heart of Washington, DC, the nation's capital, there were major inconveniences connected to segregation in schools, which were subjects in the *Bolling v. Sharpe* case.

> *On September 11, 1950, Consolidated Parents founder Gardner Bishop led eleven black youngsters to the brand-new John Philip Sousa Jr. High School, a lavishly equipped building open only to whites in Southeast Washington. Although many of the new school's classrooms were empty, when Bishop's students, including Spottswood T. Bolling, Jr., tried to enroll, they were turned away. James Nabrit, a Howard University law professor, promptly brought a suit against Melvin Sharpe, president of the D.C. Board of Education. The Bolling v. Sharpe suit was unprecedented, for it attacked segregation as unconstitutional.*[35]

That year, children like Kinard were used to help desegregate schools in the city; however, the Kinard children personally were never involved in the protests. They observed other children's involvement. Their parents, although supportive of the movement, actively discussed the topic of integration and equal rights in the home through most current events. All over the city, there were schools that Blacks lived in closer proximity to, but because they were Black, they were turned away instantly. They were forced to attend the segregated school a further distance away. Kinard faced having to attend Dunbar High School when Eastern High School, an all-white school, was closer to his home. In another Black neighborhood in Washington, DC in the Anacostia and Barry Farms community, there were similar issues with segregation. With eyes filled with emotion, Freda Alston remembered:

> *There was an elementary school like a block and a half or two blocks away but because it was prior to desegregation, Ketcham Elementary school on Good Hope Road, I was not able to go to that school because I was a black child or of the colored race. So I had to attend other schools. I did attend Douglass Junior High School named after Frederick Douglass.*[36]

This victory of full integration would later change the nation and give many options to Black America. Kinard's younger brothers, who graduated from the integrated Eastern High School in Washington, DC, were able to take advantage of this new integration. Washingtonian Marjorie Williams remembers vividly the importance of schools and the myriad impacts of community residential patterns on school attendance:

> *By the time I got to Coolidge there weren't many of us Black students at Coolidge. I lived near Coolidge near Quackenbos and Rittenhouse (streets), and so Coolidge was two blocks away from where I lived at that time and, of course, when we moved up into that area we were one of few Black families there at that time.*[37]

In 1955, John Kinard graduated from Spingarn High School. His graduation came just one year after the United States Supreme Court ruled that segregation in public schools was unconstitutional. In the Spingarn High School yearbook, surprisingly under John Kinard's ambition, was placed the word "Aviator".

Kinard's brother, George Ellis Kinard at age 16 in 1962. Kinard Collection.

Kinard's brother, William Douglass Kinard at age 17. Kinard Collection.

Like many Black Washingtonian families, church was an integral part of their development representing the extended family or community. The church was politically active in the Civil Rights Movement, starting early day care centers for single mothers, and organizing constructive and creative activities like Boy and Girl Scout troops for members' children and community youth.

> *The highest spiritual values are always to be found where there exist the highest social values. We are sometimes not aware of the fact that many of the ordinary uses of the church building are, at least in part, recreational... The church realizes its highest recreational expression in its informal features. The Sunday School with its occasional special program, the church social, choir practice, casual entertainments, class meetings, men's clubs, etc., are the chief activities of the average church that supply recreation.*[38]

It also reinforced positive stereotypes that were absent in mainstream media and recreational outlets for African American youth. This outlet produced assistance and support in improving the status of African Americans. Kinard looked to his father, who was an example of hard work and determination. However, Kinard's father did face a lot of disappointing times in his life, and imbibed in alcohol, which was commonly used by Black men as a mechanism to escape the pressures they faced in their efforts to conform in America. William Kinard's deep-set eyes filled with strength as he stressed:

> *...he (Mr. Kinard) had experienced much more segregation than I did. The only segregation that I experienced as a growing child was that I realized that I couldn't go to the white boys' club and the theaters downtown.*[39]

Raised to respect religion and spirituality, the Kinards held membership in the African Methodist Episcopal Zion (AME Zion) Church. Many young Black men needed other role models outside of the home in order to develop a wider community of support to help guide their future. Kinard's parents believed in the possibilities of Kinard having a strong foundation built in spirituality, education, and community to assist him in becoming the first in his family to reach higher heights in life and obtain opportunities they could only dream of aspiring to when they were his age. They attended Metropolitan Wesley A.M.E. Zion Church located in Washington, DC and raised their three children to participate in the Children and Youth Choirs, Buds of Promise Missionary Society, Sunday School, and Acolyte Guild.

Knowing early in his life that he wanted to be a minister, Kinard gravitated to the mentorship of his pastor, Dr. Collins Lee, and preached his trial sermon at the age of sixteen. The pressure was placed on Kinard to break major barriers. He found strength in spirituality as a way to accomplish this task. Although groomed by the best teachers in his schools, Kinard enrolled in Howard University in the fall of 1955 and found that it was quite overwhelming. College life for John Kinard, during this period, was challenging. His close friend provided a lens into his feelings at the time:

> John initially went to Howard [in fall 1955] and I remember there is a place called Douglass Hall ...at the time I went there that's where you go, you play cards; it's where you flunk out of Howard... I had a locker there ... I was a city student, John was a city student, too. And I remember seeing him and he saying ,"Clennie, I've got to get out of here. This school is too big for me and too impersonal and cold." And he left; he wanted to go somewhere he could feel ... a family.[40]

Dr. Collins Lee was an alumnus of Livingstone College, which was founded in 1879 by members of the A.M.E. Zion denomination with the purpose of educating African Americans in the state of North Carolina. The first President of Livingstone College, Joseph Charles Price, world-renowned orator, philosopher, clergyman and civil rights crusader, studied theology at Lincoln University. Schools like Howard University, Fisk University, Shaw University, and later Livingstone College were able to lay the foundation the future schoolteachers, doctors, lawyers, and ministers of the Gospel needed for instruction, professional work, religious studies, and leadership of the Negro in rural and urban communities.

Under Price's leadership, Livingstone College excelled in teaching the fields of liberal arts, theology, scientific training, political science, and social responsibility.[41]

Joseph Charles Price's ability to cultivate this school of self-sufficiency illustrates the central role of education as a means for uplift of the race to a greater degree.

The star of achievement to which Joseph Charles Price, a black boy of those days, hitched his wagon was the founding of a school for colored youth a sort of black Harvard.[42]

This school produced the finest graduates, for example, Dr. Collins Lee, pastor of Metropolitan Wesley AME Zion Church; Dr. James E.K. Aggrey of Ghana, West Africa; and Bertha Kincaid Whittington, talented musician and mother-in-law to John Hope Franklin. Through the influence of Dr. Collins Lee, Kinard was able to bounce back from his rocky first year and a half at Howard and start over, gaining a football scholarship to attend Livingstone College in the spring of 1957. Kinard, being the first in his family to go to college, adjusted quickly. A history major, Kinard excelled in all of his courses:

American History, European History, American Government, Negroes in American History, American Literature, New Testament, Fundamentals of Speech, American Race Problems, Regional Geography, Principals of High School Teaching, Educational Psychology, and History of Social Thought.[43]

Kinard loved to learn and often attempted to improve himself by developing his skills. He encouraged others like his college roommate, Rev. Vernon A. Shannon, to take advantage of self-enhancement activities that were available to them. According to Shannon, Kinard had a big heart and sparked his interest in striving to use the college years to evolve. With profound and lucid insight, he outlined the friend he knew:

John was versatile; John was well read. He was articulate... I remember, not only were we classmates, we were roommates at Livingstone College... John ordered

these records and he said, "Shannon we have to listen to these records..." They were
records on enunciation and diction and reading. It was a record of someone reading
and we listened to the pronunciation records and we learned how to speak, and
other people became surprised because I came from a rural section... a country boy
and some people thought I was from Boston... John and I sat up late at night just
listening to someone else read and enunciate and we did that on our own. That was
not an assignment from an English teacher. We did that on our own... John could
stand before any audience.[44]

This small college town suited Kinard, providing fewer distractions
than Howard University. It allowed him to focus on achieving a college degree. In addition to excelling academically, Kinard was active in
college life and social activities early on. He lettered in track and football and was an All-Eastern Intercollegiate Athletic Conference guard.
He was also a member of the Student Council, and member of the campus chapter Lambda Psi of Omega Psi Phi Fraternity, Inc. which was active in leading the civil rights marches and protests in Salisbury, NC.

**John Kinard at a football game with Livingstone College friends wearing his
Omega Psi Phi Fraternity, Inc. sweater.** Kinard Collection.

As a student at Livingstone College, students on the campus were protected within the African American community of Salisbury, NC, as were most students in college towns around the country. According to students, during the fifties and sixties there was a special route followed in order to safely walk from campus to town. To buffer themselves students knew an unspoken reality.

As quiet as it's kept, in small college towns, in those days the people who were working in student activity and college affairs offices tried to protect us. In other words, we couldn't go off the campus in those days. We could not leave the campus unless we were in groups, and in our freshman year we were told that there were certain streets we could walk on and there were certain streets we could not walk on. For example, to go to town, which may have been about eight blocks from the campus, there was a certain route we had to go. We didn't understand that we had to go that certain route because somebody might do something to us as far as the racial tones were concerned... We just did what we were told to do... We were told that we had to go up Monroe Street, to Ellis, over Ellis to Innes and then walk up Innes. Know that was keeping us from going into the residential areas because Livingstone was situated in a very nice part of town...There were a lot of white people that lived around the campus and they didn't want us black children walking in front of their homes, so that's why they gave us a certain route to walk and we couldn't just go wherever we wanted and walk wherever we wanted to walk to go to town just those few blocks that was sort of protecting us...[45]

Black Students and the Civil Rights Movement

States like North and South Carolina were well known as the homesteads of white supremacist groups. The grip and actions of these supremacist groups, the anchor of white supremacy connected to old American values, was practiced all over the South, especially in Salisbury, NC. Its beliefs were still entrenched in the Civil War confederate values, retaliating against the consistent boycotts that were being staged and the groundbreaking decision of *Brown v. The Board of Education, Topeka, Kansas.*

Deepset in the Southern mystique is the notion that the South is more than just "different," that it is distinct from the rest of the nation, a sport, a freak, an inexplicable variant from the national norm. The South, so it goes, does more than speak differently; it thinks differently. Its apartness goes deeper than the visible elements of soil and sun and large black populations, into the innermost values of the region, into what Wilbur J. Cash called "The Mind of the South." The South as we are drawn to agree by each ugly headline has its own set of characteristics. Racism tops the list of course. But the South is also provincial, conservative, fundamentalist, nativist, violent, conformist, militarist.[46]

In 1955, most Black youth were affected by the Montgomery Bus Boycott led by the Montgomery Improvement Association and Dr. Martin Luther King, Jr. The catalyst of this boycott was an incident involving Rosa Parks, a seamstress, who, as she was returning home from work, was arrested for sitting in the front of the public bus that was reserved for white patrons. Another incident that significantly impacted Black youth was the murder of Emmet Till, a young African American teenager who was severely beaten and drowned for whistling at a white woman in Money, Mississippi. These movements inspired young educated college students all over the nation to get involved in the Civil Rights Movement. The grassroots efforts of the Civil Rights Movement were led by the convergence of the Lawyers' Committee for Civil Rights, Congress of Racial Equality, Student Nonviolent Coordinating Committee, Southern Christian Leadership Conference, National Association for the Advancement of Colored People, Legal Defense Fund, Negro American Labor Council, National Urban League, National Council of Negro Women, in addition to the divine nine black fraternities (Alpha Phi Alpha, Omega Psi Phi, Kappa Alpha Psi, Phi Beta Sigma, Iota Phi Theta) and sororities (Alpha Kappa Alpha, Delta Sigma Theta, Sigma Gamma Rho, Zeta Phi Beta).

A series of civil-rights laws were passed by Congress in the 1950's and 1960's, spurred; it appeared, by the intense black protest of those years: the Montgomery bus boycott, the sit-in movement, the Freedom Riders, the mass demonstrations in many southern cities. These laws forbade voting discrimination against blacks, banned literacy tests where a voter had a sixth-grade education, and enabled the registering of voters by special federal officials where a pattern of discrimination existed.[47]

Throughout Kinard's college years, the country was in an uproar of tension caused by racism and Jim Crow, which Kinard and others at Livingstone College and around the nation could never escape, and they all became involved in the struggle. The suffering and bitterness endured by Blacks all over the South led to anger and frustration that set in motion an organized movement with roots deeply ingrained in the theories of nonviolence.

Nonviolence as a method has within it the demand for terrible sacrifice and long suffering, but, as Gandhi has said, "Freedom does not drop from the sky." One has to struggle and be willing to die for it. J. Holmes Smith has indicated that he looks to the American Negro to assist in developing, along with the people of India, a new dynamic force for the solution of conflict that not merely will free these oppressed people but will set an example that may be the first step in freeing the world. Certainly, the Negro possesses qualities essential for nonviolent direct action.[48]

There were a series of incidents that occurred at Livingstone College that escalated the students' level of frustration. Dr. Samuel Varner, one of Kinard's fraternity brothers while at Livingstone College, remembers with keenness and heartfelt honesty:

We had a white teacher on campus. I used to play tennis with her early in the morning and the bread man used to come and bring bread to the campus... They came early in the morning, and every time they would see us playing tennis they would come up to the tennis court and look and they didn't say anything to us, but the college president got a letter from the bakery saying if the college wanted to continue to get bread from that bakery that white teacher could no longer play tennis with the black student on campus. Now that was one of the things. Another thing that happened was the music teacher at Livingstone would take us over to Catawba (White College in Salisbury) and if we had somebody on campus that the white students wanted to see (entertainer) they would come over from Catawba. The president got a letter about that. We had an exchange student from one of the Mennonite Colleges. A white student was sent down to Livingstone and he was a

*student on campus because his uncle taught at the seminary. So this white student
was on campus... the president also got a letter about that and after that a cross was
burned on the campus. There may have been other letters that I don't know about...
but we saw the cross afterwards. We didn't see it burning.*[49]

Crosses were burned to instill a level of fear in Blacks throughout the
South. The emergence of an urgency for Blacks to improve their conditions
as college students all over the state of North Carolina, including Salisbury,
was ignited by Dr. Martin Luther King, Jr.'s teachings and the success of the
Montgomery Bus Boycott, and the protests at North Carolina Agricultural
and Technical State University.

*On February 1, 1960, four students at North Carolina A& T College in Greensboro sat
down at a lunch counter in the F.W. Woolworth five-and-dime store in downtown
Greensboro, a facility at which service was available only to whites. The students
protested against being allowed to shop in the store but not being permitted to eat
at the store's lunch counter. The sit-in was peaceful. The four students Joseph McNeil,
Franklin McCain, David Richmond, and Ezell Blair, Jr., were not served, but they
remained at the counter until the store closed.*[50]

Like a wildfire, communities all over the South risked their lives to protest
injustice. Richard Stewart was a student at Livingstone College, member of
Omega Psi Phi Fraternity and President of the NAACP Livingstone College
campus chapter. He played a leading role in urging Livingstone College students to protest against disenfranchisement in Salisbury. This activist recalled the clear need for action in the region. He viewed the racist policies as
wrong and took action to demonstrate his responsibility as a student-leader:

*I was the organizer of the Livingstone Chapter of the NAACP. We had a relationship
with all of the college chapters of the NAACP. We would have various meetings and
held one state meeting at Livingstone College where students from all over came to
Livingstone, and then we would go to other college campuses for various activities.
Salisbury was the headquarters for one of the Klan groups. So they were known to
be in the area. John Kinard was in a class ahead of me. He worked with all of the
ministerial students. [John Kinard] was very supportive of us doing different things.*

He wasn't there to be arrested, but when we had boycotts and marches, he would participate. We were supposed to go march in Selma, Ala., but the teacher that was supposed to go as a chaperone backed down at the last minute, so we weren't allowed... Back in that day, students were very mannerly for the most part and if the school told them not to do something, for the most part, they wouldn't do it. But we sent telegrams when different things happened. We had a number of marches from the campus downtown to the main square, just general protesting of the segregation patterns.[51]

As a student at Livingstone College, Kinard and Vernon Shannon, his roommate, witnessed a lot of strong activism in the community of Salisbury, NC. As young ministers-in-training, they remember observing the leadership of the then President of Livingstone College, Dr. Samuel E. Duncan, as the voice of the college during this era. His support and protection of the students was vital in North Carolina, which most college presidents of Historically Black Colleges and Universities faced during these changing times. The students from Bennett College, Shaw University and Saint Augustine's College were also involved in the social injustices faced in their respective locations. He thoughtfully stroked his face and his strong jaw while reflecting matchless strength on issues that could not be ignored, Shannon's quiet fury explained in detail how:

Samuel E. Duncan was the president of Livingstone College during those years, and he was the one who interceded and intervened between the students and the public officials... We remember the KKK in large numbers in a large caravan driving down Monroe Street, which is right in front of the college... We saw that and we became enraged that the KKK would have the audacity to display their racism and their pretense of violence in our own campus community... And of course, several of the students from Livingstone College who participated in the demonstrations were jailed because of their participation ...[52]

In 1960, after graduating from Livingstone College, Kinard enrolled in graduate school and entered Hood Theological Seminary, also administered by the AME Zion Church located in Salisbury, NC. While at the seminary,

Kinard was ordained a minister and served as pastor of Pleasant Hill AME Zion Church in Wadesboro, NC. Wearing an impeccable suit and an above reproach stare, Shannon related how

> *John was the pastor of a congregation... He saw his role as that of empowering the people that he served, and I think that is leadership... His leadership was in the area of opening the eyes of the people that he served so that they will know and recognize the barriers that were before them—both visible and invisible—to arouse within them a discontent and dissatisfaction with the circumstances and conditions on which they had to live out their lives... John served that role well.*[53]

John Kinard with Hood Theological Seminary classmates: Vernon Shannon, Milton Williams, and Joe Lavie with Dr. Frank Brown, Dean of Hood Theological Seminary. Kinard Collection.

Many of the Hood Seminary students were active in the marches led by the school. The movement gained widespread momentum as students developed new forms of protest. Mass participation at the grassroots level was quite successful in the organized efforts of the movement. Read-ins at public libraries, wade-ins at public swimming pools, and kneel-ins and pray-ins were methods used by protestors.[54] Like many college and university students, strides were taken in militant protesting. Livingstone College student, Rev. Benjamin Elton Cox, was heavily involved in the militant group called the "Freedom Riders," that aggressively served like prisoners of war fighting against Jim Crow.

Ben Cox, who had spent four years at Salisbury's Livingstone College in the mid 1950's and who had vivid memories of the town's rigid color line, was as surprised as anyone. From Salisbury, the buses continued southward, through Rowan Mill, China Grove, and Kannapolis, and on to Charlotte.[55]

On May 4, 1961, two buses filled with CORE Freedom Riders set out on the route to desegregate southern towns beginning their journey in Washington, DC and arriving in New Orleans, LA. on May 17, 1961.[56] The efforts Livingstone College students made on February 28, 1962, were critical. The students of Livingstone College and Hood Theological Seminary brilliantly strategized the ways to desegregate this small town's movie theater adopting methods of militancy and civil disobedience as a means to challenge the segregated system. Rev. Richard Stewart was one of the activists, adamant in his memory of the past, who resolutely recounted in these words:

A native Buffalonian, I went to Livingstone in 1958 as a freshman theological student. By the early sixties, I was heavily involved in the Civil Rights Movement. I was one of those people who led the movement. I was one of seventeen students arrested in February of 1962 for trying to integrate the movie (theater) there in Salisbury. There was seventeen of us who went to jail on that evening. Following our release, all the movies, the hotels, the restaurants, just about everything was integrated because of the efforts of the students at Livingstone College and Hood Theological Seminary. Some of us were enrolled in the college and some of us were enrolled in the seminary. The women weren't arrested; that is kind of our fault. We probably kind of acted like male chauvinists. We didn't want the women to go through what we had heard about when you went to jail. The beatings and the abuse and those kinds of things, so the women we kinda had them there with us, but they didn't rush to be arrested for various reasons. After there were seventeen arrested the jails were full. They didn't arrest anyone else. We had been going for a month or so. We had been going to the theaters and to the restaurants... we were going like every day. We would go down and it came to a climax on that night. February 28th, is when we were told to leave the theater grounds or we would be arrested, and we chose not to leave. And after about an hour, they called the police on us, and four of us were taken to jail first. Word had gotten to Livingstone that we had gotten arrested and the entire school ran downtown to the movie theater and they joined the picket lines. Thirteen more were arrested and the police finally gave up, and so it was big news in Salisbury.[57]

There were also acts of violence that some of the nonviolent protesters faced. According to one protester he was burned by a white female patron of the movie theater in Salisbury:

And I was one of the students who went down to protest against the theater. Where we had to buy our tickets in the front and go to the back. I bought a ticket one day in front of the theater and stayed there, and a white lady came by and took a cigarette lighter and opened it and poured all the oil in her cigarette lighter on my head and lit it. I had a big Afro and it burned down to my scalp. Because of the protest movement, we were never to fight back or to do anything. I had to allow my hair to burn up; I couldn't put it out. That was part of the protest that we had to make.[58]

We had a student from Ahoskie, NC who was a light-complexioned student ...it was difficult to distinguish her from the whites... I remember the owner of the segregated theater walking up to that lady saying to her, "You don't have to demonstrate with these people; you don't have to go to the balcony. You can sit downstairs." And I remember how enraged she became. She said, "These are my people. I am one of them, and I might not be as dark in complexion as they are, but we are of the same DNA, the same hue..." And she continued to demonstrate with us. I remember those days.[59]

Women were just as active as men on the campuses of colleges during this era. A young woman, Marjorie Williams who entered Livingstone in 1960 from Washington, DC, was eager to take part in the struggle for equality. She admits to being somewhat naive to the Civil Rights Movement and her place in it as a protester until she became aware of her role in making a difference as a college student. She remembered the many incidents that clearly reflect on the concerns of every student—male or female.

When I went to college...I began to participate in the Civil Rights movement. We would have sit-ins, and in the state of North Carolina I'm sure you are familiar with A&T and the bus boycotts... sit-ins at the various department stores and lunch counters ... we were a part of that on the campus... While I was in high school I didn't pay that much attention to it... We were allowed on occasion to go to the theaters to the movie houses, but we had to sit up in the balcony ...during those days the black people in the South were used to doing certain things. They were used to sitting up in the balconies, so we just went up and sat on the balcony. As far as the lunch counters initially, we knew that we could go to Woolworth's, but we had a certain place we had to go around the back...[60]

Affecting change in using public facilities was influenced by the students of Livingstone College in Salisbury, NC, especially the out-of-state students. In the travel to college, she noted an important pattern. It was the tenor and tone for Marjorie Williams future role as a student civil rights advocate.

When we came into Salisbury on the train, those of us from New York, New Jersey, Philadelphia, Washington, most of us traveled to Salisbury on the same train and we knew when we got to Salisbury, to the train station there was a certain area where we could sit, and go to the bathroom, and drink water. But we couldn't go to another section, so we just did what we had to do and we didn't rock the boat. But when the Civil Rights Movement came, and the movement for college students came, we were right in there and we made a difference. We changed the whole tone and character for not only Salisbury but for the state of North Carolina, and it just traveled all over the country.[61]

Most northern Black students were able to use the same facilities as whites; however, not so in the South, where the law resisted the integration of public facilities. The support from many northern Blacks was effective due to the acceptance of the unfortunate conditions many Blacks faced.

Though plagued by separate and unequal housing, schools, and life chances, blacks outside the South seemed incapable of convincing local and national media, politicians, or even civil rights leaders that their concerns were as compelling as sharecroppers registering to vote for the first time in a century or as inspiring as college students sitting in at coffee shops and lunch counters. Free to use public accommodations and exercise their voting rights, northern blacks struggles seemed both less urgent and farther removed from the Deep South's civil rights battlefields. Ironically, the stark gap in white America's perceptions of black life in the North and the South during the early1960's was reflected in increasing support from northern liberals for southern civil rights organizations activism that included financial contributions, support from prominent intellectuals and artists, and the active participation of hundreds of white volunteers from far-flung parts of the nation who travelled south to join the movement. Down south the face of white resistance to waves of civil rights demonstrations, boycotts, and sit-ins could be seen in the frowning expressions of men and women, children and teenagers, the middle-aged and the elderly who wished to make the increasingly regular spectacles of black protest disappear.[62]

Williams, a young woman from an elite family in Washington, DC was no stranger to the importance of education, it was expected. She represented the few African Americans in the nation that could boast of being the third generation of degreed African Americans. Remembering leadership and responsibility, they were a daily part of her entire life. And she was committed to these values during her time at college. Without hesitation, she explained:

My family was somewhat unique in that my mother went to college. All of her sisters and brother went to college... My grandmother and grandfather went to college... They went to Tuskegee at that time... I guess it was Tuskegee Institute, which is known as Tuskegee University. I guess you would say I would be the third-generation college graduate in my family. There was no question about education. We knew that was expected of us, to go to college... After me, Livingstone became our family college. My brother went there, my sister went there. I had two cousins to go there, and other relatives... Livingstone at that time was a very small college... I learned independence there, I learned that I could succeed, I learned that I was capable... In my high school, at the time I went, black students didn't have that much of an opportunity in leadership positions because it was the early onset of integration. So, we had to sort of take the back seat, and maybe we were allowed to be a hall monitor or something very insignificant. But at Livingstone, we were able to take leadership positions. And of course, I started out as a leader on that campus. I didn't know I was going to be a leader, but one thing led to another and I enjoyed it so much... My experience there was just so meaningful and I think I came into my own personhood there at Livingstone College. I was president of the Women's Assembly, I was the secretary of my class, I belonged to Delta Sigma Theta Sorority there, and went on to be president of Delta Sigma Theta there...[63]

Like many female students, Williams faced sexism from different directions. As a popular young lady, she set an example that although women were the producers of babies, they could also produce ideas. She was often encouraged by other female leaders in the school's administration to excel and reach her fullest potential, thus changing campus stereotypes and generating more female campus leaders. So, when faced with opposition from the opposite sex, Williams tackled it head on. With a firm smile she expressed her understanding of the close link between her beliefs and her personal life:

If anything was going on, on the campus, Marjorie Williams was a part of it. As a matter of fact, one young fellow that used to try to make some time with me-we would call it boyfriends, I guess you would say-said, "You are in too many organizations. And when we get married you are not going to be able to do anything." And I said, "Brother, that's right, because I'm not marrying you, and don't you even look my way anymore... I am here to do business, I am here for leadership, I am here for an education, and you better get out of my way."[64]

Aspiring young Black women often faced attacks from men. They were scolded for being overly ambitious or when they were encouraged to succeed primarily for social mobility. Some males became domineering and easily offended by leadership traits in women and discouraged women. Other men did not believe women were born to lead. These sexist ideologies, overcome by Williams, led to weaker women of this same era on college campuses around the country to be overturned and affected by sexism. Many brilliant women with high expectations faced issues of early pregnancy, which forced them to leave school abruptly to become mothers or support their husbands' educational efforts gained through the college experience.[65]

With no rationale for achievement save material gain, they worried about how they were perceived as women at a time when their white peers were staying at home, having children, and scanning the shelves for the latest appliances. Negro women felt guilty about the education that they did have. [66] They were more conscious of the fact that accomplishments may prevent them from getting married. Yet economic exigency and the combined forces of sexism and racism kept propelling Black women forward. [67]

Conclusion

This period was instrumental in impacting many young men and women of all races, religions and nationalities. Of course, Kinard was involved in the causes of ending racial injustice, learning grassroots activism, organization and leadership skills, and using his voice as a minister to make a difference. The results of this development and proven militant strategies used during the Civil Rights struggle were integrated into Kinard's leadership characteristics that he utilized to become an effective leader. This turbulent era of his youth, growing up in Washington, DC and young adult life as a college student, shaped his destiny of activism.

Chapter 2

THE GREAT AWAKENING: PREPARATION FOR LEADERSHIP

Courting a Woman of Substance

Among the maples and oaks on the campus of Livingstone College, romantic relationships were developed and nurtured into marriage. Both hailing from the same hometown, John Kinard and Marjorie Williams met in Salisbury, NC. Then a graduate student at Hood Theological Seminary, earning a Masters of Divinity, Kinard worked on the campus as the dormitory director of Dodge Hall. Marjorie Williams was smooth spoken and gracefully effortless as she revealed meeting John Kinard:

> *John was a student at Hood Theological Seminary when I arrived on the campus of Livingstone College. I did not know him; he did not know me, but in those days, men who worked and attended Hood Seminary were given jobs on the campus if they wanted to... Some of them had churches, some of them had little odd jobs around town. But John was the dormitory director of the freshman (boys) dorm that was Dodge Hall, so I would see Mr. Kinard in the dormitory with the boys, telling the boys what to do, giving them direction and giving them instruction, monitoring*

them. And of course, I didn't think anything of him other than the fact that he was Mr. Kinard. That's how I met him as Mr. Kinard, the young man who was in charge of Dodge Hall.[1]

Both members of the African Methodist Episcopal Zion Church (AMEZ) (Kinard from Metropolitan Wesley and Williams from Galbrieth & Trinity, both located in Washington, DC), they often saw each other's familiar face when they went to worship, which was required for students on the campus. There was a close link between church and the academic community. One day at Moore's Chapel AME Zion Church the opportunity presented itself for Kinard and Williams to meet, socialize and become friends.

One Sunday I went to church at Moore's Chapel AME Zion Church down on Partee St., and he escorted some of the young men from his dormitory down there ... They were walking behind us and he would make little small talk to me. I would turn my head and make little small talk to him. It wasn't any big deal... I was with my friends. We sat in the front and after church he asked me if he could walk me back to the campus, and I said yes...We stood around talking. Then we went and had dinner in the cafeteria, and after that, we came out on the campus and talked some more. And that's how we began to develop a friendship—and of course, one thing led to another.[2]

From this point on, the friendship that developed was central to the later success of John Kinard. Kinard immediately recognized this woman of substance, and was captivated by her inner and outer beauty. It is further stated in Martin-Felton and Lowe's, *A Different Drummer: John Kinard and the Anacostia Museum 1967-1989* (1993), that during a two-year courtship, Kinard and Williams shared a loving relationship that would later lead to marriage on November 14, 1964, at Albright United Methodist Church in the District of Columbia. Kinard saw in Williams a female equal. She was one who shared similar views, values, life interests, a thirst for knowledge and global exposure. A member of the Black middle-class where tempered activism was a part of her family growing up, Williams witnessed her parents and grandparents as active participants in Washington, DC branches of organizations like the National Association for the Advancement of Colored People, National Urban League, National Association of Colored Women's Clubs, and the National Council of Negro Women. Her mother, Novella Sneed Williams-Martin (stenographer for the Department of Navy, Bureau of Medicine and Surgery), was a member of the Order of the Eastern Star and held a high position as Worthy Matron in the Gethsemane Chapter. Her father, Thomas Williams (claim supervisor for the Department of Treasury), and grandfather, William Moses Sneed (photographer for the US Department of Agriculture), also were actively involved in the Acacia Lodge of the Prince Hall Masons in Washington, DC. Williams was prepared early on to recognize the importance of leadership, global awareness and Black liberation, and she encouraged Kinard to walk into his destiny while courting her at Livingstone College and throughout their relationship. Williams, although younger than Kinard as a college student, was challenged to become an exceptional force, learning the uses of education as a strategy to reverse racial politics Black men and women faced throughout the country. Prior to their marriage, Kinard was

Pictured with co-workers, John Kinard serving as a wildland fire fighter with the USDA. Kinard Collection.

encouraged to explore the country as a wild land firefighter in California with the US Forest Service, helping to integrate the agency through the efforts of the presidency of John F. Kennedy in 1961. His expanding desire to serve the world can be seen geographically.

> *His summers have been spent working with the U.S. Forest Service in Northern California in 1961.*[3]

As a student at Livingstone College, in the midst of the John F. Kennedy administration in which President Kennedy challenged the country to "Ask not what your country can do for you, — Ask what you can do for your country,"[4] many African Americans yielded to this call to break the glass ceilings of exclusion they faced chiefly in education and employment. On the campus of Livingstone College, faculty member Dr. Berta Hamilton, a white female anthropologist, provided assistance in breaking these ceilings by offering students opportunities to integrate the federal government.

William Kinard on patrol in the Grand Teton National Park.
He was one of over forty African American students recruited from HBCUs that
integrated the professional Park Ranger series in 1962. Kinard Collection.

She also made other unique assignments available to students, that otherwise would never have sought out the employment of African American college students like Kinard, who would later become part of the great leadership of this country. This professor encouraged a world view Kinard had always embraced. He was a person who understood the need to experience the world, and all it had to offer, in new ways.

John and I pledged Omega the same time. John was behind me. I was number two and John was number three on line for Omega. John went to Crossroads the first year and then he gave me the book, the autobiography of Dr. Robinson, the man who discovered Operation Crossroads Africa. And I read that book, and after reading that book, I wanted to go. John F. Kennedy the president at the time wanted to buy out Crossroads but Dr. Robinson said, "No, don't buy out Crossroads. Start something similar to Crossroads." And he started the Peace Corps. So the Peace Corps was based on Crossroads and I became interested in Crossroads when John returned.[5]

We had a professor on campus, Dr. Hamilton, a white anthropologist. She came to Livingstone College to get black students involved in things that black students were not involved in. In those years, no black students were ever recruited to fight fires out in California. So she recruited John and got him going out there. The year before that, she recruited John and I to be counselors at a Jewish camp in Penn Yan, NY on Lake Seneca. And no blacks had ever been camp counselors in a Jewish camp before. So these are the kinds of things she did for us. When we went through the orientation for the camp swimming, canoeing, horseback riding, John could always pick up on things quicker than I could. I think the first night I was there, they taught us how to play chess and John got it quicker than I did. So then John taught me how to play chess, and then the next morning I think it was horseback riding—how to get on the horse, how to saddle a horse... He taught me. John was very smart. He just caught on to things quicker than I did. He knew about things that I didn't know about and he would help me a lot. I had a lot of respect for him because he was so smart, and he would teach me a lot. I would latch on to people I could learn from and John was one of them.[6]

In addition to these diverse opportunities in the United States, with the exception of the Deep South, Dr. Hamilton exposed Livingstone College students to rare opportunities that broadened their horizons, like traveling abroad. The following summer in 1962, after mourning the loss of his father, Robert Francis Kinard, Kinard became the first student from Livingstone College to be selected to participate in Operation Crossroads Africa. He was awarded a sponsorship through a special program sponsored by Hood Theological Seminary and the AME Zion Church.

AGGREY MEMORIAL DINNER AND
FELLOWSHIP

Sponsored By

THE OPERATION CROSSROADS AFRICA, INC.
COMMITTEE

WEDNESDAY, APRIL 24, 1963, at 7:30 P. M.

DR. JAMES E. K. AGGREY, 1875-1927

AGGREY MEMORIAL STUDENT UNION BUILDING
LIVINGSTONE COLLEGE
SALISBURY, NORTH CAROLINA

"Whoso Stoppeth His Ears At The Cry of The Poor He Also Shall Cry
Himself But Shall Not be Heard". PROVERBS 21:13

**Program from the Aggrey Memorial Dinner and Fellowship honoring
John Kinard from Washington, DC and Joyce Johnson from Buffalo, NY.
Livingstone's representatives to Operation Crossroads Africa, April 1963.
Kinard also went back to serve in 1964. Kinard Collection.**

THE GREAT AWAKENING: PREPARATION FOR LEADERSHIP

John Kinard became the first African American student from Livingstone to travel to participate with Operation Crossroads Africa. This was a singular honor that had a profound effect on the rest of his life. Founded by the late Reverend James H. Robinson, Operation Crossroads Africa takes students from the United States and Canada to Africa, where they work, study, build, and learn with African counterparts. That summer Kinard worked with American, Canadian and African students in Oldonia, Sambu, Tanzania, building a dining hall and dormitory at a youth leadership training center for the Masai people.[7]

Kinard and Operation Crossroads Africa

Operation Crossroads Africa (OCA) was founded by Dr. James H. Robinson, an African American and graduate of Lincoln University in 1935. He was an exceptional leader and heavily involved in the Civil Rights Movement in Harlem, NY. As a 1938 graduate of the Union Theological Seminary, Robinson later founded the Morningside Community Center and the Church of the Master the same year.

His first real kingdom for creative leadership was in Harlem. As soon as he graduated from Union Theological Seminary, he founded the Church of the Master, with his first congregation consisting of four adults and six children. Under his leadership it grew to three thousand men and women, and children of different races. As one inspiration led to another, Operation Crossroads Africa developed from one of the many projects of the Church of the Master. It has become his major interest, and he has recently resigned from the Church of the Master to give Crossroads his undivided attention.[8]

Dr. James Robinson, despite growing up poor in Knoxville, TN, was one of the many dynamic religious leaders of Harlem. As a result of Dr. Robinson's vision, mentorship, and energy, and the opportunity to work directly with him in Operation Crossroads Africa, Kinard's life was forever changed. This example of servant leadership, displayed in Robinson, provided Kinard, as a growing ministerial student, a different opportunity to serve mankind and to embrace multicultural forms of cultural education. Professor Leonard Jeffries was unambiguous in his memory about the era.

Founder of Operation Crossroads Africa, Dr. James Robinson.
Amistad Research Center.

John Kinard and I were on as leaders, we were also the field reps. And Rev. Robinson gave us this enormous task when you think about it; a tremendous responsibility for young black men dealing with the New Nations of Africa and the crisis that was there everywhere. The fact that we were given these positions was extraordinary. So, Africa was divided up in East Africa and Southern Africa was the realm of John Kinard. And West Africa and Central Africa particularly the French speaking areas was the realm of Leonard Jeffries. So, these two young black men were running around the African continent organizing programs in bringing over white and black Americans and Canadians to work in youth camps with Africans.[9]

... I was a leader of a group that went to Kenya. We worked with the Christian Council of Kenya on the Indian Ocean in Mombasa, building an athletic field and house for the caretaker of this conference center. After that, I enrolled at American University to work on a Ph.D. in Ethics in Washington. I had not gone to school more than a month, I believe, when Dr. James Robinson, the founder of Crossroads Africa, called me and asked me if I'd like to go to work for Crossroads Africa. I thought it was too good an opportunity to turn down, so my responsibility was to develop projects from Cairo to what's now Zimbabwe for American and Canadian students to work on with African students during their summer vacations, to get to know something about Africa. Now the basic philosophy of this program, as Robinson, who was a

black American born in Knoxville, Tennessee, as far as he was concerned, he felt that America had a backward view of Africa in terms of jungles and people living in a primitive style. That's the American vision as he saw it, and he wanted to create a situation where Americans, young people in America, could get together with young people in Africa and exchange ideas, because these young people in Africa would be leaders in those countries in the future. He wanted them to have a good relationship with Africa. So that's why he started this program among college students. So, I went to work developing projects, and the projects ranged from building dispensaries, hospitals, cutting roads, brick work, building a dormitory and a cafeteria. There were athletic programs; there were nursing programs. I mean I ran the gamut from A to Z.[10]

During this summer abroad, Kinard, a leader of his OCA group, wrote letters to Williams to nurture their relationship, capturing his greater appreciation for Africa and its people. He shared the amazing life experiences that OCA offered of which he took full advantage. In a letter written by John Kinard to Marjorie Williams, on July 21, 1962, he conveys some of his not-so-pleasant first experiences in Africa. The letters of John Kinard to Marjorie Williams Kinard have significance that transcend their utilization as historical documents. Indelibly, they are revealing on myriad personal levels. They are without equal as personal, social and cultural lenses into African American history at that time.

**John Kinard laying bricks to construct a building
for villagers in East Africa.** Kinard Collection.

My darling sweet (wife) Marjorie,

Honey I know that you must be bored especially during the day. I received three letters from you today and they were quite revealing. I don't remember telling you that I was having a good time. I must have been dreaming when I wrote that letter. Yes, I really was. Every day is a workday here; there is always something to take up my time. I returned from Uganda last night and discovered that the father of the girl who had the break down had come out here to get her. I was not alerted of his coming. He looked high and low for me but he couldn't find me because I was 400 miles away from her in Uganda. So, all day today was spent getting the two of them prepared to return to NY... I wish that I was coming myself. Honey I'm glad that you are taking care of all the things that need to be done for a marriage, because I wouldn't know where to begin. I'm lucky to have such a wonderful girl to get married to. All of my friends tell me that I'm a lucky man, and I am. I am very concerned about your being alone; if you had some little babies to take care of you would have more company. I know what you're thinking now, that I'll be making little trips all of the time. Well you're absolutely wrong because I intend to be there with you. I want our children to know their father and know him well. Surely you would want them to know, what a wonderful guy I am now wouldn't you sweetheart... Did you register for any diapers, I'll be glad to see the silver that you're interested in, it must be elegant to suit your taste...[11]

Campers and villagers washing dishes at Operation Crossroads Africa-East African campsite. Kinard Collection.

He also expresses in the next letter, dated August 1, 1962, his observances of indigenous African women, and the other African American students who were women on his team from Spelman and Dillard. The letters of John Kinard dispel one of the important myths about African Americans—the lack of love men had for women in their lives. In these letters, there is evidence of respect and high moral integrity for African American females. One example is the letter below in which negative conceptions about African American females are dispelled:

Dear Margie,

Seriously the girls here are quite shy, few of them are educated and they hold a subservient position compared to the boys. An African girl here would hardly ever start a conversation with a boy even of her own age. They are taught to respect men at all cost. The girls in our own group are quite hard workers. There are two Negro girls among us, one from Spelman and the other from Dillard. They are all nice girls, but not as nice and sweet as you are of that I am certain. We have just about completed one of the buildings that we started. Today we put the rafters of the roof on, by the end of next week we will be finished. We have many discussions here in the evening about everything and these African Teachers are very keen. I admire them very much, I think that in them Africa has a glorious future. I am confident that you are keeping yourself well and in your spare time reading a great deal. I realize now more than ever before that I must do much more reading on politics and world affairs than I have been in the past. Many questions I am unable to answer simply because they are of a precise and technical nature. People want to know things and it's my duty to be able to tell them. While working here I have a great deal of time to think about many things. I am happy in the thought that if a man or woman wants to they can become anything that they desire; however, discipline and common sense are to be greatly considered for one mistake can be fatal. It won't be long now before we shall be together and I feel that my experiences here in Africa have enlarged my love and concern for people and made me a much better individual of these things I am proud. I hope that you are working hard and learning all that you can for it will be important to us in the future. In certain areas, I see now where I should have studied much harder. Please give your family my fondest regards and remember that Africa is not some far off place where people are radically different...it is (culturally so much) nearer to us and Africans are as similar (as) the people around the corner in many respects.[12]

The experiences in OCA helped Kinard become exposed to the politics and history of Africa, which were much like America. The disenfranchisement of African Americans was similar to what the indigenous Africans faced during colonized rule. The leaders of this movement to decolonize during the 1950s and 1960s were attempting to reclaim their heritage taken during colonial rule.

British, French, Portuguese, Belgians, Spanish, Germans, Italians, all at one time or another, ruled parts of Africa or still continue to do so. Their methods might have varied, but their purpose was the same: to enrich themselves at the expense of their colonies.[13]

To finally realize decolonization, the indigenous African nations had to unite much like the Blacks in America. Just as African Americans grew tired of oppressive systems designed to paralyze growth, among the indigenous African people similar injustices were fought to overturn government through decolonization.

On the eve of the Second World War, only Liberia, Ethiopia and Egypt were independent. But by the end of 1959, that is twenty years later, there were nine independent African States: Egypt, Sudan, Morocco, Tunisia, Libya, Liberia, Ethiopia, Ghana, and Guinea. In 1960, Nigeria, the Congo, French Togoland, French Cameroons and Somalia achieved independence. They were followed, in 1961, by Sierra Leone, Tanganyika, Uganda, and Nyasaland. The independence of Kenya, Northern Rhodesia and Zanzibar cannot long be delayed.[14]

Kinard and Pan-Africanism

In order to achieve in the fight against this horrid system, brave leaders organized to unite Africa much like Blacks in the United States. To establish linkages between the African and African American suffering during this period of decolonization, one must look at slavery and its crippling impact on the psyche of the African slave throughout the African Diaspora. The energy found in Pan Africanism inspired a greater measure of cooperation between Africans and their descendants throughout the Diaspora to support the movement for self-government. The works of Marcus Garvey, with the Universal Negro Improvement Association (UNIA), and W.E.B. Dubois through the Pan African Congress developed the bridge for dialogue among the working, middle, and upper-class members of the race, engaging them all with exposure to the ideologies of Pan Africanism. Garvey, a West Indian leader from Kingston, Jamaica, made a unique impression nationally and internationally, which inspired leadership that would later give credence to the work in decolonizing Africa.

Garvey's near miraculous rise was a result of his ability to construct an interpretation of world events, particularly the First World War, which would suggest solutions to the problems blacks faced and counteract the increasing despair among blacks in the United States. He presented his ideas before a generation of blacks whose circumstances made them particularly receptive to his view of the world. His world was divided into race groups and distinct nationalities, struggling for preeminence. The First World War, in his view, had been a fratricidal war among Europeans for control over colonies in Africa and throughout the nonwhite world. He reasoned that in the future blacks in the vast Western Hemisphere diaspora that European expansion had created would find themselves in rapidly declining circumstances.[15]

The failure of the Garvey movement in the 1920's and the coming of the Depression forced the attention of most Negros in the United States closely upon their own country. Yet, if there was a decline in interest in Africa, coloured American influence on emerging African nationalism did not cease. Negro American missionary activity, orthodox and unorthodox, continued to influence the African political scene. Negro American schools and colleges still attracted increasing numbers of African students. As in the period before the First World War, this was one of the main ways in which Negro American ideas and methods of political organization entered Africa. This is obvious from the careers of Kwame Nkrumah, Nnamdi Azikiwe and Hastings Kamuzu Banda. Furthermore in South and Central Africa a glorified image of Negro American as the liberator of Africa from European imperialism developed between the 1920's when Aggrey visited Africa with the Phelps-Stokes Commission

THE MAN, THE MOVEMENT, THE MUSEUM

and was seen as the spearhead of a coloured American invasion of South Africa to the 1947 Madagascar Rising...[16]

Kinard, quite inspired by Garvey and his writings, eventually met Amy Jacques Garvey, Garvey's widow, on the many vacations he took to Kingston, Jamaica later in life. Influenced by the strategies of Black leadership and scholarship found through the works of W.E.B. Dubois, Paul Robeson, Ralph Bunche, Carter G. Woodson, and Marcus Garvey, African Nationalist leaders like Kwame Nkrumah and Nnamdi Azikiwe, were educated in America at Lincoln University and were hugely inspired by Pan-African ideologies. Azikiwe spent some time at Howard University and was a member of Phi Beta Sigma Fraternity Inc. Other African Nationalist leaders, greatly influenced by African American leaders, but uneducated in the American system like Jomo Kenyatta and Tom Mboya, were also great leaders who played a major role in bringing the reality of decolonization to Kenya. Nkrumah, considered the father of African Nationalism, came to America in 1935, and ten years later, used the education and experience gained to lead Ghana successfully to independence.

In May 1945, a few days after war ended in Europe a penniless black graduate sailed out of New York. Kwame Nkrumah was returning to the Old World after ten years in the United States. Two years later he arrived back in his native Africa and four years after that became "Leader of Government Business" in the newly created parliament of the Gold Coast. He was on his way to becoming the first black prime minister of a modern democracy. His success heralded a transformation of the face of Africa. In little more than a decade colonial governments gave way to independent ones in all but five white dominated states of Africa's Deep South. The Gold Coast, rechristened Ghana, led a cohort of the thirty-five African countries into the United Nations. Black people everywhere began to walk tall. The name of Nkrumah became familiar across the world.[17]

According to David Birmingham, in *Kwame Nkrumah: The Father of African Nationalism* (1998), President Nkrumah during the 1960s had a strong desire to see the rest of Africa liberated from colonial and settler domination. As African Nationalism penetrated the continent, the cross-cultural exchange of language was a barrier against the struggle for unity to quickly bring about decolonization in Africa and gain the wide indigenous support, as well as the hope gained through African American leadership. The emotional struggles faced in Ghana obtaining liberation from colonial rule were celebrated in 1957 (a year before the founding of OCA) with achieved independence. Captured in the writings of Dr. Martin Luther King Jr., who expresses his reflections on the independence celebration in which he took part in Ghana, further confirms how the strong connections of the global African diasporic achievements inspired Black civil rights leadership.

The minute I knew I was coming to Ghana I had a very deep emotional feeling. A new nation was being born. It symbolized the fact that a new order was coming into being and an older order was passing away. So, I was deeply concerned about it. I wanted to be involved in it, be a part of it, and notice the birth of this new nation with my own eyes. The trip, which included visits to other countries of Africa and several stops in Europe, was of tremendous cultural value and made possible many contacts of lasting significance. Struggling had been going on in Ghana for years. The British Empire saw that it could no longer rule the Gold Coast and agreed that on the sixth of March, 1957, it would release the nation. All of this was because of the persistent protest, the continual agitation, of Prime Minister Kwame Nkrumah and the other leaders who worked along with him and the masses of people who were willing to follow. So that day finally came. About midnight on a dark night in 1957, a new nation came into being. That was a great hour. As we walked out we noticed all over the polo grounds almost a half million people. They had waited for this hour and this moment for years. People came from all over the world's seventy nations to say to this new nation: "We greet you. And we give you our moral support. We hope for you God's guidance as you move now into the realm of independence." It was a beautiful experience to see some of the leading persons on the scene of civil rights in America on hand: to my left was Charles Diggs, to my right were Adam Powell, and Ralph Bunche. All of these people from America, Mordecai Johnson, Horace Mann Bond, A. Philip Randolph, then you looked out and saw the Vice President of the United States. [18]

The freedom of Ghana was realized, and although other African countries were hoping to follow suit, there were divisions that hindered their independence. These divisions were present in class, sex, education, religion, and language. Class, education, religion, and sex are four distinct dynamics, which are fought against constantly on a global level. Throughout colonization, in Africa, language barriers and traditions were lost through ancient styles of dialect. The thought process and teaching of indigenous African languages in adapting to imperialism has been a unique shortfall to overcome; however, decolonization neutralized the ability to reclaim what was once lost. Cheikh Anta Diop, a great African historian, has analyzed the importance of language on the African continent and its linguistic unity which once existed:

There is also a common linguistic background. The African languages constitute one linguistic family, as homogeneous as that of the Indo-European tongues. Nothing is easier than to set down the rules that allow transfer from a Zulu language (Bantu) to one of those of West Africa (Serer-Wolof, Peul), or even to ancient Egyptian (cf. L'Afrique Norie pre-coloniale, Part II). However, the old imperial languages, Sarakole in Ghana, Mandingo in Mali, Songhay in Koaga (Gao), have had their areas of extension sharply reduced today. At the apogee of these African empires, the imperial tongues, the languages of trade and government affairs, were the African languages themselves; even after the advent of Islam, Arabic always remained only the language of religion and erudition, as did Latin in Europe of the same period. With European occupation in the nineteenth century the official African languages were replaced by those of various "mother countries." Local dialects surfaced and vied against the older national cultural languages which had virtually submerged them. It became less and less necessary for civil administration, politics or social intercourse to learn the latter. The demands of daily life required learning the European languages; the disrepute of the old linguistic unities in our day reached its depth. While we may be able to build, a Federated African State covering all of the Black Continent on the basis of historical, psychological, economic and geographical unity, we will be forced, in order to complete such national unity and set it on a modern autochthonous cultural base, to recreate our linguistic unity through the choice of an appropriate African tongue promoted to the influence of a modern cultural language. Linguistic unity dominates all national life. Without it, national cultural unity is but fragile and illusory. The wranglings within a bilingual country, such as Belgium, illustrate the point.[19]

Being an African American, Kinard became familiar and empathetic to the lost culture. As a Cross roader, and scholar, Kinard learned to converse in some of the indigenous languages, and became fluent in Swahili and other East African languages. In addition to becoming familiar with the Black consciousness movement in America, Kinard also followed the African Nationalist movement while in Kenya. Taking part in building African communities, Kinard helped to provide and expand resources. Through this effort, Kinard and others answered Kennedy's call to represent the best of America. He accomplished this by aiding African communities through the efforts of James H. Robinson and Operation Crossroads Africa, founded in 1958. Explaining the prime motivation for John Kinard, Professor Leonard Jeffries noted with uncompromising personal insight:

The finished building project Kinard led in East Africa. This is an example of the work Operation Crossroads Africa did for the communities they served. They built a tropical storm-proof building for educational and community activities. Kinard Collection.

THE MAN, THE MOVEMENT, THE MUSEUM

Pan Africanism was the spirit that moved myself and your father (John Kinard), and others and particularly the preacher Rev. Dr. James H. Robinson who started the Operation Crossroads Africa program. He was motivated by thoughts of Pan Africanism.[20]

This integrated program founded on Pan Africanist ideals successfully completed multiple goals of leadership development, multicultural advocacy and aiding indigenous Africans to reclaim and rebuild their land. During the OCA application process, Crossroads students and leaders had represented all aspects of the United States and Canada. Selection was designed to provide a cross section of the most well-rounded and brilliant youth to represent the OCA program.

Cross roaders come to Africa not as missionaries or adventurers but as students who want to share ideas, expand intellectual vistas, examine cultures. Each group builds something with African colleagues a rest home, a clinic, a schoolroom which the Cross roaders leave behind as a symbol of friendship but the work project is really only a vehicle. The real goal is a chance for Africans and Americans to meet on a day to day, dirt-under-the fingernails relationship in which the carapace of custom and nicety is eventually pierced. From America come members of the Protestant, Jewish, Negro and Catholic tribes. In Africa, they work with Ibos and Kikuyus, Moslems or animists. For Africans, this provides a close-up look at young representatives of the world's most powerful and affluent society working with their hands and backs. To most Africans this is an eye-opener.[21]

In this program, the uniquely integrated setting of Black and white students interacting and living together outside the pressures of American society, aided further cross-cultural exchange in this experience. This became a source of rebirth and exposure to dispel myths through the separation of segregationist views found in the best universities involved in the OCA program. According to the OCA brochure, *Operation Crossroads Africa: A Decade of Achievement* (1968), undergraduate and graduate students, from over 105 schools found in America and Canada, were from:

THE GREAT AWAKENING: PREPARATION FOR LEADERSHIP

Albion College, Alma College, Amherst College, Atlanta University, Austin College, Barnard College, Bennett College, Bishop College, Brown University, Bucknell University, University of California Los Angeles, Cedar Crest College, Chatham College, Claremont College, Claremont Men's College, Clark College, Colgate University, Colorado State University, University of Colorado, Connecticut College, Cornell University, Dartmouth College, Defiance College, University of Denver, Dillard University, Emory University, Fisk University, Georgetown University, Goucher College, Hampton Institute, Howard University, Langston University, Lincoln University, Livingstone College, Massachusetts Institute of Technology, Morehouse College, Mount Holyoke, University of Notre Dame, Oberlin College etc. to name a few.

These schools contributed to a diversely populated program. As students applied and trained for OCA, they participated in orientation at different locations; however, the more popular locations were Rutgers University or the Washington National Cathedral. In preparation for the trips, reverse culture shock courses for the African American students were mandatory. Due to the enormous amount of indigenous Africans in Kenya, some of the white students faced emotional breakdowns coming from a majority environment to a minority setting. The training and empathy of the African American students was central to their emotional strength. Dr. Samuel Varner, one of Kinard's Livingstone College recruits, shares his experience with reverse culture shock first hand. With crystalline memory and incomparable personal insight, Dr. Samuel Varner recalled:

All fourteen of us met at Rutgers University. And we spent a week on campus and there were Africans who came to talk to us about Africa. We spent a lot of time working with the non-whites in the group on culture shock because that was what they were going to experience and it was interesting at how they experienced that, too. We left Rutgers University by plane from John F. Kennedy Airport. We went from there to Paris, France. We got off the plane in Paris, walked around and had a great time, then flew from Paris to Athens, got off the plane in Athens had a great time. We then landed in Egypt and couldn't get off of the plane because of the war that was going on. After that the plane landed in Kenya. When we got to Kenya we got on buses and on our way downtown. First of all, getting out of the airport, Kenyans stamped our passport, Kenyans put us on buses, Kenyans drove the buses, all the way downtown. The police were Kenyans. We got to the hotel; Kenyans were our host; and everybody was to go to their rooms, put their stuff down, and come back down to the lobby for lunch. We came back to the lobby for lunch, and the white kids couldn't eat, they couldn't talk. They were shell-shocked. For the first time, they were in a minority world—a non-white world. Everything was black. And it dawned on me that, that was what was going on. And that was my job to help them with the culture shock. Me and the two other African American girls were beside ourselves. We were so thrilled, so happy, so excited to be in Africa... I thought we were all that excited and happy, but they were not so. What I had to do was to tone down my excitement and help them to adjust. It was not easy. It was difficult because I had lived in a white world where I was the minority, and coming from Alabama, where I had been surrounded by the Ku Klux Klan and lived in terror. I wanted to laugh at them, really, but I couldn't do it because I was the leader of the group and they were my responsibility. These kids were sick; they were terrified. So, I had to help them to adjust. And the host bought us trays of fresh pineapple-all kinds of fruit, and delicacies to welcome you to Africa-and they couldn't eat it; and I was eating my head off. It was a great lesson. All of these kids were presidents of their student body, presidents of organizations back at their colleges. They were "A" students, and some of them had it in their minds, "How can a little black boy from Alabama lead them anywhere?" They really had that attitude. But when they got to Africa, they had to relinquish all of that. And I became their leader, they became dependent on me, and I realized that, too. And I needed that, because I had in my mind it was going to be difficult to lead some of those kids. One of those kids was the president of Toronto University's student body, and you know he knew it all. He spoke French and English, and one or two other languages. And he had had a crash course in Swahili, and he was anxious to get to Africa to show off his languages. And I thought it would be difficult for me to control a guy like that, but once he got to Africa and he experienced that shock, he was as meek and as mild as the rest of them.[22]

Rebuilding New Nations

Like the Peace Corps founded by President John F. Kennedy in 1961, Operation Crossroads Africa was used as a blueprint, of sorts, just as were other religious foreign mission programs that existed prior to the nineteenth century in America. In an address in June 1962, President Kennedy invited Cross roaders to the White House and stated in a tailored speech:

> *This group and this effort really were the progenitors of the Peace Corps. What this organization has been doing for a number of years led to the establishment of what I consider to be the most encouraging indication of the desire for service, not only in this country, but all around the world, that we have seen in recent years... So, I want you to know that in going to Africa you represent the best of our country. I know they will welcome you and I think that you will have the feeling of having served this country and in a broader sense the free community of people in a very crucial time.* [23]

This most effective model of cross-cultural exchange found in Operation Crossroads Africa, a privately funded organization, was used to help build a foundation for the Peace Corps. The design using the best of America's diverse youth population, and efforts, to successfully promote grassroots community development work through international collaborative efforts was studied by President Kennedy's administration. Dr. Robinson served as a valuable member of the Peace Corps Advisory Council, helping to guide its development and providing access for the Peace Corps to recruit students who completed summers abroad working within the OCA program.

Operation Crossroads Africa student construction crew that was supervised by John Kinard. Kinard Collection.

THE MAN, THE MOVEMENT, THE MUSEUM

In essence, OCA acted as a main reservoir for recruiting applicants into the Peace Corps. Robinson's recruitment of college students for the OCA summer experience made his program unique, unlike the Peace Corps requiring a longer commitment. This experience, working on a grassroots level, helped Kinard and other Cross roaders recognize the global struggle of which Blacks in the African Diaspora were victims. Knowing his efforts, in a small way, would aid in achieving the struggles of freedom in building modernized community resources, gave life meaning. Because of his relationship with Africa and Marjorie Williams' level of exposure, Kinard was excited to share his love affair with Africa and its people, and knew she would genuinely appreciate his journeys both intellectually and emotionally. In a letter to Marjorie Williams, Kinard shares some of his thoughts and experiences about Africa and its beauty of wild animals and game. He was most eager to recount his opportunity to meet and personally interact with African Nationalist Julius Nyerere, a powerful force in the fight for the liberation of Tanzania:

Dear Margie

I am miles away from the place I normally read your letters. If you can imagine it I am now resting in the attic of Lutheran Mission Station writing by the light of a flash light. We had a well spent day today. We are now on the edge of a crater where there is a high game reserve. Today for the first time I saw a lion resting in a tree, I was about 30 yards off. They were just as unconcerned about us as they could be. Honey I am so anxious to see you, however there is much to be learned here in Africa. I am certain that the prayers of people who love me have brought me this far along my journey. I have learned to love life with an affection that makes me want to help everybody. I feel that God has brought you and I together for an important occasion, and what that is I cannot imagine nor yet understand. I don't remember whether I told you or not but I had the pleasure of meeting Prime Minister (Rashidi) Kawawa and Julius Nyerere the top man here who led Tanganyika to Independence. The one high problem here is education presently is going so slowly sometimes it makes your heart ache to know that so much talent is being wasted and that's not all. South Africa and South West Africa will probably end up in massive violence and fighting on every street corner. I fear that day but I know that things must get worse before they ever get better. Honey it's going to take the sweat, toil and blood before our world becomes a peaceable place to live in where men and women will have no fear for their lives and possessions. Of this one thing, I am certain we will never see it in reality. Africa is the home of my forefathers, of this I am certain. Africans long for the day when their brothers in America shall return to Africa and help develop the land. [24]

Julius Nyerere was born to a tribal chief and his fifth wife in the region of Tanzania called Lake Victoria. Nyerere addressed the UN several times and finally, in 1961, gained his country's independence. Nyerere was well educated and attended Makerere University in Uganda and Edinburgh Universities.[25]

Kinard became familiar with the philosophies and dialogued with the then past Prime Minister Nyerere of Tanzania.

In traditional African society, everybody was a worker. There was no other way of earning a living for the community. Even the elder, who appeared to be enjoying himself without doing any work and for whom everybody else appeared to be working, had, in fact, worked hard all his younger days. The wealth he now appeared to possess was not his personally; it was only "his" as the elder of the group which had produced it. He was its guardian. The wealth itself gave him neither power nor prestige. The respect paid to him by the young was his because he was older than they, and had served his community longer; and the "poor" elder enjoyed as much respect in our society as the "rich" elder.[26]

The same enchanting and rare wildlife Kinard witnessed in Tanzania and Kenya was the same species Europeans had become fascinated with through the years to hunt for sport. One such American president, Theodore Roosevelt, safaried in this same area Kinard found himself.

President Theodore Roosevelt went on safari in Kenya. A preeminent conservationist, who greatly expanded the United States National Forest system and created many wildlife refuges, "Bwana Tumbo" or Mr. Stomach, as he was known in Kenya, was also a prolific hunter. The safari he mounted in 1909 was at the time the largest in scale and cost ever seen. It was financed by industrialist Andrew Carnegie...the Smithsonian Museum for whom he shot specimens for their collection and that of the American Museum of Natural History in New York. With hundreds of porters, gun bearers, cooks, and tent men, Roosevelt's safari traversed across Kenya, during which time he collected and shipped back to the museums specimens of nearly 5,000 mammals, 4,000 birds, 2,000 reptiles, and 500 fish, some of which are still on display. Roosevelt the hunter not only shot randomly at animals that he wounded and never finished, but in one location he killed nine white rhinos that included four females and a calf at a time when they were already extinct in southern Africa and nearly so in East Africa.[27]

Witnessing the natural habitat of Africa, and experiencing the traditions and culture of the native people was captivating for Kinard. While in Uganda, Zanzibar, Tanzania and Kenya, Kinard directly became familiar with the diverse offerings found in the geography, culture, and languages. The cuisine, architecture, art, traditions, music and dance were a refreshing change from the United States. These larger than life experiences would later benefit Kinard's leadership and understanding of multiculturalism. In this role as a participant in Crossroads, Kinard was able to work with indigenous African high school and college students on work projects. As the workdays passed, discussing, interpreting and exploring Africa through the life experiences of indigenous Africans offered Kinard a different view and perspective from the American propaganda displayed in negative and animalistic images depicted in Hollywood films. Kinard and other Americans grew up being only exposed to derogatory African portrayals in movies like *Tarzan*, which was filmed in Kenya.

I remember that when I was a boy I used to go see Tarzan movies on Saturday. White Tarzan used to beat up the black natives. I would sit there yelling, "Kill the beasts, kill the savages, kill 'em!" I was saying: Kill me. It was as if a Jewish boy watched Nazis taking Jews off to concentration camps and cheered them on. Today, I want the chief to beat the hell out of Tarzan and send him back to Europe.[28]

In the letter below, dated August 15, 1962, Kinard shares his excitement in getting an opportunity to climb Mt. Kilimanjaro and meet African Nationalists Jomo Kenyatta and Tom Mboya. He noted how his interest in African leadership was central to his trip to Africa:

THE GREAT AWAKENING: PREPARATION FOR LEADERSHIP

Dear Margie,

I received your letter and was thrilled as always to hear from you. I am now in the Post Office at Arusha. My time is very short. I am on my way to climb Kilimanjaro. By the time that you receive this letter I shall be down and in Nairobi. The trips up and down the mountain will take four days. Of course as you know this is the highest mountain in Africa going up 19,321 ft. I have just supplied myself with plenty of warm clothes. Please forgive this shabby writing. I am trying my best to do many things. Today I am having a meeting here with the Rotary Club. Please remember me to your parents. My love for you grows with the growing of age. I shall be with you soon. I'll be in Nairobi for a week where we'll hear Kenyatta and Tom Mboya. Be my love. Yours Forever, John.[29]

During the summer of 1962, Kinard was exposed to political problems and became sympathetic to the issues Africans faced as a whole after meeting with Jomo Kenyatta, Tom Mboya, and Julius Nyerere, three of the most phenomenal African Nationalists in this region of the continent. As a young, impressionable graduate student active in the Civil Rights Movement on a grassroots level in the States, this meeting with Jomo Kenyatta provided Kinard with a greater understanding of the legacy found in Pan-Africanism through the vehicle OCA. As an American learning about the ideologies of Pan-Africanism at Livingstone College through the efforts of Black Nationalists Dubois and Garvey, the shock of its use placed in action in another continent was remarkable to witness. This led to a wider thirst to inquire and investigate the political process in Africa, and to find similarities in the political suffering of the American Negro. After the summer of 1962, Kinard was recruited to promote OCA. Interviews and lectures were conducted. To spread the word of OCA was routine expectation when participants returned to the States. In the interview conducted with Kinard by the *Washington Post*, there are distinct differences in the way indigenous Africans interacted and discussed their African Nationalist ideologies with white Americans as opposed to the Black Americans. This was evident through the dialogues of John Kinard and David Davis, another Cross roader who worked in Somalia in 1962. Their very different views are precisely captured in the following quote:

Two area men have just returned from a summer in Africa, where one helped build a dormitory for a female police force and the other helped construct a soccer field. They enjoyed their trip so much they hope to return. ... The two men are John Kinard 26, of 712 12th St., S.E and David H. Davis 21 of Broad Brook Dr. in Bethesda who were in Kenya and the Somali republic respectively under the auspices of Operation Crossroads Africa. The organization sends young people to Africa each summer to help construct needed facilities...Both men said they had spent many hours discussing the American racial question. Kinard said many Kenyans are baffled by the apparent contradiction between what they hear about race prejudice in this country and the behavior of Americans who visit Kenya accepting Africans freely. Kenyans, he said are naturally attracted to Americans because of their openness and sociability. He said the English, who have governed Kenya as a colony for decades have never developed a rapport with the natives. David said Somalia "doesn't really want to come into the modern world." Its people, he said are most concerned with their pride, bravery, and generosity.[30]

Marjorie Anne Williams, John Kinard and Jessie B. Kinard at the graduation of John Kinard from Hood Theological Seminary in 1962. Kinard Collection.

THE GREAT AWAKENING: PREPARATION FOR LEADERSHIP

After returning from Africa to Hood Theological Seminary in the fall of 1962, Kinard gave interviews and lectures on his trip to recruit other students from Livingstone College and Hood Theological Seminary to become a part of the Operation Crossroads Africa experience. Explaining the benefits of this program through his broader view of the world, Kinard was able to recruit Samuel Varner and Joyce Johnson. On April 24, 1963, the college hosted the Aggrey Memorial Dinner and Fellowship sponsored by the Operation Crossroads Africa, Inc. Committee, named after Dr. James E. K. Aggrey, longtime professor at Livingstone College and native Ghanaian. He is memorialized at the college where the student union carries his name. At the Aggrey Memorial Student Union where this event was held, Kinard and Joyce Johnson (also a Kinard recruit) were highlighted as the 1963 Livingstone College Cross roaders to represent Livingstone College. Joyce Johnson, a native of Buffalo, NY, and an exceptional student, was a candidate for graduation that same year. The program for this important dinner noted:

> *Miss Johnson is an honor student, has been active in student life affairs, has proved herself to be a leader, and has, exerted a tremendous influence for good on the campus through her love for ideas and passionate concern for other people. Her memberships include, among others, the Women's Athletic Association, Julia B. Duncan Players, Student NEA, College Yearbook Staff, Dormitory Council, Senior Counselor, and Delta Sigma Theta Sorority Inc. Each summer during her college tenure she has taken special on-the-job training through the Office of Special Services to Students. She plans a career in teaching.* [31]

Kinard, during his lectures, exhibited the charisma of a preacher, connecting with his audience by sharing his personal experiences in Africa where he bonded with the indigenous African tribe, the Maasai people. He even shared the experience of drinking the blood of a bull to fully take part in embracing the cultural practices of indigenous Africans. He expressed his experience with celebration in order to recruit students to become a part of the OCA program. Several interviewees confirmed how Kinard was able to masterfully relate his experiences with everyone he spoke to about Africa.

I got involved because of some upper-class student named John Kinard, who had gone to Africa and who came back and talked about it. [He] made it seem exciting and that they wanted more students to go; and they wanted someone else to represent our school. And at the time, I thought I wanted to be a missionary like Missionary Jackson, who I thought was the most outstanding woman I had ever heard of in my life. And it seemed like an opportunity. [36]

After graduating in 1963 from Hood Theological Seminary, Kinard was invited to work with Dr. E. Franklin Jackson, the pastor of John Wesley AME Zion (the National Church of Zion Methodism), and well-known local civil rights leader who pastored one of the biggest and most influential churches in the city of Washington, DC. According to Pinkett's *National Church of Zion Methodism: A History of John Wesley AME Zion Church Washington, DC* (1989), Dr. Jackson was connected to the NAACP of Washington, DC and helped support local protests and boycotts, and more importantly, the integration of Glen Echo Amusement Park.

In 1959, Dr. Jackson was elected president of the District of Columbia Branch of the NAACP. Many members of John Wesley Church became active in the civil rights struggles of this organization under their pastor's leadership. Four of them Betty Holton, Emmer M. Lancaster, Dorothy Maultsby, and More D. Tolbert became members of the branch's executive committee. During the Jackson presidency the membership of the branch increased; some sixteen committees were appointed to work in various areas of civil rights efforts; numerous complaints were handled in areas of housing, employment, education, police brutality, and public accommodations; more blacks found employment opportunities in jobs that had previously been closed to them; and in August 1963 some 50,000 Washingtonians were largely mobilized by the branch to participate in the historic March on Washington that brought the civil rights movement to a climax. [33]

Kinard was thrilled to join the ministerial staff of such an influential minister; however, Kinard chose to pursue another opportunity to work with OCA. During this historic summer, so many young people—like Kinard's fiancé, Marjorie Williams—were striving to get involved in the March on Washington, one of the most historic events in American history.

> *As congress and the nation debated the proposed civil rights bill, the "March on Washington for Jobs and Freedom" occurred. Those who regarded the march as an idle threat were astounded to discover that even in the planning stages it was receiving broad support from many sectors of American life. The skillful organizing work of veteran labor leader A. Philip Randolph, ably assisted by Bayard Rustin, a young civil rights and peace activist, quickly produced a national demonstration that captured the attention of the American people. All major civil rights groups were joined by many religious, labor, and civic groups in planning and executing the gigantic demonstration. The American Jewish Congress, the National Conference of Catholics for Interracial Justice, the National Council of Churches, and the AFL-CIO Industrial Union Department were among the strong supporters of the march. On August 28, 1963 more than 200,000 blacks and whites from all over the United States staged the largest demonstration in the history of the nation's capital.* [34]

Hearing the speeches of Dr. Martin Luther King, Jr. and other civic leaders who marched in peace and solidarity with men and women of different races and creeds, Kinard, though busy in Africa becoming a community builder, was at the March on Washington in spirit. In a letter dated June 30, 1963, Kinard shares his travels to Mombasa, Kenya and anticipated independence for the decolonization of Kenya. In unclouded words he wrote:

My dearest Marjorie,

Sorry I've taken so long to write, I know however that you are waiting to hear from me. It has taken me some time to get settled and to start our work. We have a very fine group of students, no problems at all. We are clearing a weeded area for an athletic field. My dear this is a perfectly heavenly place just off the Indian Ocean, I can hear the waves roar and feel the wind blowing. Mombasa is a fine city however I haven't been in it since we arrived. We had church today and I preached... We met 6 African students and some Europeans today. We also met an American Missionary. Africa is not far and people are no different than people anywhere. They just do things different. You just must see Africa... We spent two days not far from Nairobi. Time is really flying and we have a lot of work to do. I do hope that we can finish some of it. It is indeed a great challenge for me to lead this group. Things are going on quite satisfactory. I am very pleased. The problems don't exceed my ability to deal with them. I am hoping for the best. Kenya should get its independence sometime this year and there is great anticipation in the country. It is really wonderful that we can live while so many advancements are being made in history. I have no news at all about the racial strife that is presently plaguing America... I love Africa and its varied cultures. I only hope that many of the problems that exist here will be readily solved. The problems are so complex and varied that they exceed the imagination in many instances.... Give all of our friends my deepest regards and say that Africa is on the move like a mighty wave and nothing on earth is strong enough to halt it, or alter its course.[35]

Kinard represents African Americans who believed that their fate was inextricably connected with the fate of the descendants of people throughout the African Diaspora. The attention of young, forward-thinking African American leaders concerned for the international freedom struggle was embraced by Black Nationalist Malcolm X. In Malcolm X's Grassroots Leadership Conference speech, "Message to the Grassroots," Kinard's work in OCA to help rebuild new African nations was made clearer:

Look at the American Revolution in 1776. That revolution was for what? For land. Why did they want land? Independence. How was it carried out? Bloodshed. Number one, it was based on land, the basis of independence. And the way they could get it was bloodshed... There has been a black revolution in Africa. In Kenya, the Mau Mau were revolutionary. They believed in scorched earth, they knocked everything aside that got in their way, and their revolution also was based on land, a desire for land. When you want a nation, that's called nationalism... All the revolutions that are going on in Asia and Africa today are based on what? Black Nationalism. A revolutionary is a black nationalist. He wants a nation... If you're afraid of Black Nationalism, you're afraid of revolution. And if you love revolution, you love Black Nationalism. [36]

Kinard had a strong faith in change and embraced this decolonization philosophy and rhetoric while in Africa. This radical and aggressive approach called nationalism was electrifying and courageously won favor in the hearts of the African leaders and people Kinard worked with as an OCA participant. In this July 4, 1963, letter below, Kinard shares his connection with the needs and desires of the indigenous people of Kenya. In magnetic words he wrote,

My dearest Marjorie,

I know that it takes about 6 days before my letters reach you, so I am writing you so that so much time won't expire between letters. I received your letter today. It was the second one. Honey, I am overjoyed at hearing from you, you are my strength, and I need you so much. You have strong faith, I can feel it. I'm glad that you are only taking one subject. I know that you will do well. I miss you more than you expect. I want so much to be near you, your companionship helps me be myself and realize my aims. I can't imagine myself without you. Honey I am working quite hard, things are progressing better than I had expected. Everybody in my group knows that you are my sweetheart. On Friday, I am going into Mombasa with one of the missionaries for a short while, to find out where the points of interest are. Tonight, one of the Educational Officers came out to talk to us about Kenyan Education and the many problems that they face. Kenya becomes independent on the 12th of December. Honey, I can see and feel the needs of the people here. One thing about exploitation is that the bitter end is not apparent. In spite of the problems you would love it here. People are like people everywhere only they perform the rudiments of life differently. It used to be bad for a man to be black however now that has changed. Now a black man can be himself without fear or intimidation. I am so glad that I am a black man for we have much to give the world. Coming into Kenya no one could get in on events as they take place from the ground floor. In 100 years, more will have happened than we can imagine. I look to the future with assurance that all will be well. The world can use us and many more like us, who want to serve mankind so that future generations will prosper. When a man is buried he can do no more here. Let's keep our lives on a firm foundation. Honey, you are right I don't hear much about what's going on in the U.S. however you can brief me on my return. Soon I'll come running back to you.[37]

In an August 4, 1963, letter to Marjorie Williams, Kinard shares his travels to Zanzibar. He is able to remark about his travels in a characteristically earnest light:

My darling Marjorie,

I am now in Zanzibar, you know the most amazing thing happened today, I spent almost $3 in stamps to send post cards and in my haste to get some things done the stamps that I had in my pocket stuck together. I sat down here to write and took the stamps out. I was shocked. I was so upset, I could have cried. I don't have much money anyway and this happens to my stamps...This is a delightful Island, many tourists come here. It used to be one of the slave ports. On Monday, the 5th I shall be on my way to Dar Es Salaam...There won't be any more parting like this again. We must be together. I hope that you are daily renewing your strength in school. You have a terrific schedule in working and going to school. I'm very proud of you honey and I always will be. There are so many things that I have to do that it gets like a circus. Nevertheless, this has been a great experience.[38]

Kinard's First Job

After leaving OCA in 1963, Kinard was inspired to seek his PhD. after graduating from Hood Theological Seminary. He headed back home to Washington, DC to attend American University and major in Ethics when Dr. Robinson contacted him and asked that he accept a full-time position with Crossroads making $6,000.00 per year.[39] According to the administrative records of OCA, Kinard worked under the direction of Dr. Robinson, assisting him with recruitment and projects. In a October 24, 1963, memorandum, Kinard's role was defined:

Mr. Kinard is being employed on this temporary basis for a period of eleven months to assist in the work of Operation Crossroads specifically to help to develop program and to supervise the program of the operation in East and Central Africa. His duty will also involve him in visitations to college and university campuses meeting with groups of clergymen, women's organizations, businessmen, etc., in developing contacts, recruitment and support for Crossroads. He will make a trip out to East Africa after the first of the year to plan the operations, to organize the projects and to meet with members of the Crossroads Committee in the various countries where we plan to have operations next summer. He has authority to explore and to recommend, but the final decision will be made back at the head office. In the summer, he will go back to Africa as Area Director in either East or Central Africa. This means that by the first of June he will be going back to Africa to check on the final arrangements before the arrival of the teams. He will work under the direction of the Director until such time as the Director deems it feasible to assign him to another staff member.[40]

Kinard had to move to New York and was the roommate of Leonard Jeffries, one of Kinard's oldest and closest friends, who would later become the head of Black Studies at San Jose State University in California. Jeffries was so inspired by his work in Africa that he left law school to attend Columbia University's Political Science program, where his dissertation studies focused on Sub-National Politics in the Ivory Coast Republic.[41] A graduate from Lafayette College, Jeffries self-confidently reminiscences about the first time he met Dr. James Robinson:

I went to Lafayette College for a football weekend in November (1960) and met Dr. James H. Robinson. When I went into the Chapel the church was run by students... I went to see the Chaplin to say hello... and when I walked in his door,

Drs. Rosalind and Leonard Jeffries met in Operation Crossroads Africa and became lifelong friends. This picture was taken on their wedding day with Dr. and Mrs. James H. Robinson, the founder of Operation Crossroads Africa. Kinard Collection.

he immediately pointed to me and said to the man sitting next to him that is the man for your program. We met. I carried Dr. Robinson's books and bag across the campus to the chapel where he was to speak before 1500 people, all of the students and the leaders of the college. But he spoke about the challenge of Africa. I'm sitting there unashamedly in tears. Because I was one of the only black persons in the audience and I was sure that that message, the "Challenge of Africa," was for me, even though he put it out there for everybody. It was a special message for me. And then those tears of joy were translated into a father-and-son relationship with Rev. Robinson. And I did not realize that now this was November 1960. I didn't know he had a daughter-father relationship with the woman that would later become eventually my wife. She had gone in 1960 to Nigeria; and how we met was in the same period of time Dr. Robinson said when you come back from Crossroads, you are supposed to speak and spread the word. So, I actually went to the Ivory Coast as a leader volunteer of the Crossroaders program, because it is a program where volunteers, they go into the field in African countries and work with African students building projects like schools, medical centers, and youth centers and what not. Rev. Robinson immediately saw me as a potential young man speaking French, who would be valuable in the French-speaking areas. So, in the summer of 1961, I went to the Ivory Coast Republic, which was French-speaking in West Africa, and was a key member of our team because I spoke French. And then when I came back at the end of the summer after the most fabulous traveling experience I could ever imagine, I was speaking and that's when I met my wife (Dr.) Rosalind Robinson Jeffries in the fall of 1961. The experience in Africa in 1961 was so extraordinary because your eyes were opened up to this wonderful world of people trying to change their lives through the new nations from scratch; and there you were on the ground floor with them participating and observing. So, my whole life was changed from that meeting with Dr. Robinson, and it is ironic and interesting that I call it the Robinson factor in my life...[42]

In 1963 and 1964, Kinard, along with Jeffries, assisted in the writing and design of recruitment material; attended meetings with colleges and universities; assisted preparing participant handbooks; and conducted presentations on OCA. In addition to soliciting funding, they also shared progress reports for existing sources like the Rotary clubs. The unique design of OCA was founded in the training in multicultural understanding. In order to confirm the transferred knowledge of the American and Canadian student participants, it was paramount that African customs be taught and respected. According to the OCA Participants Handbook, the use of courtesy when in Africa was of utmost importance.

Immediately upon arrival in each area, you should familiarize yourself with local conditions and conversations. Your African co-leader and your African counterparts in the project will be more than happy to help you in this task. Under no circumstances should you take liberties with these conventions and customs that are deeply rooted in the society in which you find yourself. There is no better way to gain the respect of Africans than by respecting their way of life. Courtesy and good manners are as important in Africa as they are in the United States and Canada. As foreigners, Cross roaders will have the added responsibility of being unofficial representatives of their countries and of walking in the glare of publicity and local attention. Your actions and your attitude will be observed by your hosts, who have their own traditions of customs, courtesy and conventions. Good taste and moderation in dress as well as politeness to and respect for your counterpart Cross roaders and indeed, all persons with whom you come in contact in Africa are the essential ingredients of a profitable and successful project and work camp experience.[43]

Kinard was excellent at custom courtesy, which is not a surprise. He was taught respect, courtesy, cultural niceties, and kindness at home from his parents. In addition to other OCA program responsibilities, Kinard oversaw the preparation of a 1,500-word research paper that had to be completed by every participant. This treatise included a bibliography divided up by country that helped to reaffirm their knowledge of African custom dynamics. The OCA Student Handbook outlined this requirement:

While it is impossible in a few months time to become thoroughly acquainted with Africa and its many facets, it is nevertheless possible for Cross roaders to receive a valuable introduction to the continent, read the basic facts of African history and geography and learn something about contemporary social, economic and political problems. A detailed, up to date bibliography is included at the end of the Handbook for this purpose. It is required that all Cross roaders submit a research paper on one of the topics proposed at the end of the handbook to us by June 1. This requirement will enable us to see the results of your independent study and will give you an opportunity to think intensively about an important aspect of Africa. The paper need not be long but it should not be less than 1500 words. It should contain evidence of thorough perseverance by the writer.[44]

At the height of militant activism during the early and mid-1960s, the American Civil Rights Movement, which fought against the inequalities and segregationist practices of American society, was still widely prevalent. Organized grassroots activism was alive and well; however, the leadership suffered from attacks and associations with communist activity. Many of the great Civil Rights leaders were accused of un-American behavior.

...Communists geared their work to Negro intellectuals and labor without realizing that the masses of Negros were unrelated...[45]

The Communist Party was alive and well all over the world. In many instances, the party exploited the use of African American civil rights leaders, which furthered their cause. This party was a threat to the United States and other republics due to the judgment and actions against the democratic belief systems. Paul Robeson, Martin Luther King Jr., Malcolm X, and many other active civil rights leaders, including Dr. James H. Robinson, were investigated by the federal government. Dr. Robinson was accused of associating with communist activities and organizations. He was also accused of teaching the OCA participants about Communism prior to reporting to Africa. In a testimony given by Rev. Robinson on May 5, 1964, to the House Un-American Activities Committee, Robinson shared his experience and background with Communism.

In his appearance before the committee on May 5, 1964, Mr. Robinson was asked questions concerning all officially cited or Communist-tinged groups with which, according to public accounts, he had at any time been affiliated. He answered all questions without resorting to constitutional privilege. Mr. Robinson testified that he was not and had never been a member of the Communist Party. He also stated that in the past he had believed in supporting and working with Communists when they were ostensibly working for things in which he believed peace, civil rights, and similar goals. He also testified, however, that his position on this subject had changed during the post-World War II years and that he no longer held this view. After explaining how he had become associated with several Communist or Communist-front organizations in the late thirties and early forties, Mr. Robinson was asked if his basic position or attitude at that time was that he would support an activity in which Communists were involved if he felt it served a cause he was interested in. He replied: I did in those days. I would not do it now. With age and experience, you learn a good many other things. But in those things, when I had just come to the Church of the Master and was involved in a great many things in the Harlem community, I did not make the same distinctions that I would now. At another point in his testimony, Mr. Robinson was asked whether, as advertised, he had been a speaker at a Forum for Victory sponsored by a Communist Party club in New York City in 1943. He said he did not definitively recall the event, but that he might have addressed the forum and if I spoke, and I may have spoken, it would have been because I was working strongly then with a great many Jewish groups against anti-Semitism. I would have spoken only for that reason and under those circumstances. I would say that at that time I believed if I could utilize the Communist Party for things that I believed in, although I knew it was a hazardous pursuit to try to do so, that I should try to do that. Mr. Robinson gave several examples of anti-Communist activities he had undertaken in recent years. In 1941, he had organized the African Academy of Art and Research in New York City, which was designed to serve as a hospitality center for African students studying in the United States. In the post-World War II years, when he learned that the Council on African Affairs, which he described as "a decided front organization," was attempting to involve African students in the United States in Communist activities, he utilized the African Academy of Art and Research to offset the operations of the Council on African Affairs. He also referred to the fact that he had written a pamphlet Love of This Land *at the request of Donald Stone, former Director of the Mutual Security Agency. This pamphlet, published in 1956, pointed out the progress that had been made in the United States in the area of race relations. It was designed to assist U.S. Government personnel serving overseas, particularly those working in Asia, in replying to criticisms about racial matters in the United States made by Communists and others.*[46]

Robinson and other civil rights leaders never thought there were possibilities of being accused of un-American behaviors when they invested so much time in making the country a fair and more civil place for African Americans.

Describing the training given voluntary workers in his Operation Crossroads Africa project, Mr. Robinson testified: We give great attention to this whole area in Crossroads when our people meet at Douglass College for Women at Rutgers for 7 days for their final preparation. We indicate what types of groups in the various countries of Africa might be leftwing or Communist and how they can answer them effectively and how they are going to avoid being pushed into a corner. We spend the whole day with the kind of problems they were going to face, what they should be reading, set up some potential situations that they might face, and help them to work out some of the answers, because they are going to be challenged all along the line, and especially by the leftwing students or the Communists. This is going to be more of a problem in the years to come, because the great wave of African students who have gone to East Germany or Moscow or Peking or Poland is just now this summer beginning to come back in any significant numbers. In 4 to 5 years that wave will reach its peak. So, we are trying to prepare our young people and our leaders, too, in what they can do to win an audience and get people to go along with them and see their view rather than just winning a battle.[47]

To accuse Robinson of connecting communist philosophies to the participants of OCA, including Kinard, Jeffries and others, was also addressed in this hearing. Robinson shared his reasons in discussing Communism to help American and Canadian OCA participants combat being questioned by African students in the African Youth Leadership Program. These students were educated in Germany and Moscow and influenced by Communism.

Referring to leaders of the civil rights movement in the United States who believe (as he does) that people can "logically" be civilly disobedient at times, Mr. Robinson stated: it is the obligation of the person who takes this stand to purge out of their ranks the kind of people who do not take it for the same good reasons of conscience and who try to use it to another advantage or infiltrate the movement for Communist ends. This is their responsibility to do this. They cannot hide under the fact that our cause is so good and our situation is so desperate that we will accept anybody on a brotherhood front movement to come in and help us. That will include Malcolm X, the Communists, and a good many other people with whom I would not agree under these circumstances. So I think the best thing to do is to prepare the minds of young people about what communism is and help them to face it.[48]

During this challenging time for Robinson, he depended on Kinard, Jeffries and others to run the OCA programs to avoid self-destruction. In this instance, Kinard provided the best of his abilities to become an integral part of his job, having a major role committed to this vehicle established to foster the tradition of Pan Africanism. Tenaciously, Kinard stated:

Those programs were without definition. It was whatever the country wanted. So, I would go out and talk to people in YMCA, YWCA, in government, in the ministries of sports activities, church ministries oh anybody who would want to talk about a project. They provide housing. We provided all of the food, and the youngsters slept in sleeping bags, so anywhere was fair game. I mean sleeping in the church! You know what I mean? Most of them didn't sleep in beds as it were; they slept on the ground somewhere. We brought our own food for ourselves and the Africans who worked with us. The youngsters also had a chance to visit another country—the Americans and Canadians. We stayed about two and a half months. We tried to finish a project. We tried not to carry these things on from year to year. So, I did that for a year. After I developed a project, the students then came to the project during the summer. Then I would go to these projects to see the problems and how they were working out. I did that for a year. I came back to Washington. As I indicated, we moved here to Anacostia in "62" and ...in September "63" to September "64"... I'm working on Crossroads. So, I began to look for a job. Robinson said, when I left New York I was in and out of the countryside. I really wasn't living in New York, but I did have an apartment there because I'd spent three months out, and if I came back here for three months, I was traveling to black colleges, trying to recruit students because that was our weakest point.[49]

Kinard was special to the OCA operation. Robinson knew his potential to inspire and gave him the most difficult job to recruit students from Historically Black Colleges and Universities (HBCUs) to become participants in OCA. As a graduate of an HBCU, who better to send than a charismatic, energetic, attractive, charming young man, who travelled all over the country to spread the word and promote OCA, a version of integrated Pan-Africanism? He inspired schools to fundraise and to send students. This crucial need to expose African American students to Africa was paramount to Robinson.

Say if we had 259 students, maybe 30 might be black students. Why? Because the student had to pay $900 at the time of what it costs to go, and Robinson felt you had to make some sacrifices. They made sacrifices, like asking sororities and fraternities on campus, doing car washes, selling newspapers, going to the businessmen in the town. That's how they raised this money, you see, so that rich students wouldn't have it over the poorer students. Usually the college minister would go by some method of selecting students to go on Crossroads. So trying to get black students to understand the value of this experience was a big job. So if I came back, it was trying to keep correspondence going with my African contacts, going to black colleges throughout the South, recruiting students, and then back to Africa and stopping in New York, that kind of thing... That was a consuming experience. But it was the experience of my life. I learned a great deal about myself, about the world as it is, how to get along with people, those kinds of things. And I am indebted to Robinson for that experience, also to Lindsey White, who suggested to Robinson that he pick me.[50]

In order to travel, Kinard was given funds to recruit for OCA. According to the administrative records of OCA, Kinard was provided with a budget for travel:

You are hereby authorized to give a cash travel advance to Mr. Kinard for his trip to Lincoln, Morgan and two or three colleges in Virginia. As he will be traveling mainly by bus and road to make his appointments, he will have to pay his travel expenses as he goes. He has been instructed in the proper accounting of the funds and will be gone for a week.[51]

Kinard also recruited at majority schools for Crossroads. According to OCA administrative records, his travel itinerary for May 1–11, 1964, indicated that Kinard traveled to Wisconsin to recruit along with Richard E. Pritchard of Westminster Presbyterian Church located in Madison, WI. Kinard attended six colleges, one in Iowa, and the Rotary Club. Stepping in for Dr. James Robinson the week of his trial with the House Un-American Activities Committee, Kinard spoke to large audiences, and was greeted with the same excitement that Dr. Robinson was given. The colleges where OCA recruited in Wisconsin were eagerly awaiting the opportunity to hear about the benefits of OCA. Kinard traveled Friday, May 1, 1964, from Newark, NJ to Chicago, IL and to his final destination of Madison, WI. Kinard visited first the University of Wisconsin at Madison, and while in Wisconsin, spoke to audiences at Ripon College in Ripon; Lawrence College in Appleton; Carroll College in Waukesha; Madison Rotary Club; University of Wisconsin at Milwaukee; and Dubuque University in Dubuque, Iowa. Kinard then returned to Carroll College in Waukesha to conduct OCA interviews.[52] According to an interoffice memorandum, the church and minister Pritchard funded Kinard's flight and shelter to recruit for OCA.[53]

Throughout his tenure at OCA, Kinard was learning, growing and developing the essence of his leadership style. This leadership prowess was manifested in his profession as a recruiter for OCA, as well as in his ability to assist his mother and his brothers, who were still in college. According to the OCA administrative records, Kinard sent a letter on January 15, 1964, to OCA's administrative director, and right hand of Dr. Robinson, his wife, in which he requested to have his earnings sent to his mother. With great care and concern he writes the following letter with very clear directions to assist his mother:

Dear Mrs. Robinson,

Will you please make out my next check to my mother, Mrs. Jessie B. Kinard; that is the check for February 1st. Instead of depositing the others, keep them on hand in case my mother should run into some unforeseen difficulty. In that case, I have instructed her to write you, however I'm rather certain that nothing will happen that can't wait until I return. Thank you very much. John Kinard [54]

With Kinard's father's death in 1962, his mother looked to him to assist her financially when needed. Jessie B. Kinard responded, in a letter dated February 10, 1964, thanking Mrs. Robinson for sending the salary of her son by mail. The response from Mrs. Jessie Kinard was revealing and straightforward:

THE MAN, THE MOVEMENT, THE MUSEUM

Dear Mrs. Robinson: I intended to have written you before now. To thank you for sending me John's salary. With 2 (two) young ones in college you can imagine how well it was appreciated. I didn't have any trouble getting it cashed. Only I had to forge his name of course as long as he don't mind it won't cause any trouble. And if you will please send me ½ (half) of his next pay. I think I'll be able to make it this month. I already know you and Dr. Robinson from hearing John's talk about you. I'm happy to know that he's affiliating with such nice very fine people, and he's doing such a lovely job, he likes it very much. Plus, it's adding so much to his education. It has been a struggle to get them where they are, it has begun to pay off. My Best to Dr. Robinson. Sincerely yours, Jessie Beulah Kinard. P.S. John requested that if I needed money you would send it to me.[55]

Kinard earned \$236.08 a month and instructed the OCA staff to send half of his pay totaling \$118.04. This lasted three months, from January to March, and possibly a longer length of time if subsequent records went unrecorded. In a letter written on February 28, 1964, Mrs. Jessie B. Kinard showed her gratitude and shared her expectations of Kinard, being the eldest son, to help provide for the home. Judiciously the mother of John Kinard wrote to the OCA administrators:

Dear Mrs. Robinson,

You're just so sweet and thankful, I certainly appreciate you arranged it so that the check was made out to me, I don't have words to express my gratitude, please accept my many thanks. I hope you will continue to send me ½ of John's pay until he arrives and I will be able to manage, what gives me consolation this struggle won't be forever. John has been, just as good as a husband, and I'm so glad that God has blessed us with you, and Dr. Robinson. I hope to meet you 2 [two] fine people one of these days. The next time he [Dr. Robinson] or you, are in Washington, I hope you can find a spare moment to drop in or call. I'll be so happy that you did. Lots of Love to you both, Sincerely, J. Beulah Kinard.[56]

Conclusion

Global unity among people of the world was the mission of OCA. Kinard found himself entrusted with huge responsibilities that contributed to the prospering development of his Pan-African education. The impact of OCA on Kinard, as well as on the other participants, was life changing and provided him with an explorer's outlook on his future. It made him realize that becoming a regular parish minister was something he would easily become bored with as a long-term career.

Chapter 3

THE BLACK CHURCH AND MODERN CIVIL RIGHTS

In 1964, Kinard moved back to Washington, DC from New York and embraced the energy of the sixties. This era brought forth a new and electrifying look, thought, and ideology channeled through its music, fashions, literature, history, and art. This period was also reflective of a surge that began to embrace the roots of Black culture. Kinard witnessed the historic changes in African freedom found in establishing new nations through decolonization, and full integration in America through the efforts of radical activism. Inquisitive and curious Blacks of this era were inspired to embrace their organic African heritage and take pride in the culture they created in America. African dresses, natural hairstyles, Black poetry and culture clubs were used as outlets of self-expression to learn about "blackness" which became quite popular around the nation.

Difficult to define as it is, the term "soul" was also used to characterize the singing and dancing and folkloric tradition of blacks, their history, the kind of cooking of a southern dish and a personal life style of staying free which was regarded as intensely and characteristically black. The concept was seen in the new appearance of blacks, which reflected their sense of identity and pride. Many blacks chose the natural look, no longer buying hair straightners. In dress, African fashions reflecting the ancestral heritage of Afro-Americans became very popular. This was enhanced by similar developments in Africa, inspired by the wave of independence of emergent African nations. Needless to say, this had an overall impact on the revival of black pride among the black Diaspora throughout the world.[1]

This new energy was also needed to help re-examine the outward image of Blacks and to take pride in their distinct African features (broad lips, nose, ears and dark skin) and recognize themselves as beautiful, unique and diverse. Thus, the internal transformation took root.

The ability to capture this powerful movement, to probe and study the image of African Americans and their self-worth and self-value changed the way Blacks viewed themselves, contrary to the historic perception of American society. This movement made African Americans face head on the historic public ridicule in art, history and the media through exaggerated depictions of negative images which caused problems within the African American community for generations.

The slogan "black is beautiful" meant that blackness and the Negro heritage were no longer to be seen as deficiencies, but as sources of pride; that oppression was a shame for the oppressor, not the victim; that strength and courage and all the noble qualities of the human race came not from superiority on an artificial social scale, but from the will to fight back, whatever the individual's social position was.[2]

This massive action, which restored dignity and an allegiance to promote Black image reform, was one of the last critical barriers African Americans defeated in striving to embrace a more acceptable image. Although the vestiges of oppression had not totally subsided, in some areas, the Black middle class forged ahead in desegregating the nation's majority white universities and white neighborhoods, while the poor among the race were still crippled by poverty and subconsciously produced apathy within.

The national government was not responsive enough, national politicians had other priorities, and by 1965 the disillusionment with both nonviolent tactics and the establishment political system was strong. Then came the mass uprisings in the urban ghettos of the North, in 1964, 1965, 1966, 1967, 1968. And "Black Power," the voice of Malcolm X, the mood of rebellion, not just against southern segregation but against the American system of racism, seen now to permeate the entire culture, its institutions, its thought, its day to day behavior, its most liberal manifestations. The new black mood expressed itself in many ways, and with a special militancy among the young. In the black colleges of the late sixties, there was a surface calm contrasting with the earlier excitement of the sit-ins, but underneath that exterior, in the attitudes of black students, dwelt an anger with the American system, more widespread, more profound, more portentous than the feeling of the early 1960's. And the young were influencing their elders, or perhaps acting out what their elders, under more constraint, found difficult to do.[3]

What was happening was not the abandonment of nonviolence as an ultimate principle; the new mood still did not lend itself to aggressive violence, and little of it was committed by blacks. Black activism was, rather, an acceptance of the self-defense against attack, and a readiness to turn to violence if it should ever become tactically feasible and if no alternatives remained. More significant, many blacks now saw neither political reforms, civil rights laws, executive orders, court decisions nor well publicized privileges for a few well-placed blacks as sufficient. The shift in emphasis was from changing laws to changing the relations of power and wealth in the society. To accomplish this goal would require a revolution in the way blacks, as well as whites, thought and felt about their racial identities.[4]

Still faced with the frustration of living generation after generation in poverty, many Blacks lacked the enthusiasm to progress. Although poor residents overcame class exclusion through the power of education, nonetheless, many Blacks embodied dispassionatelessness, lethargy and indifference. All over the nation, the mood of Black America was elevated with tension due to the lack of full justice throughout the collective Black community. In order to respond to the need for justice, a revolution was brewing within the urban Black community. Both Washington, DC and Newark had African American majorities. One-third of Philadelphia's population of two million people was

African American. "Inner Cities" in most major urban areas were already predominantly African American, and with the white rush to suburbia, African Americans in the next three decades would control the heart of our great cities.[5] Among the major cities like Harlem, Chicago and Los Angeles, none was as powerful as Washington, DC, the center of political protest, the headquarters of preeminent civil rights organizations, and home of Howard University, one of the leading institutions of intellectual and radical activism in the nation. This institution alone inspired the world to reignite its energy of activism through the Black Power Movement, led by Howard University's own, Stokley Carmichael, also known as Kwame Ture. In 1966, he was a leader in the Student Nonviolent Coordinating Committee, prior to his involvement in the Black Power Movement. The revolutionary ideologies among Black militant leaders and groups spoke of a new readiness created through the Black Power Movement. This ideology was built in the precise foundation that believed American society must make radical changes in economic and political institutions, in the value structure of society's culture, and develop strong efforts to heal the racial divide for a better understanding.[6] This movement, which some identify as a rebellion, was used against the marginal system of American government. During this period and prior, most civil rights activity focused on the South, and not on the problems of the poor in rural and urban America.

Malcolm X, the famous leader known for his sophisticated, yet poetic style of oratory, made an indelible mark on the consciousness of America by emphasizing the need to think critically about the current state of human rights and equality on a global level. He emphatically spoke out to Black America about Black pride, cultural understanding, community preservation and becoming your own master through intellectual liberation. This great awakening of Blackness—and the move to breathe new life into a generation of youth that embodied true progress and defined their own destinies based in activism—was not always the opportunity which Kinard embraced.

For these same youth have been shamed into distrusting his own capacity to grow and lead and articulate. He has been shamed from birth by his skin, his poverty, his ignorance, and even his speech.[7] Although the Black middle class made efforts to gain opportunities through the use of desegregation, the decay of the African American community rapidly spread, which destabilized the community within African American neighborhoods. Middle-class Blacks, who served as the only role models and links to resources some poor Blacks had growing up in segregated neighborhoods, were moving into the white communities in record numbers. Going to schools together with whites, even socializing together in the same movie theaters and restaurants, led to the deterioration of the African American community. This once economic and socially cooperative environment for African American residents that once provided highly used resources that profited from serving the Black community, was abandoned for the new and polished majority facilities. Although African Americans in record numbers flocked to majority communities across the nation, most of them were met with new barriers in these communities. They were unwelcomed by most established white residents.

> For almost a hundred years, Far Southeast had been a rigidly segregated area. White and black residents lived in separate districts with their own schools, churches, and clubs. In 1950, eighty-two out of every 100 people living in the section where white. In the next twenty years, a dramatic turnover of population took place. By 1970, only 15 out of every hundred people were white. The change took place as white families moved to suburban Prince Georges County, Maryland, and thousands of black families filled up the vast new apartment complexes and public housing projects recently built in Far Southeast Washington. The city government did very little to regulate urban growth in Far Southeast. It was slow to provide adequate city services to the area. Large sections had no sidewalks, schools were obsolete and overcrowded. Mass transportation across the river to downtown Washington remained poor. Large families needed places to play, schools, and medical services. When these services finally came, thousands of children had already grown up without them.[8]

In the midst of this tension, President Lyndon B. Johnson, who became the thirty-sixth president of the United States on November 22, 1963, after Kennedy's assassination, was the driving force in passing the needed legislation after much pressure induced by civil rights organizations. This helped to support the causes fought in Mississippi and other southern states, which made it difficult for American citizens of the African American race to vote in local and national elections, as well as full integration and equal accommodations. President Johnson worked hard with civil rights leaders to support the Civil Rights Act of 1964. This great celebration led to the first meeting of Dr. Martin Luther King Jr. and Malcolm X, who linked up at the US Capitol in Washington, DC.

After nearly eight years of verbal sparring through the media, two great African-American leaders, Martin Luther King Jr., and Malcolm X, finally met for the first and only time in Washington, DC, 26 March 1964. Both were attending the U.S. Senate's debate of the Civil Rights Bill. Initiated by Malcolm following Martin's press conference, the meeting was coincidental and brief. There was no time for substantive discussions between the two. They were photographed greeting each other warmly, smiling and shaking hands. The slim, six foot three inch Malcolm towered over the stocky, five foot eight-inch Martin. They walked together a few paces through the corridor, whispering to each other, as their followers and the media looked on with great interest. As they departed, Malcolm teasingly said, "Now you're going to get investigated." Although the media portrayed them as adversaries, Martin and Malcolm were actually fond of each other. There was no animosity between them. They saw each other as a fellow justice fighter, struggling against the same evil racism and for the same goal of freedom for African Americans.[9]

In 1965, the Voting Rights Act gave Blacks their rights to function with a sense of full citizenship, which affected Kinard and those in his community who were future leaders of the country and its ideals. After these acts were passed, it was clear to the nation that the Movement and its efforts had been realized. During this same period, in 1964 and 1965, the Johnson administration faced decisions to go to war. Many served the country well, just as they did in other ways to defend America.

At the end of December 1965, more than 20,000 African Americans were in Vietnam, including 16,531 in the army, 500 in the navy, 3,580 in the marines, and 908 in the air force.[10]

THE MAN, THE MOVEMENT, THE MUSEUM

The reaction to America at war in Vietnam led to one of the largest integrated mass protests in the nation. Protests were led by religious groups, college students and those "inductees" drafted to serve in the war.

One of the most sustained and effective forms of antiwar protest was the draft-resistance movement. Most poor whites and blacks stayed out of this movement; they found their own quiet ways of avoiding the draft, or they went into the service, despite a lack of enthusiasm for the war, because it was expected of them, because for many it meant economic and training opportunities that were closed to them in civilian life. White middle-class students formed the core of draft resisters... From mid-1964 to mid-1965, according to Justice Department figures, 380 prosecutions were begun against those who refused to be inducted; by mid-1968, the figure was 3,305. Mass protests were held outside induction centers with many of the demonstrators attacked by police and many arrested. The number of people trying in one way or another to avoid induction was much larger than the number prosecuted. In May 1969, the Oakland induction center, which had jurisdiction over draftees for all of northern California, reported that more than half the young men ordered to report for induction did not show up and refused to serve.[11]

Many mass anti-war demonstrations occurred across the country, especially in Washington, DC, to protest against the reasons America was involved. According to Kinard family folklore, the Kinard sons were overlooked to enlist due to a unique protest led by their mother, Jessie B. Kinard. Her decisions were calculated based on her political beliefs and her strong belief that her sons' education, which she worked so hard to support financially and emotionally, should not be interrupted. She wanted her sons to live and make a difference, and she refused to see her sons killed or to return home with disabilities. Jessie Beulah Kinard (affectionately known as "Tata" because of her love for sweet potatoes) was destined to protect her sons from harm. Digging deep into her South Carolinian roots, she, like many southern-raised Black women one generation removed from slavery, resorted to a unique cultural belief system found in root practices. She consulted a "root doctor" in order for her sons to be overlooked and not selected to enlist. Kinard was serving on and off in the State Department as an interpreter and was in Africa at the time of his physical for the military. William and George failed their physicals, both having flat feet. These three timely coincidences led to the Kinard sons, especially John who was newly married, to be exempt from death, psychological scars, or becoming a drug addict, which affected soldiers serving in the Vietnam War.

The Kinard Family members at Christmas from left to right: Kent Williams, Jessie B. Kinard, Novella Williams Martin, Robert Stanton, Marjorie Kinard, William Kinard. Kinard Collection.

Jessie Beulah Kinard was determined for her sons to be exempt from carrying this burden for America, for she knew of the burdens they had to carry just being Black men in America. Kinard's new wife, Marjorie Williams Kinard, had landed a job in the District of Columbia Public School System as a teacher at Goding, Brent, and Truesdall Elementary Schools. She was also becoming active in John Wesley Church, the NAACP and Delta Sigma Theta Sorority, Inc. She planned for the thrills of motherhood, and while Kinard decided to support her efforts, he became an active member in the NAACP and Omega Psi Phi Fraternity, Inc., holding membership in the Washington, DC Alumnus Chapter. His brother, William had graduated from Livingstone

College with a degree in chemistry, and landed a job as one of the first African American chemists to work for the US Department of Treasury, Alcohol Tobacco and Firearms Division; and George, who obtained a degree in business from Livingstone College, became a leading financial planner and bank manager for years at the Bank of America in San Diego, CA prior to his death.

> *When I first came back to Washington, the first job I got was an escort. I worked for the State Department, and I did one job. I took around the Attorney General from Sierra Leone. He wanted to go all over this country. He wanted to look at law schools and make contacts for students, his law students, to come to America for their graduate education. He also wanted to go to the Virgin Islands and Jamaica, so I had to go with him everywhere he went.[12]*

Kinard, well-travelled, well groomed, articulate and educated, worked with the State Department as an escort from January to August 1964, according to correspondence he wrote to Marjorie Kinard. With his work in Africa, his trained knowledge of African culture made him the perfect interpreter for African diplomats coming to the United States and its territories. Kinard continued his employment working with foreign diplomats with the State Department off and on prior to his death in 1989.

Investing in People: Preacher and Teacher

Kinard served as an assistant minister at Galbraith and John Wesley AME Zion churches in Washington, DC. According to Martin and Lowe (1993), in 1966, he was given the assignment of assistant pastor at John Wesley AME Zion church. This assignment and mentorship gained through Dr. E. Franklin Jackson, pastor of John Wesley Church at the time, was a quintessential opportunity for Kinard.[13] The church had a history of attracting the elite of Black Washingtonians as members, as well as prestigious presiding clergymen, such as James Edward Ellington, the father of Duke Ellington; Florence Letcher Toms, one of the founders of Delta Sigma Theta Sorority, Inc.; Ada Wormley of the Wormley family; and the families of distinguished war veterans like Clennie Murphy, Sr. and his wife Etta Murphy.[14] Kinard was mentored by Dr. E. Franklin Jackson who had been pastor of the church since 1952.

> *During Dr. Jackson's pastorate, John Wesley Church served as an important training ground for young pastors, who received opportunities as assistant pastors... In accordance with his strong interest in promoting interracial understanding, Dr. Jackson appointed three white assistant pastors, while they were students at the Wesley Theological School of American University. They were Rev. William G. Thompson, Rev. Douglass Harton, and Rev. Glenn Cannon.... Rev. Kinard and Rev. Robert L. White were assistant pastors during the final years of Dr. Jackson's pastorate.[15]*

As a member of the church's ministerial staff, Kinard observed it as a major hub for political activity, which helped him capture a rounded view of church dynamics and its use in the broader progression of Civil Rights. It is safe to say that Kinard, although young, was quite ambitious and well-rounded with a bright future. This opportunity only refined his skills and gifts. This church prepared Kinard to have a solid and prosperous ministerial career, to obtain his own church appointment as pastor, and to work as a community activist.

> *The term "church-based activism" usually refers to very extroverted forms of religious presence forms that somehow benefit not only congregation members but people who do not belong to the church. Churches with food pantries and shelters for survivors of domestic abuse, or that build homes and run welfare-to-work programs, or whose leaders organize marches and protests, are considered "activist." This understanding of religious activism is partly the legacy of the civil rights movement, during which African American churches transmitted a powerful normative message about the ability and necessity of religious institutions to work in some way for social change.[16]*

This church provided any minister in training a great advantage to learn at the helm of a remarkable theologian well known throughout the country. Dr.

THE MAN, THE MOVEMENT, THE MUSEUM

Jackson possessed the magnetic appeal and allure to maintain a membership of over four thousand. Most of the affluent pastors of John Wesley followed a pattern where they became AME Zion bishops. Jackson's ability to preach on a grand scale, lead a large affluent membership and engage in local civil rights activism in Washington, DC made him stand out among the greater theologians who preceded him.

> *It is agreed that the Negro church and its leader, the preacher, play an important role in community leadership. Many leaders during slavery and Reconstruction were ministers. "In practically all rural areas, and in many of the urban ones, the preacher stood out as the acknowledged local leader of the Negroes." Yet there is also general agreement that the Negro cleric given the relatively extensive resources of the church has failed to realize his potential as a race leader.*[17]

As president of the NAACP local chapter elected in 1959, Jackson helped Kinard understand the cost of commitment, sacrifice and dedication to the cause for African Americans. Jackson merely re-emphasized the teachings of Pan Africanism taught to him by Dr. James H. Robinson, which was to stay involved and make a difference by collective restoration. Jackson taught Kinard the sacred mission of activism. It was under Jackson's leadership in the NAACP that he reinstated his membership in organized political activism from his college days as a member of the Livingstone College branch in Salisbury, NC.

> *Although most black clergymen remained uninvolved in the civil rights movement, the impressive minority who were involved were of crucial importance to it. Ministers played significant roles in voter registration drives, sit-ins, marches, selective buying campaigns, civil rights organizations, etc. The frequent bombings of churches and homes of black clergy during the 1950's and 1960's indicate the importance of ministerial activities in civil rights. The ministers involved in civil rights were typically younger and better educated than those uninvolved. In recent research, education was consistently shown to be a crucial variable in civil rights involvement. Also, the role of the well-educated, the intelligentsia, was shown to be crucial in revolutions and social movements. There is no doubt that the black*

ministers "contributed both techniques and ideology to the current civil rights movement." These ministers are the "modern day abolitionists," the Nat Turners and the Denmark Veseys of our times.[18]

According to Harold Pinkett, John Wesley Church historian, Jackson was originally from Pensacola, FL and was educated at Florida A&M College, Edward Waters College, Tuskegee Institute and the University of Buffalo. At John Wesley, his community outreach efforts flourished with members' support. As a service to the community, the church initiated a Head Start Program and preschool that served sixty children. There were also senior lunch programs, which were very successful.[19]

The Kinard Family at the John Wesley AME Zion Church Pastor's Appreciation.
Kinard Collection.

After Dr. Jackson's death in 1975, Kinard served as the pastor of John Wesley AME Zion Church for a month and helped the new pastor, Rev. Cecil Bishop (who later became Bishop) to transition to his role. Kinard served as the assistant pastor until 1989, working with the membership directly as time progressed.[20] He was a favorite of the membership because of his longstanding connections with the older families of the church and his impact as a spiritual teacher. Barbara Murphy, a longtime member of John Wesley Church, viewed Kinard as a consistent force within the body of the church. The worship service and the effectiveness of Kinard's Bible teachings had a huge impact on how she raised her family. She was effective, compelling, and forceful as she shared her appreciation for John Kinard's spiritual mentorship:

> He would always be on programs, and I can remember him in prayer meeting. John was very serious. One thing I learned from him, usually you hear ... people who have been to church service, they would say, "Oh you missed the service today. It was good." And they would ask you, "What did they talk about?" And you couldn't remember, but it was a good service. With John, he used to question me. He would say, "Well what was the sermon about?" And I said, "I don't know," And so he said, "You ought to write it down." And from that point on, whenever I'm in church, and there's a sermon, I am always writing down what the sermon is about, from that point on. And it makes sense because it's not that you didn't remember, but I could not tell you verbatim what the person said.[21]

Barbara Murphy, a native Washingtonian and member of the John Wesley Church since childhood, had a special connection to the church holistically. Because of her dedication and longstanding walk with Methodism, Murphy shares how Kinard's sermons were an inspiration. She also shares experiences of how he would get so emotional about his message, he would cry. In keen and revealing words she noted:

> He was very serious about his sermons and he was serious about the African American race. Sometimes he would get very filled up when he started to talk about us as a race, and how we should stick together, and how we should help one another and he would get filled up with it.[22]

Kinard's actions were also an impetus for real change to the church members:

I used to serve the homeless...with my family. And there was Central Union on R Street, and some of the men would come over there. So, I met Anthony Wright and two other guys. So, John would mention and said you wouldn't have them out to your house, and it would bother me because I thought I was a Christian and this particular time...

It was the Fourth of July and I said, "Would you all like to come to our house for a picnic?" There were three of them, and they said yes. And I invited them out, and I was kind of uncomfortable because I said, "Hey, I don't know them." But then I just said, "They're human beings and you have to trust them." This was from John's sermon.

So, they came out, and from that point on Anthony Wright we got so close, I just sort of adopted him like a son. And he still comes by. So that was an experience that I got from one of John's sermons. He inspired me... He awakened my conscience because if I claimed to love all people and to be a Christian and was following God's word, then I didn't want to be a hypocrite. So, I listened to his sermons and I know he was sincere, and that was one of John's patterns. He helped everybody.[23]

Kinard's service as a minister far exceeded just preaching in the pulpit and mentoring the membership. He conducted weekly Bible study and served as an adviser during crisis intervention. One example of this unwavering investment in helping people was the family neighbor, Mrs. Gaston, a Thirteenth Street resident. According to James Banks, John Kinard insisted that he help save the home of his mother's neighbor. In vivid and meaningful terms James Banks expressed how Kinard changed the lives of people on a personal level:

I was privileged to serve as co-chairman of the Anacostia Coordinating Council [an organization that] John served as the chair-person... This organization under John Kinard's leadership helped to get the Metro started in Anacostia and organized a plan to make sure that would happen. As a consequence the Metro was good for the community and the interest of the residents was protected. The main thing that I remember about John was the concern that he showed for others consistently, and I want to share with you a story. One night at about 11:30 when I was sound asleep, John called me. And he said, "Hey Jim, I got a problem and I need your help." I said,

"John, do you realize that it is 11:30 at night and I was asleep?" He said, "Yeah, but this is an emergency." I said, "Okay. What it is?" He said, "I ran into a former neighbor of mine in the Safeway tonight and her house is going to be put up for auction tomorrow at 10:00 a.m." He said, "I want you to do something about it." I said, "John what do you want me to do?" He said, "I want you to save the lady's house." He said, "You can do it." So, I said, "Okay, I'll see what I can do." The next morning when I got up, I called somebody that I knew, and sure enough by 10:00 a.m. the auction had been called off. And I went out to see the lady, and together we worked out a plan and she ultimately paid off her mortgage and she moved from a mortgage to no mortgage. But the main thing is, not so much that the lady saved her house, which was of course important, but John offered an opportunity for me to be helpful to a lady that I didn't know, and he offered her an opportunity to know me, and together we became neighbors, and I found that to be the story of John's life.[24]

On another occasion, Kinard stepped in when a church member and daughter of a family friend, Stanice Anderson, daughter of former DC City Councilman Stanley Anderson, was struggling to end her battle with drugs. She called not the pastor of the church but the assistant pastor, John Kinard. Anderson grew up in an upper-middle class home. In a heart-wrenchingly honest memoir, she tells her journey from addiction to triumph. Stanice found herself in a violently abusive relationship, which made her soul weep for a way out:

I always thought of a bathroom as a safe place until the day it became my prison. As my T-shirt clung to my body with sweat, I gasped to find enough of the hot air in the tiny windowless bathroom to fill my lungs. I sat on the toilet lid and strained to hear John's movements in the other room. He was my dealer, my lover, and later became my husband. My stomach cramped. My head throbbed. My bones ached from the inside out reminding me that it was time for my next shot of heroin. I had to figure out a way to get past John and make my buy since he was determined not to give me any more dope. Holding me hostage in the bathroom was John's idea of an addiction treatment program. Every time I opened the door and attempted to walk out, he would beat me with his fists back into the bathroom.[25]

During this pivotal juncture in the life of Stanice Anderson, she dug deep for a gleam of hope. The high road she chose, filled with adversity and temptation, was achieved. She succeeded with the help of John Kinard and a larger support system she had abandoned for years.

> *Although now with the Lord, I thank God for Reverend John Kinard, assistant pastor of John Wesley A.M.E. Zion Church in Washington, DC, who when I placed a desperate call for help many years ago canceled all his appointments and got me into a drug treatment center.*[26]

On other occasions, Kinard served as a mentor to young, emerging leaders entering into the community, such as Butch Hopkins. Hopkins was assertive and affirming when he spoke about Kinard's contributions to his life:

> *I had the pleasure of meeting John Kinard in 1969, which was about two years after he had taken over Directorship of the Anacostia Museum. I came to know John sort of as a privilege initially because John was one of my board of directors at the Anacostia Economic Development Corporation. And John had been formally with the Anacostia Citizens Emergence Association, which was the organizing body of the Anacostia Economic Development Corporation. I used to refer to John as one of the big four. Those were the people in the Anacostia Community that I thought, that if I didn't touch base with them, I shouldn't do anything. And that big four consisted of Jim Speight, Theresa Jones, Doug Moore, and of course, John. But it soon became a pleasure to know John, because he was always there for us. It became a time in late 1974 when we did not have any funding to continue our programs, but there was a proposal pending with the federal government to enable AEDC to become a community development corporation. Well the federal government kept saying, "Does your group meet on regular basis?" And at that time, I was practicing law downtown and I would call John, and I would say, "John, do we meet on a regular basis?" And John would say, "Of course we meet on a regular basis, Butch. We meet whenever you say we should meet." So, I said, "Well John, they want to come out and take a look and see if we are still active and meeting and taking care of the economic issues that relate to Anacostia Far Southeast." And John, of course, said, "That is not a problem. We will schedule a meeting when you say so." And of course we did so, and he got the board members together. And shortly thereafter the federal government saw fit to provide us in 1975 with a planning grant to become*

a community development corporation. That is just one of John's efforts on behalf of AEDC and on behalf of the Anacostia Community. I think we are all pretty well aware of what John has meant to the Anacostia Community and what he has meant to the greater Black society and culture, but those of us who had the privilege, and the pleasure of knowing him on an individual basis—of seeking his wisdom and counsel, and his advice—we have sort of come away with a little bit more. And I think what we have come away with is the fact that John did not tolerate any BS. If he thought you were saying something to him that did not make sense, he told you it didn't make sense. When you sought advice from him, he didn't tell you it didn't make sense. He didn't tell you that which you may have wanted to hear, but he would tell us, what he believed was right, and what he knew to be the right course of action to take. His honesty and integrity and his respect for the people that he knew in the community in which he lived, is something that we should all emulate.[27]

In addition to these and other heroic acts that go unrecorded, Kinard stepped in and helped troubled youth. As a community activist, working with misled youth, he made a difference as a mentor, role model and resource who used his talent as an advocate to make a difference to the people of Anacostia. At times, he got people jobs and out of jail. In a tone that was fervent and deeply-rooted in devotion an interviewee verbalized Kinard's qualities as a community leader:

He had an uncanny love for people and a commitment to whatever he set out to do. He was just a committed person and he generally loved people. And I guess that was his uniqueness because, many a night people would call John because their son would be locked up. He would get up out of the bed and go over to the jail to talk to boys, to talk to girls. Girls would be on drugs, and parents would call John. John would get up out of his bed and go to minister to people. I mean he was an unusual kind of person. He just had a commitment to life and he had a commitment to others. He was a born leader.... When we got married, of course you know he was a minister, an AME Zion minister in addition to being the director of the Anacostia Museum. He worked at Southeast House before the Anacostia Museum was even a concept. He led international dignitaries around the entire United States, he worked for the State Department, so his leadership was unparalleled.[28]

Lastly, Kinard helped to support other activists within the community who fought against injustice. Theresa Jones, another organizer in the community, was a leader of a tenant association within the public housing areas located in Anacostia and far southeast. She worked with Kinard on many committees, boards and coalitions. He supported her efforts in leading a rent strike during the late 1960s to the early 1970s. She insisted that:

...when I was very young, just out of school and had gotten married and was having children, I lived in public housing. And one of the things that made me mad, was the way people were getting treated and not told what their rights were. And as my awareness grew, I started to organize tenant organizations and because there is power in numbers. We had gotten to the place where we had gotten so many groups together, so we would talk back to the public housing authority. And I think one of the first projects we took on was we wanted them to install screen doors, and they said, "No, you have to pay for those doors." And we said, "No, the doors have been on long enough to wear out, so you have to replace them." Well anyway, that was a big fight that we won. And then I kept the organization of the tenant association and fighting with the public housing people, and I participated in the first rent strike in public housing. Everyone said we were going to jail; we are not going to let you do this. But we won that, too, because the public housing authority did not have the proper things to sue us for and they didn't repair like they should. And the judge said, "If you don't repair the property, you don't get the rent." But they did everything trying to tick you off, but the first 127 people that went into the rent strike won. And the judge said, "If they don't collect their money in two years suspend." ... The first place I lived was 1906 Stanton Terrace, and that was in Frederick Douglass Dwellings on Alabama Avenue. I moved from there into a larger house and only stayed there eighteen months, and that was in the Knox Hill Dwellings. And then I moved from there into Woodland Dwellings and only stayed there about two years. By that time, I had gone to work full-time and we bought a house, and that's where I live now.[29]

This serves as a testament to the aid Kinard gave to his community, as a beacon of comfort during a tragic time of change to the hopeless, troubled and lonely. His training as a minister drew people from many walks of life for relief and assistance with life's tribulations. The virtuousness and unceasing desire to give of himself, benefited society and gave birth to a legacy, rich in commitment.

The Anchor of John Kinard's Life: The Kinard Family

The Power Couple

Three months after he returned from his service with Operation Crossroads Africa, Kinard married Marjorie Anne Williams (affectionately known as Margie by friends and family), the day after his twenty-eighth birthday, on November 14, 1964.

John and Marjorie Kinard on their wedding day, November 14, 1964.
Kinard Collection.

Following their wedding on November 14, 1964, at the Albright United Methodist Church in the District, the couple moved into the Kinard family home at 2115 Thirteenth Street, S.E., in Anacostia.[30]

Together they raised three daughters, Sarah Marie, Joy Gabriella and Hope Rebecca, all graduates of Livingstone College, following in the

The daughters of John and Marjorie Kinard: Sarah Marie, Joy Gabriella, and Hope Rebecca Kinard. Kinard Collection.

family tradition. As a father, Kinard was quite effective in balancing family life and the demands of his career. Trying hard to beat the stereotypes African American fathers faced, Kinard found it easy and took pride in being the head of his beautiful family. He affirmed a sense of emotional and financial support to the family and loved his children and wife. He served as a consistent role model of leadership and protection for his wife and girls. Many times he found time in his busy schedule to complete grocery shopping, manage a vegetable garden, cook daily meals, and attend PTA meetings. By these acts, Kinard refuted the image of absent Black fathers prevalent throughout the African American community. These images have been showcased on television, in cinema and in popular African American magazines and journals for study, analysis and reflection. During this era, the media consistently regurgitated negative images quite common in the Black community, which have served as a constant reminder of how the Black family has been interpreted and portrayed as dysfunctional. Unfortunately, those positive images have purposefully been omitted. Many African American men like Kinard, who were intentionally left out of the media, made vital contributions to heal the ailing problems of low self-esteem tied to enhancing the existing deficiencies connected to self-worth found in the Black family nucleus.

Their instability, promiscuity, aloofness, and abandonment of paternal responsibilities make them culpable for the myriad circumstances that disproportionately impact African American children: high school incompletion, teen pregnancy and child birth, poverty, membership and violent activities in gangs, and the use and sale of drugs.[31]

Although well aware of this image in America, John Kinard was a product of a two-parent household, where his father provided and his mother nurtured. His parents raised three boys to be responsible, to follow through and to be committed to the community.[32] Kinard's father, Robert Francis Kinard, did, however, early in life produce a child out of wedlock. His mother provided a stable home, without the emotional and financial support from Robert Francis Kinard. Isaiah Benson, Kinard's older brother whom he never met, grew up in Cleveland, Ohio, served in the US Army, and worked for the US Postal Service until his death on August 30, 2002.

John Kinard's 50th birthday party with his brothers, George and William Kinard.
Kinard Collection.

Although statistically supported, such reports fail to describe and explain the many healthy and stable black children parented in the noncustodial father family form.[33]

As a community leader, Kinard made sure his children were raised in the Anacostia neighborhood among the haves and have-nots. Sarah Kinard, Kinard's eldest daughter, shares her perspective on growing up in the Anacostia community. In well-expressed words, she conveyed her beliefs:

I think being raised in Anacostia benefited me in a variety of ways... Growing up in an area of working class people, you saw some families who would go on their jobs, and were pretty upwardly mobile, but at the same time you saw the many families who were impoverished. Some of them probably didn't know where their next meal was going to come from. After walking through the neighborhoods and catching the buses, you really see a dichotomy because you see a bit of the haves and have-nots, but mostly the have-nots.[34]

In addition, with exactness she pointed out personal sentiments:

I can remember feeling oddly ashamed about how much we had and how much other people didn't, even though we didn't think we had a lot. It was just that the people in the community had so little, it made it seem like we had a lot. I really enjoyed my time in Anacostia. I feel like it helped me get in touch with my people. Even now, I think I am most comfortable around large communities of African Americans. It was a close-knit community. Once crime got out of control, they started the Orange Hats, and we used to go out there [with Marjorie Kinard] and they used to go out there with their orange hats and write down the license plates of people that used to come and buy drugs, and I think they rolled it [drug dealing] out of a many of neighborhoods.[35]

In 1969, his daughter Sarah was born, and six years later, in 1975, Joy was born. Last but not least, Hope was born in 1977. Their first teacher was their mother, who was the director of the Key Daycare Center, and then Albright Daycare Center, where they attended daycare and preschool. She opted to build a foundation of education for her children, and chose to forgo having a career in the district's public school system until her children were well adjusted. She raised her children and, as they grew, earned a Master's in Education and Supervision, with an emphasis on Early Childhood Education from the University of the District of Columbia. After her youngest daughter, Hope, enrolled in grade school, Marjorie Kinard reentered the workforce, working for Community Health Care, Inc., a company run by family friend, James Speight. She held the following positions: Coordinator of the Teenage Pregnancy Prevention Program; Director of Adolescent Health; Director of Marketing; and Executive Assistant to the Director.

Kinard and his wife, embracers of the blackness ideology, remained in the African American community to be members of the small group of the Black middle-class who helped improve upon the disenfranchisement of the African American community in Anacostia.

> *Those who lived through those years can't forget them. It was a time when blacks called each other brother and sister and meant it. The 1960's were an era of discovery and revelation. African Americans took pride in their past. They were confident about the present. They had a sense of destiny for the future. They believed they could make America a better place to live for themselves and their children. The spirit of the past should be the spirit of the present.*[36]

Although the Kinards could afford for their children to attend the best private schools in the nation's capital, they all attended the District's public schools, just like their parents. They were also trained to ride the local bus at the age of eight, to attend ballet and tap dance classes, choir rehearsal, and choice educational enrichment programs.

> *We could have moved anywhere. But he wanted to stay here (in Anacostia) with the people. Our kids were going to go to the same schools as the other children in the neighborhood. No private school for them. And I concurred.*[37]

One scholar suggested:

> *Devotion to their children often becomes the one human tie that is sincere and free from the competition and artificiality of the make-believe world in which they live.*[38]

Growing up in a sheltered environment and possessing an education and manners were paramount. Church was a refuge, organizations were outlets for social and civic engagement, and cultural events were frequented, for example, the Alvin Ailey American Dance Theater; Ebony Jet Fashion Shows; Delta Sigma Theta Sorority, Inc., Self-Awareness Self Esteem (SASE) workshops for young girls; cotillions; Livingstone College Homecoming celebrations; museum openings; Kwanzaa and Black History Month celebrations; receptions; and lectures to hear Ivan Van Sertima and Leonard Jeffries were a part of everyday life.

> *Some of my fondest memories include going to church as a family, times when we would go out of town. I do remember taking Sunday drives after church around Rock Creek Park, going out to different restaurants, trying different types of food. Dad always wanted to expose us to different cultural activities. So, I do remember going to hear African drummers or speakers, or plays and stuff like that...*[39]

In the Kinard household, the Pan Africanist ideals embraced through Operation Crossroads Africa resonated. Entertaining foreign houseguests who Kinard interacted with on trips to the Motherland was normal. They found refuge in the family's seventeen-room Queen Anne style home, less than two blocks from the Anacostia Museum.

> *Over the years, the door of the museum, like that of his home, swung open wide to welcome countless African visitors, students, top-level government officials and heads of state, museum personnel, friends of friends of friends...*[40]

The welcome also extended to the Kinard home:

> *I remember Emily from the Ivory Coast. I remember this man named Mussah from Africa. I don't know what part of Africa he was from. I just remember we constantly had people from other [African] countries coming to stay with us. One thing that stands out the most I remember is peanut butter soup...*[41]

115

Guests bearing gifts and foreign houseguests cooking traditional African food were common for the family to enjoy. A favorite was a West African peanut soup. The Kinard residence on 1303 Mapleview Place, SE, was also enjoyed by extended family and friends.

Old Anacostia is a unique Washington neighborhood, a place where a buyer can find a rambling, country style home with a large yard, just 10 minutes by car from the Capitol and at an affordable price. John Kinard, director of the Anacostia Museum moved to his home on 13th Street S.E. in 1964. He recently bought a 17-room house for $30,000 nearby, where he plans to move once he has renovated it. "I tell my friends that (if) you're looking for a good house, come to Anacostia. The sun rises and sets on Anacostia for me." [42]

Reading and vocabulary building were normal and common for the Kinard girls. More importantly, learning about African American history was emphasized. Having black dolls, culturally centered games and enormous amounts of the latest books and encyclopedias to read and study were the norm for the Kinard children. After attending daycare and becoming school-aged, the Kinard children attended Ketcham Elementary School. The eldest daughter, with mastery, reflects on her experiences at Ketcham Elementary School:

I went to Ketcham Elementary School from the first grade to the sixth grade. That's in Anacostia. Then I went to Sousa Junior High School, which although it is in Southeast, technically it is not in Anacostia. And then I went to McKinley High School. One of the benefits, (I don't know if it was the D.C. Public School system) by it being predominantly Black (with the teachers and the students), we learned a lot about Black people. I can remember at Ketcham in the primary grades we learned all stanzas of "Lift Every Voice and Sing." We learned about Harriet Tubman and great inventors. It wasn't just that Martin Luther King had a dream and George Washington Carver had a peanut, but we learned about Jan Ernst Matzeliger. I can still remember a lot of the inventors and famous Black people. I think it is attributed to going to school in Anacostia. I remember when going to Ketcham, a teacher, I can't remember who the teacher was but she had us, as a class, to go out in the neighborhood with trash bags and we would pick up trash. I guess after having done that, I was careful about throwing my trash on the ground, because I knew it was going to make the neighborhood look junky or someone else was going to take their time to try to pick it up.[43]

To graduate at the Frederick Douglass home at Ketcham, it was a tradition. So we knew that in June, the classes that came before us, we couldn't wait until we could get a chance to go to walk up all of those stairs and graduate on the grounds of Douglass' house.[44]

The principal of Ketcham, Romaine B. Thomas, the wife of a long-standing, respected City Councilman Harry Thomas, was instrumental in providing a stellar learning environment. She often shared her appreciation for the Kinards and other community parents for their dedication as active members of their children's school. An award-winning educator, she was captivating and winsome in her ideas about the role of schools and community improvement:

I felt that both of those aspects of trying to establish an environment for children was important in terms of gaining the kind of confidence and kind of respect in order to use the skill in which I had been prepared to teach children. I felt very comfortable trying to establish a relationship with the parents in the community in order to be able to become a respected leader in the community in terms of working with the teachers who were there to create an environment that would foster the kind of learning that we wanted to provide for those children... I would say without speaking selfishly about it that it was important to have the educational leaders in the community. When I needed to, I spoke up and spoke out for the children at that school. I had influential parents, and I must say and I'm not trying to personalize it, but Joy, your father happened to be one of them. I always had that support and I could have a very profound committee to go with me to make necessary demands to bring to their attention what we felt we were not getting our equal share in terms of providing for those children. I look at people like Rosa Hart; her children attended Ketcham. She was very outspoken on behalf of the children and on behalf of the community, and you had people around like Calvin Rolark and I always felt like I could go to him if I needed to, and people like Marion Barry, were very supportive. Other people living in Anacostia who you knew were there, you could go to them when you needed their support. People like Almore Dale, Bernard Gray and his wife, they were very outspoken, and they would make a difference, and I even had the support of Willie Wilson and Union Temple, that church in the community. So, all of that was very helpful in terms of demanding respect and attention in terms of following through with the school. And we had Mr. Johnson and Rosa Hart, they were like the PTA presidents and that's when PTA really worked; it really meant Parents and Teachers working together. They were there to really support the kind of belief that we had for the children without fear and not necessarily in anger but without fear and belief and dignity and that we could make a difference in the lives of the children.[45]

Kinard was able to represent the many African American males who chose responsibility, and not abandonment as a father. He often sought refuge in his family. He took pride in being a parent, and enjoyed the thrills and trials of parenting with his three outspoken daughters. He and his wife went out of their way to expose them to a world beyond Anacostia. bell hooks noted:

In 1960, just over two thirds of black children under the age of eighteen lived in a household with two parents. By 1991, the percentage had dropped to just over one third and has continued going down since.[46]

She also divulges:

... the belief that male parenting is not relevant continues to be a norm in black life because it obscures the reality that so many black men are biological fathers who have no desire to parent. Until black people of all classes are able to place value on the active participation of black males in parenting, black boys and young men will continue to believe that their manhood in a patriarchal sense by making babies, not by taking care of them.[47]

Although the Kinard parents were quite hands-on parents, they were heavily involved in local DC politics on a grassroots level, and often traveled together in the United States and foreign countries.

I was on the Women's Committee of the Smithsonian. All of the wives of the directors, were a part of this organization and I enjoyed that very much.[48]

Marjorie Kinard also noted:

I was more of a support. I would go to the various functions. I would accompany him to the various receptions, openings and dinners, and all kinds of things he attended. Sometimes I traveled with him.[49]

With a strong knowledge and vision, Marjorie Kinard stated:

One thing I enjoyed very much was when John had to speak in Grenoble in France one time; and I accompanied him and heard him give this wonderful speech. And it was translated in French because everybody there spoke French. And here my husband was up there speaking to the French people. He was speaking English, but there was an interpreter to repeat everything he said. To me that was very significant, John Kinard of Anacostia presenting a paper in Grenoble, France, about museums with all of these outstanding leaders.[50]

Marjorie Kinard also called to mind another trip:

Another time we were on the Dioxides *ship and toured nine Greek islands and we lived for twelve days on the ship. People were on the ship, such as Arnold Toynbee, Jonas Salk, and Margaret Mead. All of these outstanding anthropologists and scientists were assembled to discuss the development of new cities around the world... I said, "Is this me on this ship, sitting next to Margaret Mead and Arnold Toynbee?" Sometimes I hear of some of the people who were on that ship...outstanding people of the world and I realize that we were there because of the significant contributions John had made with the new concept of community involvement in museums.*[51]

Judgments about his ability were wide-ranging:

As Bruce S. Gelb, director of USIA put it: Overseas, John was liked and respected for his candor and his humor. His down-to-earth approach reflected American values. Never one to shun the hard issues, John projected both honesty and decency; he made us proud to be associated with him.[52]

John and Marjorie Kinard served on the board of directors of Greater Southeast Community Hospital, the local NAACP chapter, and were involved in the Howard University Institute for Urban Affairs and Research through the International Women's Annual Observance. His wife served on the Women's Committee of the Smithsonian (group of Smithsonian Institution directors' wives) and Delta Sigma Theta Sorority, Inc., Washington, DC Alumnae Chapter. Marjorie Kinard served as president of the 400-plus member chapter of the sorority. Under her direction, the erection of Delta Towers, a senior citizens' housing complex with 149 units, was begun.

Pictured with Dr. Gwendolyn E. Boyd, 22nd National President of Delta Sigma Theta Sorority, Inc., are: Marjorie, Joy, and Sarah Kinard at the 50th Anniversary of the Beta Kappa Chapter of Delta Sigma Theta Sorority, Inc. Anniversary Luncheon where Boyd was the keynote speaker. Kinard Collection.

In 1987, she received recognition for raising money for college scholarships. She was an alto soloist in the Chorus Choir; President of a Missionary Society; Editor of the church newsletter; and, vice president of the Metropolitan Area Ministers' Wives Alliance. Many times, her daughters would tag along and entertain themselves or have play dates with other children of the accomplished society women belonging to these organizations. In addition to many other organizations and boards, the Kinards were actively involved in committees at John Wesley Church. Marjorie Kinard was an active philanthropist and fundraised to solicit money for Livingstone College's Alumni Association and the African Methodist Episcopal Zion Church's Academy in Monrovia, Liberia, raising thousands of dollars for the foreign missions of the AME Zion Church.

Kinard was the Chairwoman of the Friends of Zion Academy philanthropic group. She served as the director of the Rock Days Camp; Mayor's Committee of Early Childhood Development; Youth Advisor of the Youth Branch of the NAACP's DC Chapter; Chairwoman of Teen Lift of Delta Sigma Theta Sorority Inc.; and Operation Sisters United programs of the National Council of Negro Women. In 1983, she was one of the ten women in Washington, DC who helped contribute to African American life, and was justly presented with an Achievement Award for outstanding contributions from the DC Department of Correction's Women's Committee. Kinard's long fingers intertwined as she spoke; and she framed each statement in an exceedingly dignified tone but always adding her dynamic style:

We women have it made. Whether we realize it or not we have it made, some of us go to the best schools in the country, and we represent some of the best educated there are. We have good jobs, and husbands. We have comfortable homes. Some of us have more than one car, we park in front of our homes, we have credit cards for everything, to every store imaginable, and we can dress the way we want, wear our hair the way we want, wear a hat if we want to, or not. We're living the good life. Some of us have chosen to get married, and are happy in that; some of us have chosen not to marry and are also very happy in that. So, we are living the good life.

But even though these are the best of times for us, they're also the worst of times for us. Because we don't have to go far to look to see that there is joblessness in this town, there are people without food to eat. I saw a man the other day eating out of a trash can, and that really made me feel bad. There are poor housing conditions. There are people still living in rat infested, roach infested homes. And you know children are being physically and sexually molested. There are adult children who beat up their elderly parents, suicides are on the increase, drugs and alcoholism are rampant, and there are various kinds of mental illnesses that not only affect those of us who are middle aged, but children are now experiencing them.[53]

So, we have a whole lot of work to do. And we need to stop jiving and we need to be about the business that God wants us to do. Lance Jeffers has a poem that I think is very beautiful, and it's very significant to us who need to stop talking and need to start doing. And this poem is "When I Know the Power of My Black Hands." I do not know the power of my hands; I do not know the power of my black hands. I sit slumped in the conviction that I am powerless. I tolerate ceilings that make me bend, my Godly mind stoops, my ambition is crippled because I don't know the power of my hands. I see my children suffering my young men slaughtered; I don't know the power of my hand. I see the power over my life and death in another man's hands and sometimes I shake my wooly head and wonder, Lord have mercy, What, can I do to free me... I don't know if you understood that poem or not, but it says to us that even though we are running around looking good, going to Garfinkel's, Neiman Marcus, Bloomingdale's, doing our thing, there are people who need us, the disenfranchised who need us, and we need to stop playing church, and start being church.[54]

Jessie Beulah Kinard, (Kinard's mother), served as the unshakable anchor helping to raise the Kinard children, who were her only biological grandchildren. (Her non-biological grandchildren, Heather and Pam, were the step-daughters of William D. Kinard's second wife, Clarice Kinard.) Although the Kinards could have employed hired help, they took pride in their southern roots, proving that women were able to rear children, cook, clean and be a wife without having a stranger coming in, but instead by enlisting the help of family. On occasion, the children went to the home of their Aunt Dottie (Marjorie Kinard's youngest sister). Dorothy and the late Fred Colding's home in Hyattsville, MD was another refuge for the Kinard children. They would enjoy playing with cousins Herbert, the late baby Darren, and Dominque, as well as going to the Silver Spring, MD home of their Godparents, who were longtime John Wesley Church members, Clennie (high school classmate of John Kinard) and Barbara Murphy. The Murphy children, Kimberly, Rhonda, Roslyn and Clennie Jr., would babysit the Kinard children. Although much older than the Kinard girls, these children had lots of energy, creativity, and imagination when entertaining the Kinard girls. There were many times that Kinard was left at home to raise his girls while his wife would attend conferences or work training. He would step in as primary parent and pick his girls up from school and planned outings. One day, he even got them ready for school pictures, which entailed picking out special outfits and hairdressing, which he proudly completed. His success was also achieved with the help of the eldest daughter, Sarah Kinard, who proudly assumed the role for her baby sisters as a role model, tutor, comforter, protector, friend and teaser. She stepped in a lot to teach her sisters how to fight and defend themselves in school against bullies, and also took the blame for things she didn't do in order to protect her sisters.

The highlight of growing up in Anacostia was playing jump rope, tag, hide-and-go-seek and many other games with neighbors, the Gastons. It was fun roller-skating around the home of Frederick Douglass with friends, and helping in the kitchen with Grandma "Tata," as she made fresh baked goods from scratch for her grandchildren to devour once coming to her home from school. The Kinard children were envied by other neighborhood children. However, Tata treated all the neighborhood kids like her own. A strong disciplinarian, Tata used the old-fashioned switch as a form of punishment when needed.

> *The Negro grandmother's importance is due to the fact not only that she has been the oldest head in a maternal family organization but also to her position as granny or midwife among a simple peasant folk. As the repository of folk wisdom concerning the inscrutable ways of nature, the grandmother has been depended upon by mothers to ease the pains of childbirth and ward off the dangers of ill luck. Children acknowledge their indebtedness to her for assuring them, during the crisis of birth, a safe entrance into the world. Even grown men and women refer to her as a second mother and sometimes show the same deference and respect for her that they accord their own mothers.* [55]

With parents who possessed impressive reputations and moral character and expected you to uphold the same image without error, some children found it hard to adjust to everyday life experiences.

THE MAN, THE MOVEMENT, THE MUSEUM

A son of Martin Luther King, Jr. declared:

My father was the standard for all of us to live by and live up to. He became the standard because he was so exceptional in so many ways. But how can you live up to the standard that by definition is so rare, so exceptional, that it is only met by a once in a lifetime human being? [56]

Some of the philosophies instilled by Kinard to his young children were inconceivably awkward to accept. For example, Kinard shared the same philosophies about celebrating the Fourth of July as Frederick Douglass: that African Americans had nothing to celebrate on this holiday. The Kinard girls never had or frequented cookouts or purchased fireworks, which were hard to accept growing up in such a patriotic city. However, they did watch the grand fireworks display put on by the nation's capital by either traveling to a popular Anacostia viewing spot on the lawn of Our Lady of Perpetual Help Catholic Church on Morris Road, or viewing it from their bedroom windows from their home, which was situated on a hillside in Anacostia. Kinard and his unwavering beliefs, through this example, demonstrated the importance of acknowledging the sacrifices of the ancestors. He exhibited a determined obligation to teach the new generation the historic struggle of African people, which began in his home with his own children. Kinard made certain his children made learning about African people a cultural manifestation found in a weekly culmination, by attending John Wesley Church. The hymns and gospel music were a constant reminder of the lasting triumph over oppression that African Americans defeated. Church was a refuge where Kinard and his family gained renewed strength and spiritual protection from the ills of life. Kinard's turbulent relationship with the Smithsonian Institution was made easier to battle through divine intervention.

When Kinard died on August 5, 1989, it was very hard for the family. Although he was respected by many around the world, his most important role as a husband to his wife and a father to his children was no more. There was an incredible emptiness caused by the loss of Kinard as parent and husband in a household where his marvelous life example made his closest loved ones remember and long for his soft tender touch daily.

Nearly 1,000 people packed a church to pay homage yesterday to a man who was as respected by the people who spend their days on the street corners in his Anacostia neighborhood as he was by the museum curators who came from around the world to seek his advice. John R. Kinard, director of the Smithsonian's Anacostia Museum, was eulogized as "a man who had the capacity to embrace everybody"; "a man who taught you don't just need a job, you need a mission"; a man who said to other blacks: "Don't forget the legacy of African people." Kinard, 53, died last Saturday. He had myelofibrosis, a disease affecting bone marrow. His funeral was held at John Wesley AME Zion Church, 1615 15 (14th) St., N.W. where he served as an assistant pastor.[57]

It was at his wake and funeral that Kinard's true impact on the world was revealed. His family stood with pride to accept the condolences paid on behalf of Kinard's exceptional legacy. An abundance of flowers, food, unexpected houseguests, telegrams and calls from all over the world were received at the Kinard residence. With gratitude, the family, through the voice of Marjorie Kinard, stood tearless at Kinard's wake and uttered brave words of thanks to the audience:

You have shown us by your presence here tonight, that my husband's life made a difference, but I want you to know one thing, and that is, John Kinard took care of home first. Now I think you need to know that because all of the lofty platitudes and wonderful things said about him really warmed my heart, and made me feel good because, we were left home alone many, many times. But you know, we knew he was coming back, and we did not mind it one bit. When he came back, we rubbed his back, when he came back we cut his toenails, when he came back we massaged him, we fed him, we are the women who took care of John Kinard. [Cheers from the Crowd] You know, some of you are concerned about us. You are concerned about me. You are concerned about how I'm going to raise these girls. But you know I believe in God. And my Bible tells me, that God is not going to leave you, he is going to take care of you. He is going to support you and undergird you and give you strength, and John taught us that. We know the power of God. So, some of you are saying,

"She looks like she is smiling," and "She looks like she is happy." Yes, I'm happy. I was married to that man, twenty-five good years, and I want you to know... [Cheers from the Crowd] [58]

The poetry of Novella Nelson was quoted by Marjorie Kinard:

...many of you know, I love poetry, and in it she says, I am not a young girl. Nor do I wish to be. I am not a young girl, except inside you see. I'm not that old as I'm sure you know, but I believe that as you live you grow, and I have lived this long, and have made it to this place. Black woman I, struggling to be brave... Black woman I... and yet, I'm a girl, afraid but I'm not a young girl, nor do I wish to be. Hey, I am a woman. I'm healthy, I'm shaped, and I'm ready... [59]

Becoming a widow was hard for Marjorie Kinard. Just as many other widows whose husbands have made a major impact in American society, she coped, and moved on with their children to provide them a meaningful life. Although Kinard died, Marjorie Kinard fashioned a blueprint of exceptional womanhood and used this to raise her children. Her life example permeated through her children, with the belief that misery was not an option. This determination provided a model of perseverance that helped her children press forward with their lives and futures. Marjorie Kinard wanted life to move at a slower pace for her children, and in an effort to accomplish this, she relocated to Salisbury, North Carolina, in 1990 to work at Livingstone College. By doing this, she ensured that the Kinard girls gained a college education under their mother's watchful eye, following in the family tradition.

Conclusion

As minister, community leader, and museum director, Kinard made the most impact on his family. Finding comfort in the supportive ear of his loving wife and helping to instill values in his children through his life experiences gave his life more meaning. A supportive neighbor, willing to help those in need was the Kinard legacy led by enormous devotion.

Joy, William, and Hope Kinard at Livingstone College graduation, 1998.
Kinard Collection.

Chapter 4

EMBRACING THE MOVEMENT AND ANACOSTIA

L ike most American settlements and communities, Anacostia dates back to 1608 as an established Native American camp recorded by Captain John Smith.

During his explorations of the Chesapeake Bay Region, Captain Smith sailed the navigable waterways of the Potomac, reaching the Eastern Branch, later named the Anacostia River, on June 16, 1608. After traveling inland as far as their ship could go, Smith and his party continued by canoe, and met Indians in other canoes laden with the flesh of deer, bear, and other wildlife indigenous to the area. Landing on the southern banks of the eastern branch of the Potomac, the voyagers entered the village of the Nacotchtanks, the original Anacostians.[1]

Historian Louise Daniel Hutchinson noted:

The original Indian inhabitants, peaceful in nature and small in number, had disappeared from their homes along the Eastern Branch within some sixty years after they were found by Captain Smith. Some succumbed to European disease, some were killed (by other, warlike Indians as well as whites) while still others retreated westward or northward. One account tells of an attack on the Nacotchtanks by whites and fifty Indian warriors, who came to take corn. According to James Mooney, an authority on Indian tribes, "after a stubborn fight, eighteen of the Nacotchtanks were killed and the remainder driven from their cabins, which were then plundered and burned."[2]

Anacostia was no stranger to the forming of a new colony in the mid-1600s governed by European imperial designees. This community was one being explored by the family members of leaders of major European conquest expeditions, for example, the first Lord Baltimore's son Cecil Calvert, and the second Lord Baltimore's brother, Leonard.[3] Prior to the creation of Washington, DC, Anacostia was historically bound, with its regional origins located in the state of Maryland.

Starting in 1671 the Maryland legislature began to sanction and encourage the importation of African slaves into the colony. There were laws to protect the investment of slave owners, while brutal and oppressive slave codes were designed to control the laborers.[4]

Louise Daniel Hutchinson's study outlined how:

beginning early in the history of Prince George's County, which originally encompassed the Anacostia region, there were contacts between the Indians and the Africans. Slaves who escaped to the forest were often harbored by neighboring tribes.[5]

Hutchinson went on to say:

The new colony had little difficulty getting started, and like its neighbor, Virginia, Maryland developed an economy based on a new crop—tobacco.[6]

This investigation went on to analyze enslavement:

Slaves seasoned in the West Indies, as well as those imported directly from Africa, were soon introduced into the colonies to support the infant tobacco economy and the plantation system.[7]

Throughout the founding of the new Washington City, which eventually became Washington, DC, the Black enslaved and freedmen in Anacostia established a presence, forming an African American community with its origins entrenched in enslavement. Overcoming this vicious institution, many Blacks within this community fled for freedom or purchased their own freedom. One unsung heroine emancipator of this community, Mrs. Alethia Browning Tanner, born enslaved and owned by Mrs. Rachel Pratt Bell (or Beale, Beall), is credited for manumitting thirteen family members. Her own freedom alone was purchased at $1,400.00 on July 10, 1810.[8]

Respected by her community and friends, Mrs. Tanner, with the aid of her brother-in-law, George Bell, also helped to save the first Bethel Church (Israel A.M.E.) on Capitol Hill. According to George Washington Williams, an early black historian, Mrs. Tanner and Bell came forward when the property was put up for sale, bid on it, paid for it, and waited for reimbursement until the church was able to raise the money. Mrs. Tanner was Thomas Jefferson's housemaid during his residence in Washington, and, according to legend, he was also one of the customers for the products of her vegetable garden.[9]

One of Tanner's prominent family members included the first African American Presbyterian minister in the District, nephew John Francis Cook and son of Tanner's sister, Laurena Cook.[10]

As the years progressed for this new city, neighborhoods were formed and Washington remained a city of neighborhoods. Growth continued in such districts as the Navy Yard, Capitol Hill, the Central City, and the White House-Lafayette Square section.[11] Rapid growth between 1850 and 1860 attracted more residents to the city. The largest segment of the population consisted of unskilled working people.[12] After the Civil War, the need for Blacks to increase their knowledge, skill and economic status was made a national priority. Aided through the establishment of the Freedman's Bureau by the federal government, this made the Progressive Era more of a reality in the African American community, establishing settlements and resources for recently freed men.

In response to the critical housing needs of thousands of blacks who had sought refuge in Washington during the war, the Freedman's Bureau helped many of these new residents to the city to relocate. Although the establishment of Barry's Farm, a free black community in Anacostia, was not within the scope of the bureau's mandate by law, General Howard believed it to be within the implied spirit of the law. [13]

With new insight Hutchinson reveals:

Howard had difficulty purchasing land for resale to blacks. His efforts to acquire property in the vicinity of the Navy Yard were spurned. Then, with a good deal of secrecy, he purchased a 375 acre tract from Juliana and David Barry, heirs of James D. Barry. The land east of Asylum Road (now Martin Luther King Jr. Avenue), hilly and covered by dense forest and underbrush, was available for development in 1867. [14]

Howard, a year later in June of 1868, purchased the flatlands west of Asylum Road, which stretched further toward the Anacostia River. In addition to the purchase, roads were developed and surveying of the land began. For $125 to $300, an African American family had the option to purchase a one-acre lot, and had enough lumber to build a house. [15] Many of these families have grown in number and strength through the years. Although in 1877, Anacostia was an all-white community, historically, the great, noble and legendary Frederick Douglass was one of its first African American residents. A regional study exposed critical data on this purchase:

In September 1877, after borrowing the needed mortgage money from Charles Purvis, an abolitionist friend, he purchased the Uniontown home of John Van Hook. This nine-acre estate, with a large house, flower and vegetable gardens, and barns, was expanded to fifteen acres in 1878 when Douglass purchased an adjoining lot from the heirs of George Washington Talbert. With more time to devote to family, Frederick and Anna Douglass enjoyed their roles of "grandpa" and "grandma." And by 1878 the Douglass' sons and daughter Rosetta, with their large and growing families, lived in nearby Hillsdale. With their twenty-one grandchildren, Frederick and Anna Douglass were able to recapture some of the pleasures of family living missed during the years of long separations when their own five children were growing up. As described by Fredericka Douglass Sprague Perry, a granddaughter, the children of Rosetta, Frederick, Jr. and Charles spent a great deal of time at the home of their grandparents, and enjoyed such childhood pleasures as climbing trees, throwing stones, and riding their horse, "Rock," bareback.[16]

The Barry Farms and Hillsdale community, historically, were areas where some Blacks, who settled in Washington, DC, raised their families. Another family, deeply rooted in this community was the Dale family. Between the 1870s and 1890s, the Hillsdale and Anacostia communities had significantly grown and expanded with the ushering in of practiced civic engagement and major productivity. The establishment of African American businesses and professional services made Anacostia a destination for Black migrants. A long-time resident stated:

Len Peyton's General Store, Henry Sayles's coal, wood, and ice establishment, Epp's Restaurant, and Samuel Lucas's nursery and hot house were well established. By the early 1900's Butler Hall and Douglass Hall housed offices of doctors, a dentist and a pharmacist, and early black entrepreneurs provided a variety of businesses and services.[17]

After World War II, this community still maintained a small, but impressive, African American business district. A historical study maintained these significant features.

Almore Dale's Grocery Store, Dr. Quarrels' Drug Store, Mason's Funeral Home, Mr. Martin's delicatessen, Williams' Grocery Store, Roberts' Shoe Shop, Saunders' Barbershop, Mrs. Luckett's Candy Store and the Carver Theater.[18]

Prior to the 1940s and 1950s, Birney Elementary and Douglass Jr. High Schools were established for African American children living in the Hillsdale and Barry Farms community. High school was attended by the African American students in the northern part of the city at the Division II high schools, which were Dunbar, Armstrong, and Cardozo.

After the end of World War II, Anacostia experienced considerable population growth and with it accompanying changes. People displaced from other parts of the city by urban renewal programs in the fifties found homes in Anacostia. Seventy-seven percent of housing in Anacostia today consists of apartment houses, in contrast to 20 percent apartment houses in the rest of Washington. For the most part, housing units are in deplorable condition and lack the most essential public facilities. "Many apartment complexes were erected on inappropriate and unsuitable sites without adequate planning for sewage, streets, sidewalks, recreation, transportation or erosion control." [19]

Prior to desegregation, segregation was becoming more and more unbearable for Blacks who were growing tired of the inconvenience of being excluded from economic exchange from white establishments and public resources, which were newer and well maintained. Historically, it was the only way Black businesses and Black economic wealth was achieved at record numbers in the nation. Meanwhile, just down the road, in Anacostia, were the Anacostia Theater, Ketcham Elementary and Anacostia High School, which were for whites only. The Anacostia Junior–Senior High School, erected in 1937, was built on a budget of $800,000 and provided wonderful facilities for students. Anacostia's African American students also took part in workshops, which gave them unique opportunities, for example, the Radio Workshop programs, musical selections and discussions of Czechoslovakia.

Almore Dale, a second-generation prominent Hillsdale resident, attended Armstrong High School, located in the Anacostia community, and graduated from Tuskegee Institute. His uncle, Dr. Fred Moten, was then president of Tuskegee Institute, which was created by Booker T. Washington. Dr. Moten served it proudly and helped to pass the torch of wisdom to his nephew with a promising future. Mr. Dale's daughter, Diane Dale, recalls the strong civic connections to their family and neighborhood that were part of the tradition and sacrifice within the Black community. In 1914, her father left a job as the business manager of Bennett College in Greensboro, NC to return home to Anacostia and run the store in the community. This family provided a service needed during segregation, when choices for shopping lacked variety and diversity. In a powerful voice with strong and vigorously related details, a key part of community history was recalled:

> In 1944, my grandfather called and said that the Jews who owned the grocery store next to where they lived on Sumner Rd.—my grandparents lived at 1269 Sumner Rd. and the store was at 1265 Sumner Rd.—were moving. My Grandfather told my father he needed to come home because the Jews who owned the grocery store are leaving and we needed a store for the community. I mortgaged the house and was told to come home and run it. So, I left Bennett in 1944 and came home to help open Dale's Market, and we ran the store until 1956.[20]

Due to chain groceries moving into the area, the Dale Market closed in 1956. Mr. Dale then became the Head of Student Accounts at Howard University, a position he held for many years.

During the mid-to late 1960s in urban America, neighborhoods were craving to develop remedies to the many problems that plagued African American communities. Poor living conditions, education, unemployment, lack of exposure for underprivileged youth, drug abuse, crime and underqualified, unskilled residents existed throughout urban and rural America. Survival was the chief concern for most Anacostia dwellers. Many of these needs were being addressed in President Johnson's administration in the creation of Anti-Poverty Programs, which is how Kinard was first employed in the Anacostia community. In February 1965, at the suggestion of Dr. Robinson, Kinard obtained local work in the Anti-Poverty Program as a counselor for neighborhood youth. He transferred many of the skills learned as a leader in the Operation Crossroads Africa Program to his endeavors in the community of Anacostia. Among the poor, there still existed bitterness in the nation, and

Kinard encountered it and attempted to make a difference. It was with this job that Kinard became a local grassroots community activist. In 1987 Kinard himself declared:

> He knew that my sense of the Christian ministry was not so much a parish minister, a parish priest. It was not that. It was more on the streets, working with people, trying to solve problems and that kind of thing. This is why he suggested this business of the poverty program. So, I came back and found that in my own neighborhood where I lived, Southeast Neighborhood House was one of the first poverty programs to get started. So, I went to work for them... I was a neighborhood worker and counselor for Neighborhood Youth Corps.[21]

Ardent and fierce responses are a vital part of Anne M. Rogers' profoundly compelling interview:

> John worked with neighborhood people in trying to help them understand the causal factors of some of our problems in the neighborhood. In pursuit of that, there came a time when my philosophy of community action differed with the philosophy of the Director. My philosophy was, "Arm people with the facts and information and let those people, if it's a welfare problem, sit around the table with the authorities to say, "Here's the history of welfare as we know it. Here's what legislation provided, and here are what the problems are as we live them each day. And here's what we recommend be done to solve these problems."

> The Director of the program was more interested in taking those same people and going to picket Senator Byrd's house or the Director of Welfare's house. Confrontation was his method, his total method.

> ...Now, I believe in confrontation, but only to bring people to the table. We don't start off with confrontation; we start off with interviews, with a request for an interview, a request for a meeting...If meetings are refused, then you make every attempt through mediators to get a meeting with the authorities. If they refuse, then you have no other recourse but some kind of action.[22]

Kinard talking with young visitors from the Anacostia community at the Anacostia Neighborhood Museum.
Anacostia Community Museum Archives, Smithsonian Institution.

Kinard was a role model to the fatherless and misled youth of Anacostia. Possessing a love for people and helping those less fortunate, Kinard faced many sad realities in the poor troubled area of Anacostia. Another pioneer in Anacostia's grassroots community activism, James T. Speight, a graduate and student activist while enrolled at North Carolina A&T State University, who worked together with Kinard and many poor black Anacostia residents to change the scope of deprived services, convincingly shares his views:

> *When I came to the UPO [United Planning Organization] Central office to run the citywide youth program, which was comprised of ten centers in ten neighborhoods, I came in contact with John Kinard. I later ran the Southeast House... I was invited by two members of the Board of Directors to accept the position as Director because of the work I had done in the community. I was director of Southeast House for eight years. I began to work with John on youth problems when we walked the streets of Barry Farms.[23]*

In some way integration provided new options for the African Americans of Barry Farms; however, it corroded the community's economic growth due to the abundance of limited options. In 1964, Kinard and his family became the first African American family to move to 13th Street in the historic district of Anacostia between W and V streets, a two-block radius from the home of Frederick Douglass. Living and working in the same community was important to Kinard, which he learned in Africa through his involvement with Pan Africanism. Respect from Anacostia neighbors, who were also clients, established a sense of trust as he worked and served the community. Despite new options afforded to them, residents gave less support to the Black resources within the community. Stan Anderson, one of the managers of the George Washington Carver Theater, and member of the Greater Anacostia People's Committee (GAP), a Black grassroots community group, shares his experience with desegregation in the Anacostia community. One historical study from the Anacostia Historical Society found:

> ...you had Anacostia Theater and you had the Congress Heights Theater. And then you had a theater in Garfield that was a white theater. But when they integrated, blacks could go to Anacostia, blacks could go to Congress Heights, and blacks could go to the one up there off of Alabama Avenue, you see. So, consequently, when that happened, that meant that Carver, which was a black theater, you know, lost all of it.[24]

Kinard and Anacostia Grassroots Activism

This community, like many across the nation looked upon churches, schools and community groups like GAP for direction. Just as Kinard helped to rebuild new nations in Africa, as a poverty program counselor, he made a major impact helping to build pride in this community, which lacked a voice and was riddled with frustration like many urban communities of this period. *A Different Drummer* scrutinized this aspect of Kinard's community focus.

> Kinard worked with the Band of Angels, a group of angry, activist welfare mothers. He named and helped counsel The Rebels with a Cause, a dozen or so street savvy black "disadvantaged" teenagers from a nearby public housing project. He honed his negotiating skills and his patience during long hours of heated discussions in endless meetings with other community organizers, neighborhood residents, and

officials from both the public and private sectors... People listened when John Kinard spoke, for he articulated his positions with clarity and logic and the force of a black preacher's passion and imagery. He appealed to the listener's reason as well as their sense of moral responsibility simply to do what was right.[25]

Working in Africa with little to no resources and communicating and negotiating as a leader on major projects was helpful to Kinard's current position. His resourcefulness, and ability to make calculated decisions with ease, to create win-win situations with respect to the needs of the program and those affected, made Kinard well respected by his peers. As a counselor, he possessed rare problem-solving skills, which set him apart from average workers, and at times he became the community's designated leader. And he never objected to this responsibility:

More than twenty-five years ago at a meeting in the Bridge, the Southeast Neighborhood Development Program's cultural arts center at 2027 Nicholas (now Martin Luther King Jr.) Avenue, S.E., Kinard listened for a long time as other staff members and community residents debated strategies to increase the effectiveness of the community organizers. He bided his time and eventually stood to say that he wished to make a suggestion. His statement took probably less than ten minutes, but in that short time Kinard argued with riveting intensity and power for a dramatic new direction. He wanted to know why the Southeast Neighborhood Development Program continued to dilute its efforts by scattering workers and trying to respond to every call for assistance throughout the entire service area. The program should, he argued, focus the energies of a small group of workers in one definable area such as the Barry Farms public housing project. After all, he continued, the social, political, and economic ills of the more than four hundred families living in Barry Farms were the same as those found in similar areas throughout the whole city and even the country. If the program could help these residents to effect basic changes in their small community, it could then provide possible solutions for others in much the same circumstances. Kinard concluded by recommending that the Neighborhood House "target Barry Farms." [26]

Kinard represented the force of African Americans which stimulated activism to protect the rights that he helped fight for as a college student. It is with this intellect that Kinard and others upheld the hope of a community though poor, disenfranchised adults with no faith in the system. These impatient and aggressive community organizers, who found favor from Kinard, brought realism and certainty through his role. Although not in charge of this program, Kinard made an impact and gave progressive solutions. He helped them verbalize their concerns in a broader context as an advocate. Instantly, Kinard recognized how the philosophies of W.E.B. DuBois transferred into his own life through the commitment of the "talented tenth" leadership legacy. Those educated few, who would lift up the rest of the race using their intellectual abilities gained through higher education, shall step in and aid the lesser educated of the race.

In just minutes, John Kinard had summed up the dilemma faced by exhausted organizers and at the same time offered an idea that met the enthusiastic approval of those present. During the following week, the Barry Farms Target Team, which included Kinard, was organized. The team was an all-male group of nine blacks and one white, led by a young social worker, Pharnal Longus. Partly because of its efforts in Barry Farms, the Southeast Neighborhood House became known as one of the most militant and one of the most effective antipoverty programs in the city. For two years Kinard refined his skills in community service. While he continued his connection with the Barry Farms Target Team from 1965 to 1966, he also worked with youths at the neighborhood house and became a counselor with the Neighborhood Youth Corps. For about nine months he opted to become a community organizer for a second antipoverty program, the Congress Heights Neighborhood Development Program, also in Southeast Washington. Then in June, he moved on to a year's stint with the U.S. Office of Economic Opportunity.[27]

After leaving the poverty program, Kinard moved to the Office of Economic Opportunity in 1966-67 working with poverty program grant proposals and fundraising projects on the Eastern Shore of Maryland as a program analyst. Kinard served eight counties on the Eastern Shore. In this job, Kinard worked as a broker of sorts, and as a middleman to garner support to rebuild and sustain needed programs for communities in his jurisdiction. He often used a well-founded community-based strategy.

I would say, "All right, if you want to have a neighborhood worker program, these people would go and talk to people on welfare, find out what the problems are. Or if they want to have certain other kinds of programs, here's the application. Here's how you apply. You send it to me in Washington, and I will negotiate, be sure all the figures are straight, and we'll get you the money for your program." That's what I was doing. Then I'd go down and check on the program.[28]

Although Kinard no longer worked directly in his community, he still remained active in the Anacostia community, organizing and planning. Learning politics in church and as a result of his Operation Crossroads Africa exposure to successful foreign leaders, Kinard became influential and an agent of change through advocacy during community meetings, much like men of leadership and radical reform found in the philosophies of Stokely Carmichael, Malcolm X and Dr. Martin Luther King, Jr. There was a resolute tone when he pronounced this policy:

We had what we called woodshed meetings (meetings on the meetings). We would meet depending on what was going on. Meetings were held at least one Saturday morning per month. Sometimes two or three...depending on what the issue was. At the woodshed meeting we would assess where we were on the issues. We would identify who we needed to bring in to talk to or get involved. We would contact them and meet with them on Saturday morning either at the Southeast House or at the Anacostia Neighborhood Museum. We took the time to inform and empower those who could be helpful to our cause, by giving them information so they could take positions in the community meetings and other places on our behalf.[29]

The Smithsonian Institution and the Urban Village: A Leap in the Dark

The experience Kinard obtained through advisement and counsel from Dr. James Robinson of OCA and Dr. E. Franklin Jackson of JWC, mixed with his background as a service-oriented community leader, gave Kinard a strong desire to lead a life of service. The next mentor to give Kinard the chance of a lifetime was Dr. S. Dillon Ripley, the eighth Secretary of the Smithsonian Institution (SI). Dr. Ripley was also a famed scientist, international explorer, and author of natural history, as well as an innovative leader with exceptional vision.

Before coming to the Smithsonian at the age of fifty, Dr. Ripley had been professor of biology at Yale University and director of the university's Peabody Museum of Natural History. He had also served on the staffs of the Academy of Natural Sciences of Philadelphia, the American Museum of Natural History, and for a short time, the United States National Museum. He was trained as a biologist, his particular love being ornithology. He had traveled widely and conducted expeditions to such places as New Guinea, India, and Nepal and had become something of an authority on the birds of Asia. He was active as a conservationist. At his home in Litchfield, Connecticut, he operated, as a hobby, a considerable aviary. When he became Secretary, Ripley conveyed the impression that he meant business and that those who did not like it could jolly well pack their bags. Some of them did. He was friendly but firm and determined. But the new image created by Ripley, although not universally admired, may go deeper than appearances. He has made his greatest contribution so far in his emphasis on the role that museums can exert in our changing culture. He believes that too few people today realize the potential educational use of museums, art galleries, and kindred institutions, which can be a real force on the urban educational scene.[30]

This Ivy League (Yale) trained scientist breathed new life into the SI establishing new ground expanding the diverse fascination of the SI. In addition to these changes, came major integration into the leadership of the SI. John Kinard and Julian Euell were part of the higher level of diversification which met a degree of opposition, but with Dr. Ripley's support, Kinard went to his grave challenging the ideals and consciousness of the old SI cultural norms that Ripley couldn't fully change. Prior to Kinard and Euell's appointments as the director of the Anacostia Museum and the Assistant Secretary of the SI, respectively, the highest position held by an African American of prominence in past years was Solomon Brown. Just as Kinard, Solomon Brown lived in Anacostia and was a prominent and respected community leader.

Solomon Brown, a clerk at the Smithsonian Institution as a settler of Barry Farm... Mr. Brown also in 1902, celebrated 50 years of service to the Smithsonian Institution. Active members of the House of Delegates and the council, Brown and Frederick Douglass (later his son Lewis) represented the interests of the entire Anacostia region.[31]

S. Dillon Ripley was the Secretary of the Smithsonian Institution from 1964–1984.
Smithsonian Institution Archives, Smithsonian Institution.

Dr. Ripley, at the helm of a rich international legacy that was founded by the great European scientist James Smithson, had strong desires to increase the knowledge of a growing country with boundless promise called America. James Smithson, born in Paris, France, in the year 1765, the son of Hugh Smithson and Elizabeth Hungerford Keate Macie of elite and well pedigreed parents, was well educated. Recognized as a scientist studying and analyzing chemical experiments, in addition to socializing in affluent societal circles, Smithson was in a category well above that of the common man. Possessing a strong fondness for edification when he died, in his will, he requested that the new nation in America receive monies to increase knowledge which birthed the well know Smithsonian Institution.

In the case of the death of my said Nephew without leaving a child or children, or the death of the child or children he may have had under the age of twenty-one year as or intestate, I then bequeath the whole of my property subject to the Annuity of One Hundred pounds to John Fitall, & for the security & payment of which I mean stock to remain in this country, to the United States of America, to found at Washington, under the name of the Smithsonian Institution, an Establishment for the increase & diffusion of knowledge among men...[32]

The Institution over which this galaxy of public servants, scientists, and multimillionaires presides is every bit as heterogeneous as its Board of Regents. Among other things, it conducts, or participates in, research expeditions all over the world (two thousand to date), and, in a complicated exchange operation, annually disseminates to learned institutions, learned individuals, embassies, and missions in every part of the globe, including the United States, more than a million packages (1,461,720 in 1966), weighing more than a million pounds (1,041,492 idem), of learned and other publications, some of which it publishes itself but most of which (the Federal Register, the Congressional Record, the Yale University Bulletin, *and the* Oregon Law Review, *for example) it merely bundles up and transmits.*[33]

Throughout the years, this precious gift from James Smithson has been an enormous source of teaching via the dissemination of science, history, and cultural studies through different mediums of research. Headed by a Secretary, Assistant Secretary, Board of Regents, and museum directors, the SI has evolved from a culturally diverse exclusive organization to politically inclusive. Bold steps were taken during 1966 to establish the Folklife Festivals, developed by Ralph Rinzler and the Neighborhood Museum Concept. In 1966, Dr. Ripley, in his introduction to the symposium *Knowledge Among Men*, wrote:

If the Smithsonian Institution has a motto, aside from the enigmatic and Sibylline "increase and diffusion of knowledge among men," it should be the pursuit of the unfashionable by the unconventional... In its history, the Smithsonian has always tried to do only what for various reasons other organizations or agencies were not doing, and to husband its resources of manpower toward the accomplishment of abstract and original study.[34]

THE MAN, THE MOVEMENT, THE MUSEUM

Liberal, open-minded, and tolerant of the changing world, Dr. Ripley challenged the SI to put aside its laissez-faire approach to the delivery of knowledge, fashioned through exhibits, and inspired the SI's cultural resources and workforce to inject creativity and clever ideas to "pursue unfashionable by the unconventional" themed research and projects.

While not challenging the preexisting interpretive framework at the Smithsonian, Ripley was gifted with a wider, more democratic sense of inclusion than previous secretaries. Becoming secretary in 1964, Ripley may have been influenced by the American–dream rhetoric of Martin Luther King Jr., who was a master at combining the language of national mythos with the demand for equal justice that was a special concern of African Americans. At certain moments of potential crisis, this wider vision of the museum aided Ripley in asserting a statesmanlike leadership. For example, as mentioned above, the Poor Peoples Campaign arrived in Washington in the summer of 1968. With folks walking and riding from the Deep South to the capital, the Smithsonian had time to prepare for the arrival of these new visitors to the Mall. A crisis management meeting was called so that the Smithsonian's administrators could determine the appropriate response to this challenge to the security of the collections. Ripley took a completely different view. Rather than battening down the hatches, he suggested that the doors be flung wide open to this new and quite visible part of the American public. Vividly recalled by many participants in that meeting, this was a triumphal moment in Ripley's stewardship of the Smithsonian.[35]

This same year, Dr. Ripley took a risk with the reputation of the SI to experiment on diversifying its museum goers and its programs. Broadening and stretching the internal culture of the SI to contact diverse demographics that never visited the museums on the National Mall, Ripley led by example to demonstrate his vision in taking the museum to the African American people of urban America, choosing Washington, DC neighborhoods. History must recognize how:

Ripley wished to place an informal, experimental museum in a low-income neighborhood for the nontraditional visitor who rarely, if ever, visited the imposing museums anywhere in the city. It was Ripley's hope that, once introduced to an interesting, hands-on museum in their neighborhood, residents would be more inclined to visit the National Mall. [36]

In the midst of the mid 1960s, Ripley, like other white decision makers, was observing the Black political revolution and the modern civil rights protests. Their militant acts pressured the governing establishment to answer the questions, "Why don't you employ African Americans in leadership roles?" "How are you ensuring the proper delivery of diverse topics to broader audiences?" and "Why don't you exhibit American artists of the African American race?" During the Vietnam War, civil rights activism continued to petition ignored issues raised through national and local activism in Washington, DC.

The decade of the 1960s was a time of local and national activism in the capital. In the Capitol Hill neighborhood, people began associations concerned with neighborhood improvement, recreation, and education. Washington's best-known local activist, Julius Hobson, took on the public-school system. His lawsuits against the schools helped equalize school funding throughout the city and led to the abandonment of the track system. [37]

All over the nation, African American people made their presence felt through activism. Both silent and vocal, they were hoping integration was the device which would make an enormous difference in the pursuit of the American dream. Countless opportunities materialized from the efforts of integration, however slowly enforced. Outbreaks of massive frustration from African Americans interested in enhancing the social conditions they faced led to the formation of revolutionary groups like the Black Panthers.

These are the conditions which create dynamite in the ghettos. And when there are explosions—explosions of frustration, despair and hopelessness—the larger society becomes indignant and utters irrelevant clichés about maintaining law and order. Blue ribbon committees of experts and consultants are appointed to investigate the causes of the riot... What has to be understood is that thus far there have been virtually no legitimate programs to deal with the alienation and the oppressive conditions in the ghetto. [38]

THE MAN, THE MOVEMENT, THE MUSEUM

Although limited in providing the daily needed resources to the community, such as hospitals, grocery and clothing stores, banks, post offices, and schools, Dr. Ripley's efforts to develop this museum were grandiose and unprecedented in nature. He did the unthinkable and granted full autonomy to the community to operate the museum. This was one of the first attempts by any organization of this stature to reverse the alienation and oppressive conditions found in the ghetto. It has helped create a central focus during the Black Studies era, having the African American community be the subject of positive reflection through a legitimate institution. Through the years, it had to fight within the institution for an identity, but made its own, managing to earn international influence, which most of the SI museums never reached. The elitist staff's views of this new SI era led to steering new visions, although holding on to romanticized depictions of American culture. In addition, the staff was lacking the appeal to embrace broader diverse audiences, especially the local African American population found in Washington, DC until Dr. Ripley challenged the institution to change.

> *The urban problem is upon us and beats on our ears or flashes out of the newsprint, or snarls at us from shattered shop fronts every day. To a large extent, people from rundown neighborhoods tend to stay there. They tend not to be mobile, or to move much out of their district, except in a transient sense from slum to slum. Such people, referred to again by slogan phrases like "disadvantaged," are likely never to go into any museum at all. Here I agree wholeheartedly with the sociologists. Indeed such people may feel awkward going out of their district, badly dressed or ill at ease. They may easily feel lost as they wend their way along an unfamiliar sidewalk toward a vast monumental marble palace. They may even feel hostile.*[39]

All over the country, there was a concern to embrace the poor people of the world. The campaign led by Dr. Martin Luther King Jr. was an inspiration for many. Although no historical record links Ripley to the poor people's campaign, it is highly likely that he wanted to make an impact, which was realized through the efforts of John Kinard. In looking at the Washington, DC area, which mirrored most urban African American communities nationwide during this era of change, it became apparent that it required much more practical and useful educational resources. In the eyes of urban youth, they could care less about the offerings of a museum. With the strong vision of Dr. Ripley, making efforts to invest within a community broken by forced exclusion based on race and class, the opportunity for a neighborhood to house a museum was seriously pursued. In 1966 neighborhoods from all over Washington, DC responded immediately to the neighborhood museum concept.

In November 1966, Washington newspapers carried an account of S. Dillon Ripley's remarks to museum directors at a meeting in Aspen, Colorado. Mr. Ripley, the Secretary of the Smithsonian Institution, told his audience to try taking their museums to the people. He suggested they rent space in low income neighborhoods and install exhibits that could be touched and operated. He noted that many people learn more easily through touching and handling real objects than through reading. This newspaper article evoked immediate response; requests for beginning neighborhood museums came in from community groups in several different low-income neighborhoods in Washington.[40]

The idea for a small satellite museum located in a low income urban setting grew out of a conference on museums and education held in August 1966. Jointly sponsored by the Smithsonian and the U.S. Office of Education, the conference sought "to begin to discover ways of making more effective educational use of the more than 5,000 museums that exist in the United States." The conference generated thoughtful suggestions for the re-examination of the museum exhibit content as well as methods of presentation. Of the several lively ideas proposed the one by Mary Lela Sherburne for a drop-in museum for drop outs caught the imagination of many.[41]

With the demands of the position as Secretary of the SI, Ripley enlisted the aid of other experts to help develop this idea. Finding the right person to develop the concept, who was familiar with the plight of the urban community, was key in its development.

Dr. Caryl Marsh was a consultant to the Smithsonian Institution on special projects and an avid supporter of the Anacostia Neighborhood Museum.
Anacostia Community Museum Archives, Smithsonian Institution.

This concept was refined in a proposal written by Dr. Caryl Marsh (at the time a graduate student at George Washington University majoring in psychology studying curiosity), a special assistant to Secretary Ripley, who helped in the sixties to integrate the parks and recreation facilities in the Washington, DC area. A remarkable and well-established museum scholar, Dr. Marsh had the ability to remember in detail her interest in museums:

I worked for the D.C. Recreation Department and there, I worked (well) initially, I was paid there, to work on the issue of how to integrate. There was a division one and a division two and I was involved in figuring out ways to integrate the two divisions, so that people of different skin colors would feel comfortable with each other. So, I met with the staff informally. We had these informal discussions and through informal discussions people began to see that they had common issues in their different neighborhoods. And in that you could initially see the White people sat on one side and the Black people sat on that side but then as they talked they began to see that they really had so much in common. Before you knew it before the second or third meeting, they sat wherever they felt comfortable with the other person. Everybody was all integrated so it worked very well.[42]

She went on to explain:

I got interested in the museum profession after I started working on the Anacostia Museum. I wasn't so much at that point interested in the museum profession at the time I started working on it, I was more concerned about integration and opening up bridges for people who weren't using the cultural facilities of the Smithsonian had some access to museums and it was only after working there with them for several years that I really realized that I wanted just to stay with museums. That's why I pulled this document out for you. This is called a proposal to establish an experimental museum. That was what I wrote in 1966 when they first hired me. And that became the founding document for the museum. And if you read it you will see that everything in there is basically what your father [John Kinard] used as a blueprint to go forward, and he took those ideas and developed them very creatively in his own way that suited the community.[43]

In summary, she was fervent and vehement in her description of the era:

In the 60's of course there was the big explosion. And when Mr. Ripley at the Smithsonian gave a speech proposing to reach out to low-income neighborhoods it seemed...real. And a marvelous idea.[44]

The proposal written echoed the desperate need of cultural enlightenment. This effort was articulated in a study/proposal which shared the core needs of the community through projected cultural enrichment. This concept would expand the scope of the SI mission and mandate it to increase knowledge and reach out to a different audience of the unrefined and misunderstood residents living in Washington's "ghetto." Although not the initial goal, this concept turned into a successful attempt to embrace the Black Studies movement through the channel of a museum. Caryl Marsh, special assistant to S. Dillon Ripley, eighth Secretary of the Smithsonian Institution, was emphatic when she explained:

The city itself is a great educational institution. One of its tragedies is the number of its inhabitants who are not really aware of the wealth of the resources that are offered, free, to anyone who cares to visit them. The Smithsonian Institution is setting an example of skill in the advertising of education, in its most attractive form, when it proposes to establish a neighborhood branch museum in an abandoned pool hall far from the building along the Mall.[45]

Ripley's concern and reason for the study was caused by staggering statistics that made him re-evaluate and analyze the institution's role in educating both the advantaged and disadvantaged. The Marsh Proposal reflected these statistics: 32,909 school children from the area took guided tours of the Smithsonian; only 1,871 or six percent of the children so served were from the schools in the District of Columbia itself. In addition, Ripley knew that the pattern of the SI visitor in no way "reflected the city's actual population characterized in a city whose population is predominately Negro (62 percent). More than 98 precent of the visitors to the Museum of Natural History on a recent holiday were white".[46]

Reasons for the infrequent use of the SI museums by most Black Washington, DC natives fell among the issues of class and deficient representations of minority-inclusive history in exhibits and exhibit development. Blacks living around the nation were beset with economic strife. Concerns of jobs, food, healthcare, and education were important and foremost on the minds of the poor. Much of life left little room for cultural study and reflection.

In Washington, DC, a city where 262,000 people, or about one third of the total population (of the District), live just above subsistence level, it is hardly to be expected that large numbers of the poor can afford the bus fare for a trip to a museum, or the clothes either. In connection with a recent PTA program in Washington to sponsor trips for children and their parents to local attractions, a number of parents in one low-income neighborhood objected to the program. The parents, it was learned, felt that they did not have the proper clothing for such a venture; they preferred not taking part in the possible humiliation of conceivably being denied admission to places they might want to visit.

If the above is true, then the only solution is to bring the museum to them. For of all our people, these are the ones who most deserve to have the fun of seeing, of being in a museum. Although private collectors may wish to keep their collections private, the responsible person in charge of a museum, no matter how recondite, esoteric or aesthetically rarefied his collection, must occasionally have at least a twinge of educational esprit, the merest modicum of egalitarianism or desire to improve the lot of his fellow man.[47]

In some areas of the city, native African American Washingtonians went to museums with schools and auxiliary group outings. However, the reason they refrained from frequenting museums was seeing false cultural depictions or the lack of seeing themselves. Clennie Murphy and Diane Dale give insight to this view. Clennie Murphy maintained:

When I was growing up in Washington, the black teachers were fantastic. They took us downtown to the Smithsonian Institute. They took us to all the places, I remember going to the art gallery. I remember going to a few other events downtown as a result of teachers. I remember us at Lovejoy (Elementary School) leaving there and going over to catch the street car at that time to go downtown to the art gallery. So, yes, I got that from black teachers at that time who were very very resourceful.[48]

Diane Dale gave voice and affirmed the entire community's feelings:

There was nothing in those museums that represented us but people standing around barefoot in grass skirts holding a spear.[49]

Substantive ideas that reflected the new directions in which America was moving helped sustain the neighborhood museum concept. This bold step forced the institution to re-examine itself through the vision of the Anacostia community to answer the questions posed by Dr. Carter G. Woodson as he spent most of his adult life exhaustively reclaiming the Negro's place in American history.

The diverse groups that make up American society have long spoken a common political language, although they have often interpreted its vocabulary in very different ways. Apparently universal principals and common values, moreover, have been historically contracted on the basis of difference and exclusion. Nowhere is this symbolic relationship between inclusion and exclusion between a national creed that emphasizes democracy and freedom as universal rights and a reality of limiting these entitlements to particular groups of people more evident than in debates over that fundamental question "Who is an American?" Today many politicians blame America's problems on an alien invasion and propose to redefine our nationality along racial and ethnical lines. But there is nothing new in bitter conflicts about who should and should not be an American citizen. We as a people have long been obsessed with definitions of "Americanness." [50]

This can be found true in the SI, which catered to an elite class engaging those who gave credence to the study of mankind and its interpretation of American history that was totally Eurocentric in scope. Defining Americanness is grounded in the reflection of objects and documents found in American cultural institutions. One institution with an enormous amount of influence, the SI, during this era of change, merged the diverse American experiences into the scope of mainstream history. Included in this merger was the neighborhood museum concept. The four neighborhood organizations that showed interest and were considered for the location of the first neighborhood museum included: Adams-Morgan Community Council; Friendship House representing the Capitol Hill area of the city; Southeast Neighborhood House in Anacostia; and the Shaw Urban Renewal administration. Although Anacostia was finally selected, the efforts to make this museum reflect the diverse American experience found in African American culture a reality required a cultural renaissnce.

Intellectual Harold Cruse took a position similar to that of the Nation when he declared that if culture is the "soul of a race, nation, people or nationality," the soul of black people in America had "lost its power abandonment of true identity, and immature, childlike mimicry of white aesthetics." He suggested that black people needed a cultural renaissance in order to secure liberation for themselves. [51]

Dr. Ripley, excited about the new venture and pressured to deliver by residents, moved at an immediate pace to establish and open the museum in 1967, just a year after his concept was delivered in Colorado. It was Ripley's hope that once introduced to an interesting, hands-on museum in their neighborhood, residents would be more inclined to visit the National Mall. Charles Blitzer, director of the Smithsonian's Office of Education and Training, was appointed to head the effort. He in turn hired Dr. Caryl Marsh, a psychologist with the District of Columbia Department of Parks and Recreation. Marsh, closely allied with the city's Roving Leader Program, began meeting with community groups to test the level of support the SI might expect in various neighborhoods. By November 1966, she drafted the original funding request to establish an experimental neighborhood museum in the District of Columbia. The main guideline for the neighborhood selected was the area's stability. Preferably they wanted a block containing a laundromat, a symbol of daytime neighborhood involvement, rather than bars. Washington, DC Councilman Stanley Anderson, a resident of Anacostia, who was then the director of the Recreation Department's Roving Leader Program, and Marsh, a consultant to the Department, shared mutual interests and concerns. The neighborhood museum concept appealed to Stanley Anderson, and the next step was to interest the Greater Anacostia People's Corporation (GAP). Although Anacostia was selected for the museum, the yearning displayed by GAP to actively organize was one of the main reasons the neighborhood was ultimately selected. Recognizing the value of acquiring the partnership of the SI, coupled with the power of cultural awareness, in addition to the autonomy of the African American community's voice, all aided in making the concept a reality.

> *The auguries seemed good. A community advisory council... chaired by Mr. Alton Jones, Chairman of the Greater Anacostia Peoples, Inc., Mr. Stanley Anderson, later to become one of the first members of the new City Council of Washington, Mrs. Marion Hope, Mr. Ben Davis, and a good number of willing volunteers, including a sergeant of the 11th Police Precinct, Andrew Salvas. My colleague, Charles Blitzer, was active from the beginning, and we depended heavily on the advice of Mrs. Caryl Marsh, who had worked with neighborhood social problems in Washington.*[52]

Almore Dale and Alton Jones, chairman of GAP, soon became prime movers in getting people to come out to meet and talk with Dr. Charles Blitzer, who was then the director of the Smithsonian's Office of Education and Training, and Dr. Caryl Marsh, consultant to the Smithsonian in planning and developing the neighborhood museum. Several meetings were held at Barry Farms, but with more people attending it was to be expected that some would lack enthusiasm about a museum in the neighborhood. They questioned why the money should be spent for such a purpose when there were other, more crucial needs that had been long neglected. People in the low-income and poverty groups mistrusted any schemes that did not promise practical results. The question of jobs kept coming up, not just jobs for those who were unemployed, but for those who hoped the museum would offer opportunities for upgrading their present job status. *A Different Drummer* narrated these crucial events:

> *Caryl Marsh recalls a rainy morning in late 1966 when she drove Blitzer and Ripley to Anacostia to urge them to select the Carver Theater on Nicholas Avenue. Already considered and rejected had been sites in Northwest Washington, in the Adams Morgan section and the lower Georgia Avenue area. Certainly, there was a predominance of low income households in some neighborhoods east of the Anacostia River. These same areas, with burgeoning youth populations, were also sadly neglected by city officials. Ripley addressed this concern when he noted that while "the concept of bringing a museum out of its stated setting is not new," he felt that all of the current outreach efforts of museums "overlooked urban areas... The urban area is upon us and beats on our ears or flashes from shattered storefronts every day." For all of our people, these are the ones who most deserve to have the fun of seeing of being in a museum.*[53]

The funds to establish the museum obviously materialized from wealthy sponsors. Groups of white, wealthy philanthropists, both anonymous, and listed sponsors, were able and willing when Dr. Ripley placed the call for funding his vision. Due to the lack of an appropriation from Congress to assure an operational budget, for the next two years from 1967-1969, the museum sought funding to operate. The Marsh Proposal was developed and used as a blueprint to seek funding from philanthropists to make the concept a reality with key points as follows:

EMBRACING THE MOVEMENT AND ANACOSTIA

The Smithsonian Institution is seeking funds to establish and operate an experimental Neighborhood Museum in rented quarters in a low-income neighborhood in Washington, DC. The purpose of this experiment is to provide an environment for open, non-directed learning through actual contact with real things which is the unique characteristic of museums for adults and children who rarely, if ever, use existing museums and other cultural resources potentially available to them. The neighborhood museum is not viewed as a substitute for use of the city's cultural resources, but as a doorway or bridge to greater use of them.[54]

Another segment articulated:

Funds are being requested from private sources to support the initial operation of an experimental neighborhood museum. If the pilot project is successful, the Smithsonian Institution will consider requesting a Congressional appropriation to provide continued support for the neighborhood museum and if feasible to finance similar additional facilities. Federal funds, however, cannot be available for use until the beginning of Fiscal Year 1969.[55]

The text expressed how:

...as a museum, the Smithsonian Institution is an educational resource, open to the general public for "the increase and diffusion of knowledge among men." While millions of visitors use the Smithsonian annually for pleasure and learning, it is all too clear that large sectors of the Washington urban community do not do so.[56]

The wording of the study conveyed the museum's functions:

This museum will have a number of functions. At one level, it will serve its neighborhood as what might be described as a "curiosity shop," to which people can come as to any museum to observe an assemblage of interesting or puzzling or beautiful things. Objects will not be displayed as in traditional museum exhibits, however, but will be available to touch and tinker with; working model and machines will be stressed over static displays. In addition to the displays of objects, the Neighborhood Museum will experiment with the use of films, slide shows, and music in connection with exhibits. To the degree that users become interested or

curious about objects displayed, the museum will provide encouragement and space for workshops, clubs, and other related activities.[57]

Also during this development of the neighborhood museum, specialists from the SI staff gave their recommendations of museum curatorial displays. Most of them mirrored the attic of the institution; however, this forced the institution's career staff to embrace the new Ripley vision.

To determine the extent of the Smithsonian Institution's available resources for exhibits in the neighborhood museum, the curatorial staff was asked, in October 1966, to suggest ideas for possible exhibits. The memo circulated asked the objects be able to withstand vigorous exploration, either because of their sturdiness or because they can be replaced frequently. Staff responses ranged from program suggestions to the offer of objects from the collections for display.[58]

In order to help devise the Marsh Proposal, Marsh scheduled meetings with the most visible Black staff of SI custodians and museum guards. They shared their views of inclusion which was crucial in finding out how the SI should delicately approach using respectability in understanding cultural and class acceptance and expectation:

When they first asked me to plan for the museum I said the first thing I wanted to do was to talk with people from the community, and looking around, I said the only brown skinned people I see around are the guards and the maintenance workers. So I said that's who I want to talk to, so they thought I was crazy. The man who was in charge of the guards and maintenance and all of that... he arranged it... he said how many people do you want to talk to, and I said seven or eight. That would be fine. He got together a group of guards and maintenance workers and they were all African Americans and we met one morning or afternoon or whatever there at the Smithsonian in the castle and we had a very frank discussion about if the Smithsonian wanted to reach out where should they go and what are the things that they need to be concerned about... How important it would be to have someone from the community be on the staff of the museum. They raised questions of dress. They said would people be turned away if they weren't dressed right. For each question that they asked me, I would turn back the question to them and I would say what do you think? How would you advise? How do you think it should be? For example on the question of dress, they said well, supposing say some kids came in there bare foot, so I said so what do you think? And they said well encourage them to wear shoes, but they didn't say turn them away...[59]

The Making of a Neighborhood Museum

Although this museum fulfilled a need of educating the community through cultural awareness, cultural expressions, and celebrations of African traditions, museums and cultural institutions did exist in the United States in the African American community prior to the early 19th century and were established in the Black church. These religious institutions provided a source of outreach for the sophisticated and unsophisticated artist and exhibited collected history. The eminent scholar Bettye Collier-Thomas detailed the following history:

Black people in America, from the arrival of the first black person to the present have sought ways to celebrate and give recognition to their African and Afro-American heritage. Their efforts to define black achievement, to celebrate their blackness and to honor individual black contributions have taken many forms. Prior to the development of specific black institutions, such as museums, the church and school performed museum defined functions. As early as 1800, free blacks in cities were sponsoring small but significant exhibitions of black art and handiwork. As black religionists physically withdrew from white churches, to form independent black worship groups and after 1816 independent religious denominations, a variety of activities and programs having essentially museum type functions were developed. Prior to 1850, black museum type functions are identifiable in simple exhibitions of local black arts, small exhibitions of pictures and documents related to Phyllis Wheatley, Toussaint L'Ouverture and other black hero figures... In the cities, free blacks sponsored exhibits and gave awards for original poetry, original compositions of sacred music, original temperance essays and oil, crayon and water color paintings. The Reverend Daniel Payne, in The History of the African Methodist Episcopal Church, *gives an excellent example of this. In 1849, in Baltimore, Maryland, the Bethel A.M.E. Church sponsored a "Literary and Artistic Demonstration For the Encouragement of Literature and the Fine Arts Among the Colored Population." From 1865 to 1900, the phenomenal growth of black churches, benevolent institutions, normal schools and colleges and independent political and social organizations, spurred an increase in the number and kind of exhibitions available in the black community.*[60]

For example, Hampton and Tuskegee Institutes both served their local communities and established museum collections, which preserved and showcased relics and historic memorabilia connected to the history of the colleges and their prominent neighboring citizens. Prior to this era, African Americans also privately collected art, cultural memorabilia, and historic documents. The earliest African American collector of note and status is businessman Thomas Dorsey of Philadelphia, PA whose son eventually expanded the family's collection.

It would seem that the colored people were too poor to become collectors in one sense of the word, and yet if a lover of antiques, a lover of historical books, pamphlets and pictures were to go among them he would possibly be surprised. The Dorsey collection is well known as a collection of race literature and souvenirs. Begun in the lifetime of the elder Thomas Dorsey, it has been constantly enriched by the son until it contains many historical works, coins and other antiques. The interest the Negro is taking in himself is shown all over the country, and especially in Philadelphia by this tendency to collect all facts of interest to the race or which show the progress they are making toward overcoming prejudice.[61]

Another scholar notes:

It is noteworthy that the two most heavily endowed Negro colleges in the private sector (Hampton and Tuskegee Institutes) were the chief exponents of this educational concept. The philanthropic sources, individual and organized, contributed generously to the building and endowment programs of these two institutions. These contributions were in sharp contrast to those colleges which emphasized other educational concepts. However, both schools, in spite of their initial emphasis, do happen to be in the forefront of Negro colleges with such resources as art museums, and collections of works of art. The locus of the vast majority of predominantly Negro colleges is in the Deep South, and many are located in rural areas. The South until recent years was a culturally impoverished region. Also, it was by custom and law,

completely segregated along ethnic lines. These conditions further isolated the Negro
college, and its constituencies from those institutional resources which the South did
possess, such as art galleries, museums, and art schools. Thus there were few or no
incentives locally that could serve as the precursors to a dynamic awareness of the
Visual Arts in the Negro college.[62]

Professor Bryant Tolles particularizes how heritage was neglected:

A large number of research libraries, archives, historical societies, genealogy groups,
and black museums share the common purpose of collecting and preserving
material on history and cultural heritage of African Americans. Their mission is to
provide a more accurate picture of a history that has been continually, and in many
instances purposefully, neglected over time. Since the establishment of the College
Museum at Hampton Institute in 1868, some 150 institutions in thirty-seven states
have furthered this mission, operating against considerable odds to document the
story of the African presence worldwide. [63]

Anacostia, the community designated to house the Smithsonian Institution's neighborhood museum, won the chance to actively organize a museum. The community organized itself and articulated the overarching needs
the other neighborhoods lacked.

A woman, who found refuge in Anacostia after World War II, Mrs. Marion
Conover Hope of the legendary Hope family, was revered in the community
of Anacostia. She was a member of GAP and was leader of the search committee for the director of the neighborhood museum. James Hope articulated
these critical historical facts about Anacostia:

My parents moved here back in 1945 or 46 right after World War II. We had just
come back from Honolulu, and my father was teaching engineering at Howard
University and where as we had an apartment at Howard University we were told
we had to move out so we came out here to visit some friends who had purchased
a house right across the street, and we stood over there and looked over and
laughed at this funny house next door which six months later became our home...
When my parents bought this house, as you probably know, or maybe don't know,
Washington, DC was just like South Africa. We had apartheid here. There were

restrictive covenants placed on the titles and deeds to property saying there were certain properties in Washington that black people could not buy... We moved here when they still had restrictive covenants on properties... This particular street (Talbert Street) was kinda low or middle class/ blue collar/ white. And my mother was a real estate broker; one of her friends bought the house across the street, Mrs. Penn, who used to be one of the dorm mothers at Howard University, and then we bought a house, and then my mother was a broker and sold three other houses on this street. She sold one to Mr. Paul Thorn, he was one of the first black motorcycle police officers here, Mr. Harry Cook, he was the head of the D.C. Police Boys Club or something like that, and then Mr. Eugene Howie who lived in the white house across the street from here who was one of those interesting people that President Kennedy found in the Post Office. Dr. Howie had an advanced degree in Political Science and History but he worked at the Post Office. He had a good job and so, she sold three houses on this street and actually elevated the street. It was a benefit to the street.[64]

Marion Conover Hope a founder and advocate of the Anacostia Neighborhood Museum. She urged John Kinard to accept the museum director position.
Anacostia Community Museum Archives, Smithsonian Institution.

Mrs. Conover Hope, a very influential Washingtonian and Anacostia resident, was solicited to locate a director for the museum along with Dr. Blitzer, Dr. Ripley's head of education for the Smithsonian Institution. John Kinard briefly worked with James Hope (Mrs. Hope's son) as an interpreter for USIA, and also discussed their foreign travel experiences at the Hope's Talbert Street home. While he visited often, Kinard never met James' parents. Kinard recalls meeting Mrs. Conover Hope for the first time. He quickly realizes she has an agenda involving his future, which he initially rejects. John Kinard recalled lucidly these essential parts of his personal history:

I met this guy who lived around the corner from me, who was an escort, named James Hope. He calls me and says, "Listen, my mother wants to meet you. Will you drop by after work?" Fine. The distance that we lived from each other is about two blocks, not far at all. So I go by their home on Talbert Street, down at the bottom, near the museum, and Mrs. Marion Conover Hope and her husband, Edward S. Hope, were there. Jim, of course, was there. Now, I had visited Jim before, but he lived in an apartment upstairs. We'd go up there and talk about our experiences and drink rum, that kind of thing, you know. So because the house was separated, I never saw them, you see. This lady's asking me all of these questions. I had no idea what was really going on. It was the first time I ever met her or knew anything about her, and she said, "Listen, Mr. Kinard, we have decided that we are going to develop a museum out here in Anacostia, and we want you to be the director of it." I said, "Well, listen, Mrs. Hope, I don't know anything about museums. I have no training. I don't even visit museums. However, I tell you what. I would like to sit on your committee, because I'm generally interested in what goes on here in Anacostia. I haven't worked here." She says, "Because of your work here all of these people who know you have said, where ever we have been they say, 'Get Kinard.' That's how we know who you are." I said, "Well, listen Mrs. Hope. I have no inclination to want to run a museum. I don't see how a museum could have any redeeming factor in the development of this community, but I want to see for myself. I want to sit on the committee. You tell me the Smithsonian wants to do this museum. I don't believe it, and I want to see and hear with my own ears." She was with the Greater Anacostia People's Corporation. She was the one charged with finding somebody. This was a loosely contracted group of individuals who represented themselves and organizations, a large group of people. They got started over a riot... So I told Mrs. Hope, I said "Mrs. Hope, listen." I always tell people, when I tell this story, she was a pushy little lady. And that irritated me too because I don't cotton I'm not a chauvinist, but I don't cotton to being pushed by anybody. So I told her I would go and see this... (she always got his name mixed up) Hitzer, Titzer, it was Blitzer. Charles Blitzer. She said, "Listen, If you go see Mr. Blitzer, he's the main man." I said, I will go see what the Smithsonian's all about on this issue. I promise you I'll do that." She said "Okay." From that point it maybe took a couple of weeks before I got this appointment with Blitzer. When I went to see Blitzer... Blitzer said "Thank you for taking the job Mr. Kinard." And that is just the way it happened. I would like to introduce you to the secretary of the Smithsonian. So I said to myself "What the hell?" "A person ought to, if he has a chance, take one leap in the dark with his life, and this is it a leap in the dark." On July 5, 1967, Blitzer gave me the keys to the old rundown theater. [65]

Kinard was asked to attend a meeting with Dr. Blitzer and was selected to be the director of the new neighborhood museum, a position he held proudly for over twenty years. Julian Euell interviewed several educated, strongly qualified people, but the Smithsonian Institution was looking for someone civic minded.[66] They specifically wanted someone who knew the community and who would know what teenagers and adults would like; someone who was exposed to the world and international issues, but who felt comfortable with all kinds of people.[67] Dr. Caryl Marsh, Special Assistant to Secretary Ripley, remembers:

S. Dillon Ripley was a mastermind at understanding the dynamics of getting people to do whatever he wanted to have done. He had a great relationship with John. The two of them got along really fine. He was very sensitive to John. Anything that John wanted and he talked to Mr. Ripley about it, he got. He thought the Anacostia Museum was very important. And he thought John was terrific and that John knew what he was doing and Mr. Ripley was going to give him all of the support that he could. Ripley tried very hard to get extra money. [68]

She also added:

Everybody knew John was a minister. His strong concern for people and his strong concern for human beings and his acceptance... he never turned anybody away. He just welcomed all people and made them feel comfortable in the museum. [69]

The task before Kinard was very difficult. He spent much time planning, studying, and training himself in the museum field. He gathered a team of outstanding people to volunteer and assist with the renovation of the

Anacostia Neighborhood Museum. The history of the Smithsonian Institution and the prestige it carried left no room for error. Kinard's family friend, Robert G. Stanton, Director Stanton is the first African American director of the National Park Service. He was appointed by President Bill Clinton and was instrumental in assisting initially with the restoration of the Carver Theater.

In 1962, while a student at Houston-Tillotson College in Austin, TX, Stanton helped to integrate the National Park Service under the John F. Kennedy administration at the Grand Teton National Park in Jackson Hole, WY. While there, he befriended another park ranger named William "Bill" Kinard (Kinard's brother), a chemistry major from Livingstone College. This friendship afforded Stanton the ability to move to Washington, DC and become adopted by Jessie B. Kinard as an honorary member of the Kinard family. During his stay in Washington, DC he resided in the Kinard's Anacostia home. Robert Stanton relished the opportunity to look back on their first meeting and the ways it profoundly changed both of their lives:

I enrolled as a student in Houston-Tillotson University in Austin Texas where I graduated in 1963 but while at Houston Tillotson, The Department of the Interior was beginning to provide equal employment opportunities and consequently were doing recruiting on the college campus of historically black colleges and universities. I was a junior at the time when the recruiter came from the Department of the Interior and I was recommended by the president along with other students to accept these new opportunities. I was selected as a park ranger at Grand Teton National Park for the summer of 1962. And it was in the Grand Teton of 1962 that I met a distinguished young man from Livingstone College from Washington, DC. William Kinard and I worked at that park together in 1962 and came back in 1963 and through those summers, we developed a very, very close working relationship. And then in 1966, I became permanent with the National Park Service in Washington, DC. At that time I was still a bachelor and didn't have a place to stay in Washington, and I wanted to come there temporarily to look around for an apartment, so I got in touch with William and he said, "Hey Bob come on to Washington. We have a place and a room for you to stay with us." So I came to Washington in June of 1966 and I stayed with William, and his mother and John and Margie, and we developed a strong relationship and a relationship with the Kinards continued from 1962 when I first met William in Grand Teton National Park.[70]

He went on to relate his Washington, DC experiences with the family and museum:

While I was working with the park service in Washington in 1966 and living there with William, John, George and Mrs. Kinard, John had gotten the new job at that time. He was working with the Office of Economic Opportunity and this was under the Johnson administration, and during that period of time the Secretary of the Smithsonian, Secretary Ripley, had the great idea to really bring the museum to the people and they decided to locate it in Southeast Washington in the Anacostia area. And they needed to have someone with strong ties to the community who was energetic, who had a vision for cultural enrichment and certainly a great love for African American history and the culture of Anacostia, and John was selected for that position and really was the pioneer in the museum field. The first site as I recall selected for the museum was the theater located, at that time it was called Nichols Ave., which today we know as the Martin Luther King Jr. Ave. in the Southeast area. And after coming from work at the interior and William coming from work at his location, we all assisted John and the people from the community and the Smithsonian in rehabilitating the museum, and it proved to be an outstanding success and I think it far exceeded any of the expectations that Secretary Ripley and others in the Smithsonian leadership had at that time and it has proven to be a jewel of an asset not only for Anacostia, or Washington, DC but indeed an accent for the nation.[71]

A clear strong voice reinforced his insight on the building and the work he performed at the first museum site. Robert Stanton never lost sight of this museum's place on the path toward community improvement.

It was an old theater (Carver Theater) located on what we call now Martin Luther King Jr. Avenue. It was called Nichols Ave., at that time and it had to be rehabilitated. We had to put in new petitions and other kinds of improvements to accommodate it being used as a museum to put in certain kinds of exhibits, audio visual presentations, paintings and what have you. So there had to be a lot of interior work done. The exterior was not being changed substantially other than to note on the marquee outside that it was the Anacostia Museum. But we worked in there in the evenings. They had a number of committees formed and I was asked to chair the exhibit planning committee as a citizen volunteer. I was also painting and cleaning the building. That was during the earlier days.[72]

The Anacostia Museum was not the only cultural institution in the neighborhood. The Frederick Douglass Home gained affiliation with the National Park Service after strong petitions from the Anacostia community and popular national organizations. Because of Robert Stanton's connections with the community, through the museum, he soon found himself to be the first manager of the Frederick Douglass Home. To help tell the story of the Douglass' initially, Stanton enlisted the help of Kinard and his talented exhibit team, although the National Park Service had a regulated exhibit fabrications office located in Harpers Ferry, WV. Stanton chose to work with the Anacostia Neighborhood Museum's exhibit team because of the research sensitivity the subject needed. Robert Stanton is a manager with a powerful voice; a muscular and athletic frame; and, is one of the most ever-present and capable historians of this period.

As I moved up in the NPS where I eventually became the Superintendent of National Capital Parks-East. Frederick Douglass' home and administrative functioning office was in my area. Consequently we developed a close working relationship with the Anacostia Museum, in terms of exhibits and what have you. And one of the most outstanding exhibits that we worked on was "Frederick Douglass: The Sage of Anacostia". It was an award winning exhibit.[73]

The Professional Historian

He said, "When I go to the museum, that's my church."

During this great period of change in the course of the Black Power Era, Kinard, as director, became part of the new movement which ushered in reflections of cultural awareness and image analysis through the Black Studies and Arts movements. Meanwhile, the main beacon for the leaders of these movements found refuge in the African American museums that existed in different parts of urban America, some that predate the Anacostia Neighborhood Museum.

In the 1950's and early 1960's, most of the individuals who founded museums were artists and/or teachers, such as Elma Lewis, who founded a dance school in Roxbury, Massachusetts, in 1950, and eighteen years later the National Center of Afro-American Artists, or Margaret Burroughs, who organized the Ebony Museum of Negro Culture in Chicago in 1961 (now the DuSable Museum). Some of these new museums were founded by people involved in progressive politics, such as the group of trade unionists who established the San Francisco Afro-American Historical Society in 1956. Other founders emerged from the politically active wings of liberal Christian churches, such as Sue Bailey Thurman (wife of the leader of the noted Afro-American Historical Society of Boston [now the Museum of Afro-American History] in the African Meeting House on Beacon Hill.) After 1964, the founders of Black museums tended to be younger people whose political rhetoric and cultural goals were informed by the demonstrations, sit-ins, and freedom schools of the Southern Civil Rights Movement. These young people, such as Charles Wright, who established the Museum of African American History in Detroit in 1965, Edmund Barry Gaither, brought in by Elma Lewis in 1968 to be the director of the National Center of Afro-American Artists in Boston, Byron Rushing, the first director of the Museum of Afro-American History (founded in 1969), and John Kinard, first director of the Anacostia Museum (established in 1967) tended to share the older founders sense of the absolute importance of preserving African American life, history, and culture.[74]

A complex organization much like the African American church, the African American museum connected various cultural disciplines. This microcosm of influence bridged the cultural movements linking cultural awareness that served as a mirror to strengthen and define Black identity much like the church. Leaders of these cultural institutions around the nation have and continue to help steer this vehicle (the museum) in which lies the workshop to create, develop, demystify, and re-define Black popular culture. For in African American museums, you saw Black people taking ownership of images no matter their disciplinary background, which resembled the "for us, by us" community of support. Those who wanted to understand the revolution and urban explosion and newly found research on African people in America came to museums. Black artists found a vehicle of exposure to express their gifts and talents through visual, written, or performed art and supported these museums. The African American museum has been the incubator of stewardship for Black identity in America. Many experts of the Black Studies and Arts movement were atheists, leaders of the Nation of Islam, Christians, profound thinkers, and others just searching for an identity. This museum, the Anacostia Neighborhood Museum (ANM) and others, became a source of direction and support much like the African American church. These institutions became and still are multifaceted vehicles, which have full autonomy to interpret the African American experience. The Black Museums Movement, which started in the 1950s has been a steward of long forgotten collections and papers, many of which pre-date the organizations that house them.

Historically, to extract themselves and conform, Black people have formed a love affair with white culture, which derived from the hierarchical system of cultural values connected to enslavement. The museums help to provide cultural outlets for the culturally deprived children, youth, and adults. Ultimately, its goal ensures and validates the existence of African people in America. Questions of cultural identity historically have been problematic when trying to define the Black experience as beautiful, or connected to the American experience. The urgency of change was ignited around the country by one of the leading militant speakers, Stokely Carmichael. In his speeches, he shares the historical views and contradictions of our heritage taught to prior generations to disconnect from their genetic beauty which was a symbol of the much needed approval of white America. Urging Blacks to embrace their beauty, Carmichael found captive audiences at African American museums like the ANM, and prided them as vital in continuing the fight for justice.

The founders of the African American Museums Association now known as the Association of African American Museums. Mr. John Kinard, Mrs. Margaret Burroughs, Dr. Charles Wright, and Dr. Bettye Collier Thomas Kinard Collection.

It is time for you to begin to understand that you, as the growing intellectuals, the black intellectuals of this country, must begin to define beauty for black people. Beauty in this society is defined by someone with a narrow nose, thin lips, white skin. You ain't got none of that. If your lips are thick, bite them in. Hold your nose; don't drink coffee because it makes you black. Everybody knows black is bad. Can you begin to get the guts to develop criteria for beauty for black people? Your nose is boss, your lips are thick, you are black, and you are beautiful. Can you begin to do it so that you are not ashamed of your hair and you don't cut it to the scalp so that naps won't show? Girls are you ready? Obviously it is your responsibility to begin to define the criteria for black people concerning their beauty.[75]

The museums can be defined as a place where collections of art, research, cultural studies, archives, and other memorabilia are properly stored, exhibited, and showcased for the general public, to observe and explore exhibits which connect with diverse age and cultural groups. Black museums face a lot of responsibility to interpret a story entrenched in sadness and succeed in their effort. The same three major problems facing all museums around the world involve weathering the following: (1) challenges with fundraising; (2) marketing; and (3) finding skilled employees with longevity and commitment. In his role as the director of the ANM, Kinard supervised a staff that included exhibit specialists, education specialists, researchers, curators, and collections managers. Unlike most museums around the world, Kinard directed the first totally federally funded African American museum in the nation.

You know, there's an old saying that he who pays the bills calls the tune. But I think that here we have a new creature. As a branch of the Smithsonian Institution, our funds come from the Federal Government...[76]

**On Friday evening, September 15, 1967, the opening night ceremonies
for the Anacostia Neighborhood Museum took place.**
Anacostia Community Museum Archives, Smithsonian Institution.

A secure budget and appropriated funding for staff training, exhibits, research, and education program development, made the museum secure in its operation; but the needs to subscribe to a structured bureaucracy afforded less freedom, having to follow rules, policies, procedures, and neighborhood advisors. Most African American museums just wrestled with a board of directors. If other African American museums had the luxury of secured annual budgets, they could have better facilities and staff. The drive and determination of a capable staff helped to make the museum respected worldwide. Although Kinard lacked formal training as a museum professional, he learned about museum management on the job. The museum developed programs, which raised self-esteem, self-respect, and produced positive self-development in its community. This museum encouraged neighborhood residents to embrace their cultural history and become more knowledgeable of their connections to American history. Edward Alexander, author of *The Museum in America,* a book that combines the history of museums since the eighteenth century with a detailed examination of the function of museums and museum workers in modern society, saw the Anacostia museum as an essential resource.

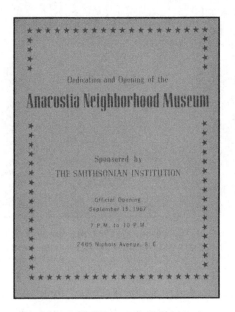

Program from the opening ceremony.
Anacostia Community Museum Archives, Smithsonian Institution.

On September 15, 1967, the Anacostia Neighborhood Museum staged a gala opening attended by about four thousand community citizens and residents of the entire metropolitan area, featuring an 84-piece band, two jazz combos, and an enthusiastic block party with energetic youngsters and adults serving refreshments.

Exhibits borrowed from the Smithsonian's National Museum of Natural History, National Museum of American History, and National Zoo included an 1895 store of early Anacostia with a post office; metal toys, butter churn, ice cream maker, coffee grinder, and water pump; as well as live monkeys, a large green parrot, other birds, and a black snake. A group of young local artists known as the Trail Blazers painted a mural of primitive life in Africa on a nearby fence, and the lot across from the museum contained a dinosaur, Uncle Beasley, on which children delighted to climb. A projector with slides was available in the museum, and show boxes of small natural history exhibits where bird and animal skins, shells, and fossils could be examined. The community accepted the new institution as its own and maintained it carefully. The museum was estimated to cost $125,000-150,000 per year covered at first by Smithsonian private funds and foundation grants. When that figure proved too small, the local community raised $7,000 to match a grant, with individual contributions ranging from five cents to one dollar. A local businessman also provided a bus to take children downtown to the Smithsonian for Saturday morning classes.[77]

The scholarly work of his staff, still respected today for their educational programs and exhibits, laid the groundwork for many creative and ingenious education programs that made the museum popular. Exhibits were created on African American inventors; Frederick Douglass; the historic Anacostia neighborhood; Anna J. Cooper; and the Anacostia Studies program which focused on community preservation and served as the catalyst for the Anacostia Historical Society.

"This place," said John R. Kinard, the director of the Anacostia Neighborhood Museum in Washington, DC "has brought people who wouldn't otherwise be caught dead in a museum." Its exhibitions often might be based on the requests found in the suggestion box, giving local residents a real feeling of 'this is our place." At the museum, neighbors could "meet to discuss local problems and try to find ways of improving them," and its exhibits and programs expressed every aspect of the Anacostia experience psychological, spiritual, social, and political. Thus such a museum could meet the practical needs of its community, while attracting a significant number of neighborhood people at all levels. And finally, Kinard asserted, such a museum should concern the common people: Our country and its museums have scandalously never told us the truth about Western society. Because

presentations were written about the middle-class white Americans by middle class white Americans who study and write about what interests them, their presentations on our society represent the life of celebration, of achievement and conquest. This is not of interest to most Americans, for our lives are lived striving to achieve self-identity, and to make something out of everyday life.[78]

Louise Daniel Hutchinson was the museum's historian and head of the Research Department from 1971-1987. She wrote the acclaimed book, *The Anacostia Story*. Anacostia Community Museum Archives, Smithsonian Institution.

This period of Black consciousness strongly supported brotherhood and sisterhood throughout the nation. Recognizing this collective communal contact with one another provided a richer, sincere outlook of those living together in the urban neighborhoods, which gave credence to the "for us, by us" ideology. Anacostia was no different. When choosing the staff of the museum, there was no reason to look outside of the museum for capable employees. Some of the first people hired were from the community of Anacostia, and professional black SI staff members like James Mayo, a well-known black exhibit designer, lived in Anacostia.

The very first person that John Kinard hired was a man that was suggested by Stanley Anderson. Stanley Anderson knew him for a long time and his family lived next door to Stanley and he was an ex-convict and, in fact, when I got his name and happened to know somebody in the courts, so I called up to find out about this man, cause I said we are going to hire him and Stanley suggested that he be hired as part of the maintenance staff and caretaker, to show the community that everybody was welcomed and they were trusted. So the guy from the court said, "Oh your man has got a record as long as my arm." He had been convicted not once but many times. He was a tall very handsome guy. And your father had no hesitation; he just hired him and he became the chief caretaker. Zora Felton had never worked in a museum before and she was somebody your father knew fairly well. The very first community meeting that we had was at the Southeast Neighborhood House, so we all were there and Zora was there. And Zora was involved from day one, and then your father hired her to be the head of education. She was not trained to be the education director at a museum but she carved it out and did a fabulous job. She was terrific.[79]

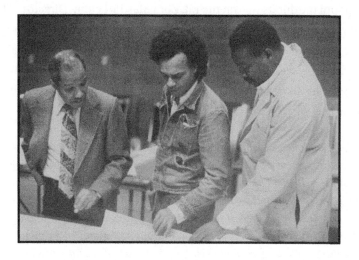

Senior staff of the Exhibit Design and Production Laboratory, 1978. Larry Erskine Thomas, Jim Mayo, and James Daniels. Anacostia Community Museum Archives, Smithsonian Institution.

Caryl Marsh added:

The first exhibit that your father did was the exhibit of sculptures from Ralph Tate. Well that was a fabulous exhibit. And people on the mall, they hissed and fumed... why was this... so on and so forth... but Tate was an African American. He had done these fabulous sculptures and it was entirely suitable. So the whole museum was turned over to the sculptures of Ralph Tate. It was brilliant... There was one incident. When the museum opened one of the things on display was a model electric train, and I think one day your father discovered that one of the youngsters carried off one of the trains. So I forget exactly how he handled, but either the same day or the next day, the youngster came back. It was so tempting to the child he just took it, but he brought it back the next day.[80]

Kinard, through this museum, was an agent of change and pioneer in Black cultural redefinition. This museum provided a unique model for American museums to set a standard to raise the consciousness of Americans, to think about their rich, diverse history, culture, and environment. One of the most popular exhibits was on the rat. Zora Martin-Felton, Director of Education for the Anacostia Museum was the creator of the exhibit, *The Rat: Man's Invited Affliction*. She is a delicate woman with clear and unmistakable brilliance, a widely respected museum innovator with many museum awards for her work. She shares the day she brought the idea about an exhibit on rats to Kinard:

When I approached John about an exhibition on the rats, I was thinking small. There was somewhat of a turf battle going on in that the exhibits people wanted all of the space. So I had carved out the children's room, which was a room where kids could come in and do all kinds of experimental things. It was their space. I said to John, "There are a lot of strange things happening with the few animals that we have in the zoo and outside of the zoo. There is a great hatred for those Canadian rats. I would really like to do something on rats. It will just take up a little corner in the museum." He leaned back in his chair and said, "Take the whole museum." The children in the community knew more about rats than I did.[81]

Although Kinard had the much-needed support of his family, Secretary Ripley, Julian Euell Assistant Secretary, Charles Blitzer, and the community, he faced many obstacles throughout his journey to carry out the unique mission of the Anacostia Neighborhood Museum. Kinard overcame these obstacles and faced rejection through faith in himself, his spiritual beliefs, and the desire to destroy the hurdles of racism, by integrating the position as the first African American director of a Smithsonian Institution museum, a position he never sought out, but which became his destiny. He joined the affiliation of many distinguished men, such as, Director Kennedy of the American History Museum. Director Kennedy liked Kinard and perceived Anacostia as a great asset to the Smithsonian Institution.

If he had been rich, white, and well connected it would have led him in another direction... I recall respectful, intelligent exchanges that were candid and did not dissemble the real challenges he had—he was too candid for some, but never I think out of any other impulse than serving the larger causes of equal opportunity in American life, and the special needs of the Anacostia community in a stressful time. I never thought he grandstanded or let his ego get in the way of the work.[82]

He added these noteworthy thoughts:

Of course —he was put in a special role starting a new venture of a novel sort. He did it very well... he was well qualified to do what he was asked to do—and he never pretended to be a historian in the academic way...[83]

As an activist he became a pioneer and major museum professional. Many residents in the Anacostia community, both children and adults lacked exposure and never had a desire to leave the comfort of their neighborhood to visit museums.

Gradually an informal set of guidelines developed from the discussions, reflecting what was wanted as well as what was to be avoided from the past disappointments with museums as well as with other public programs. "We were told that for the proposed museum: It was important to have adequate funding and paid staff. The exhibits should be something special and really unique, not dull and boring. Visitors should be able to come in not only to look and touch but also to do. There must be a chance to become familiar with new skills. There should be exhibits on "Our Negro Heritage." There should be space for the display of neighborhood talent and of exhibits produced by neighborhood people.[84]

The task of funding this project in its first year was sponsored by a number of sources. Most of them contributed annually to the Smithsonian Institution to fund research and special programs.

The Carnegie Corporation of New York, Eugene and Agnes E. Meyer Foundation, Anne S. Richardson Fund, Irwin-Sweeney Miller Foundation, Stern Family Fund, and the Cafritz Foundation. The budgetary cost for the ANM in its first year of operations totaled over $100,000.[85]

In 1967, Dr. Martin Luther King Jr. launched the Poor People's Campaign. The idea for this campaign was to organize the nation's poor to demand action from the United States government to respond to their grievances and to secure jobs and provide economic resources for all.

We intend to channel the smoldering rage and frustration of Negro people into an effective, militant, and nonviolent movement of massive proportions in Washington and other areas. Similarly, we would be calling on the swelling masses of young people in this country who were disenchanted with this materialistic society and asking them to join us in our new Washington Movement...We decided to go to Washington and use any means of legitimate nonviolent protest necessary to move our nation and our government on a new course of social, economic, and political reform.[86]

This dream, realized in Anacostia with key leaders of the community coming together to plan a strategy to transform a community through a museum connected to resources, gave a voice to the poor people of southeast Washington, DC. Although King was assassinated before this protest of social, economic, and political reform came to fruition, King remotely breathed life into the purpose of this neighborhood museum.

During the establishment of the museum, President Lyndon B. Johnson held office. His wife Lady Bird Johnson was a leader in environmental education and national initiatives promoting the beautification of America. She encouraged Americans to plant flowers to make communities more enjoyable and attractive. Lady Bird Johnson's idea was embraced across the nation, even in Washington, DC and, in 1966, supported the development of Project Pride, a program community activist Marion Barry worked closely with.[87]

> *The Project Pride committee was formed; staff help came from the National Capital Housing Authority and headquarters opened at 913 P Street, N.W. Twenty Howard University students were employed through a Department of Health, Education and Welfare grant, and eighty high school students worked on the project through the Neighborhood Youth Corps.*[88]

Refusing to relinquish the project, Lady Bird Johnson sought help to fund it the following year.

Washington, DC Councilwoman Polly Shackleton and John Kinard.
Anacostia Community Museum Archives, Smithsonian Institution.

Polly Shackleton, Democratic National Committee woman in 1961, and a Washingtonian, supported Project Pride and assisted Lady Bird Johnson in seeking funding to keep the summer programs for DC youth functioning in 1967. In Anacostia, the summer program funded by Laurance Rockefeller, similar to Project Pride, was called the Trail Blazers. These youth helped to restore the Carver Theater, as well as other beautification projects in the Anacostia community.

To underwrite her idea, Shackleton approached Laurance Rockefeller who agreed to make a $50,000 gift to the society for a summer project to be called Project Trail Blazers, which would enlist "low income young people living in areas east of their neighborhoods." The project "eventually enrolled 110 youths 95 boys and 15 girls; aged 13 to 15, many of them came out of a background of extreme deprivation which often makes its mark physically and emotionally." Their work included the reshaping of a shuttered movie theater into the Anacostia Neighborhood Museum, as well as the creation of play spaces near the Frederick Douglass Home. In late 1967 Mrs. Johnson toured the project with Henry Diamond of Rockefeller's staff. "It was just great" Shackleton noted, "for the youngsters, the staff and the Anacostia population in general to have her go out there." The youth, which made up the Trail Blazers, were also involved in the (Anacostia Neighborhood Museum's) Youth Advisory Council.[89]

To fund the Trail Blazers program, the money Polly Shackleton received from Laurance Rockefeller was in stock shares. Getting the stock shares transferred into an account to underwrite the program was slightly delayed but ended up working out. According to Caryl Marsh, Polly Shackleton shared the story of the strange encounter receiving the suitcases of stock shares.

Mr. Rockefeller gave us $75,000. We got a budget for it and so on. Polly told me the story about the money. They called her up from New York, and said that a messenger was coming and so somebody appeared at her doorway with these two suitcases and in them were these, I guess it was this big gasoline company's $75,000 worth of shares of the stock. So she had to call up this woman that she knew who understood about all those things. She took the stock, and got the cash for it.[90]

In an effort to involve the youth of the community, the museum continued the efforts of the Trail Blazers and established the Youth Advisory Council (YAC). This volunteer group of teens who lived in the community was an invaluable asset to the museum. Zora Martin-Felton developed this future leadership extension of the museum to help keep youth off the streets and provide an opportunity for them to give innovative input into the operation of the museum. The impact of the YAC's representing the museum in their community and abroad resulted in the success of the experimental neighborhood museum from a different perspective. In the fifth anniversary report created by the (ANM) staff, Debbie Jones expressed her experiences as a member of the Youth Advisory Council:

As a member of Youth Advisory Council (YAC) I have learned the importance of responsibility. When you are on your own in another country (YAC has traveled to Africa, Puerto Rico, Nassau [Bahamas], and New York City), many people depend on you to give a good impression of where you came from, to establish and maintain a reputation as a responsible citizen. Being a part of YAC means a lot to me. It gives the perfect opportunity to be active in the workings of the museum. Being a member of YAC also presents some worthwhile and exciting opportunities for example, meeting important people from other museums as well as from other parts of the country and of the world. Being exposed to people from all walks of life is a good way for one to develop a sense of awareness of oneself. [91]

Volunteers in the YAC group were instrumental in exposing other youth in the community to a world filled with culture and opportunity. They represented the disenchanted youth of the African American community who needed to see new creative ways of thinking through life options and career choices being opened up to Blacks. One of the members, Debbie Jones, whose mother Theresa Jones was involved in leading the rent strikes at Barry Farms, raised her children to be active in the community. As a member of the YAC group, she worked as volunteer staff, assisting with education programs. Debbie Jones had fond memories as a YAC member:

The past few months we have learned to do all of the demonstrations in the children's room, which incidentally we helped plan and physically put together. If after school groups came in, we helped with the tours and demonstrated how to make soap, taffy, candles, and ice cream. This year, again, we are silk screening our original black Christmas card to sell for our Travel fund. [92]

Youth Advisory Council Coordinator, Zora Martin-Felton, explains the Youth Advisory Council concept started by the community youth:

The Youth Advisory Council was founded by Gregory Reynolds and another student from the Barry Farms Housing Project. They came to see John one day and Kinard challenged them to go and come back with a plan for youth involvement in the ANM. They returned and said that they wanted to form a Youth Advisory Council to help run the Anacostia Museum. This was revolutionary to have teens helping to run the Museum. They used to come to the museum every day after school and they would come to my office and "tell me what to do" and "tell John what to do." They learned a lot of skills. They learned about exhibit design and production. Some of them are now employed by the Smithsonian. Ahmad heads an exhibits department at one of the museums.[93]

She was categorical as she made known these significant pieces of information:

Kids from the neighborhood gained excellent skills as they developed their own programs and exhibits. They traveled out of the country to Puerto Rico and the Bahamas. Because of John's influence with Crossroads Africa, Trish Jones went to Haiti to work on a project. Michael Battle went to Botswana and Gail Pettigrew went to Ghana.[94]

This outlet became a vital part of the museum's operation and further justified the need to have this museum be led by the community. This also enabled the community to discover other alternatives of honorable employment. Although not in existence today, this program assisted in changing the stereotypical opinions of the Black deprived youth in one community and gave hope to families all over the community of Anacostia.

Behind the Scenes: The Image Makers and Breakers

Museums have traditionally been organized to contain exhibits, research departments, and educational programs tailored to certain age levels and historic events centered on visually appealing exhibited research. The Anacostia Museum was a one-of-a-kind museum, in that it met the needs of the community for which it was named. It also employed one of the most capable and competent staffs of any museum, Black or white. Uncommonly found in any mainstream museum, African American exhibit designers made major strides in image control within African American museums. These persons figured prominently in the Anacostia Museum.

Jim Mayo, now he did work for the Smithsonian. There were African Americans behind the scenes like Jim Mayo who worked in the shops. I never saw them so I met Jim Mayo. Jim Mayo came out from the very first day he came to the community meetings. He was mad at the Smithsonian because they wouldn't do this and they wouldn't do that. So everything he said that they wouldn't do, I saw to it that they did. Initially, Anacostia didn't have an exhibits shop of their own. The exhibits were all made down at the Mall. Jim Mayo was down at the Mall. One of the things your father wanted was his own capability, so finally when they began to have regular budgets, he got a budget for exhibits and carved out a place in that building. It was converted into an exhibitions production facility and Jim Mayo was in charge.[95]

James Mayo, the Exhibit Specialist; Larry Erskine Thomas, Research Department; and Zora Martin-Felton, the Education and Development Department Specialist were encouraged to be creative and think outside of the conventional sphere to connect and relate to museum education and exhibit designing within the fundamental scope of collected research.

Zora Martin-Felton, a native of Bethlehem, PA was the first African American graduate of Moravian College, the sixth oldest college in America. She migrated to Washington in 1958. Prior to joining the museum, Felton was field counselor at a school for delinquents, director of teenage activities for the Dayton, OH YWCA and director of group work and education programs at the Southeast Neighborhood House where she first met and worked with John Kinard. Felton directed all activities of the Education and Development Department at the Anacostia Neighborhood Museum. She played a major role in the creation of the Children's Room, the Mobile Division, the YAC group, and the exhibit on rats titled *The Rat: Man's Invited Affliction*, and many other special projects. Felton, the museum Educational Program Coordinator, recalls in a low-pitched voice a unique program offered by the Anacostia Neighborhood Museum:

> *Community involvement made the ANM different from other museums. Who would want to be bothered with convicts? Who would think about going into the penitentiary and sitting down and working with them? We made arrangements for inmates to leave the penitentiary and come to the museum. We would have rap sessions. Some of the inmates became tour guides. That was really revolutionary. They were brought from Lorton every day. They conducted demonstrations. People did not know about the "Inner Voices" until they came to the museum. This was a wonderful dramatic group, which portrayed life at Lorton. They were so powerful. They had a band. We did many, many programs with Lorton.*[96]

Between 1959 and 1965 James Mayo was exhibit specialist supervisor for the Museum of History and Technology of the Smithsonian Institution. During a leave of absence in 1963, he designed and produced the installation of the Robert Woods Bliss Collection of Pre-Columbian Art for the Dumbarton Oaks Museum, located in Washington, DC. Mayo was a freelance designer and fabrication specialist contracting with museums and private collectors from 1965 to 1967. He designed and supervised the installation of an exhibit on *The Evolution of Afro-American Artists: 1800-1950* for the city of New York. Early on, the Metropolitan Museum.

> *...became very concerned about the African American population in New York and they decided to have an exhibition called* Harlem on my Mind, *and somehow we were invited up to New York. So John and a man named Bob Mason (The Special Assistant to Secretary Ripley) and I went up to meet with Tom Hoving, the director of the Metropolitan Museum. The first question he asked was to your father, he said where is Jim Mayo. Jim Mayo had a great reputation being the best person working with plastics. At that time they were just beginning to make glass cases out of clear plastic and apparently it was difficult to glue the four corners together, and Jim was the genius at that, and Mr. Hoving wanted Jim Mayo to make some special plastic cases for the Metropolitan Museum, he didn't really care about us all he wanted was Jim Mayo.*[97]

Larry Thomas was a leading figure in technical art procedures and graphic arts training in Africa. He was a teacher for eight years and developed comprehensive curricula in technical illustrations and mechanical drawings for

EMBRACING THE MOVEMENT AND ANACOSTIA

the Ethiopian Ministry of Education and Fine Arts. He also served for five years, at the request of Emperor Haile Selassie I, on the advisory committee for special cultural exhibitions. He supervised the design and production of cultural exhibits honoring the visits of President Tito of Yugoslavia and King Paul and Queen Frederica of Greece. Studying cultural anthropology at Haile Selassie I University, Thomas designed the pictorial map of Ethiopia that was presented to President Eisenhower during the Emperor's visit to the United States in 1954. Balcha Fellows, Special Projects Assistant, wrote and coordinated proposals for Museum programs and projects. Previously, he was Assistant to the Director for Public Relations, a staff photographer, and producer of graphics and audio-visual material for the Museum. Prior to joining the museum, Mr. Fellows was assistant sales promotion officer for the Cotton Company of Ethiopia, the founder and sales manager of the Ethiopian Publishing Company, and circulation and advertising manager for the Voice of Ethiopia. Mr. Fellows produced numerous graphics including "The Age of Innocence" for the National Trust for Historic Preservation; a hall display for the Federal City College dropout Prevention Program; and the "1970 All-Pro Games Sports Exhibition" for the Southern Christian Leadership Conference.

Fletcher Smith, Program Manager of the Mobile Division was responsible for dissemination of mobile services and programs. This included portable exhibits and speakers as well as educational materials for schools. Prior to joining the museum, he was playground director for the DC Recreation Department and guidance counselor with a manpower training program. Renny Parziale, pottery artist, conducted pottery demonstrations and workshops privately and at numerous DC schools. Barbara Bryant, Museum Technician, conducted guided tours of the museum. Prior to joining the museum staff, she was with the Museum of Natural History and Smithsonian Oceanographic Sorting Center. Carolyn Margolis, Research Assistant, performed research, wrote scripts for exhibits and slide/tape shows, and organized and wrote catalogs for major exhibitions presented by the museum. James Campbell, Exhibit Specialist from the Museum of Natural History, was assigned to the

THE MAN, THE MOVEMENT, THE MUSEUM

Anacostia Neighborhood Museum in May 1967. Michael Guido Fischer, Visual Information Specialist and photographer, recorded the museum events and worked on documentaries and motion pictures.

The museum's Mobile Division van took exhibits and books to sites throughout the Washington area. Pictured is Ahmed Mbalia (Fletcher Smith) who operated the jitney bus purchased with funds from the Junior League of Washington.
Anacostia Community Museum Archives, Smithsonian Institution.

Together, these masterminds assisted the Anacostia Neighborhood Museum plan the approach to sensitively exhibit African American culture with delicate urgency. The work at the Anacostia Neighborhood Museum was respected all over the world:

> There are those who have seen Anacostia as nothing more than a recipe for organized chaos, a museum version of a popular American Negro church. Certainly Anacostia is as different from the British Museum as a service in a popular church would be from Evensong in Westminster Abbey or High Mass in St. Peter's, but this is a superficial judgment. Any community museum will necessarily take on the flavor of the district in which it finds itself. There is no fixed pattern. Anacostia, however must be given the credit of pioneering the concept of a museum without walls to keep it

within bounds, a museum with a creative flow of ideas, exhibits and people between itself and the outside world.[98]

Entering new horizons with the ecomuseums of the world, the community concept was embraced and nurtured. In 1979, Pierre Mayrand, director of the Haute-Beauce Museum and Regional Interpretation Centre, introduced the concept but not the name to the residents of his community. Haute-Beauce is a remote rural Appalachian plateau in Canada. In this remote and isolated area where no cultural facilities existed, this resource would fulfill a need for learning together with its residents, much like the Anacostia Neighborhood Museum. Sheila Stevenson, an ecomuseum enthusiast from the Nova Scotia Museum, Halifax, found that the most highly valued element of this sort of museum is the interaction of people. The fact that the neighborhood museum concept started to reach foreign lands regardless of color, proves cultural and community preservation was important. Working together in developing an effective plan, the departments of the museum had to devote major time, creativity, and effort to draw in visitors. The design of the exhibits, education programs, and research were crucial and took long hours to achieve the desired goals. Exhibits on *Historic Anacostia, The Rat: Man's Invited Affliction, Bethune and the Black Cabinet* and other diverse cultural subjects were of great community interest. Carolyn Margolis, a volunteer who became a paid member of the research staff vividly recalls:

The camaraderie and the family spirit that prevailed in those days: There was never an exhibit we opened when we didn't work until an hour before the show opened on Sunday. John would come in at 2 am to clean the bathrooms, then go out and buy Kentucky Fried Chicken, and come back with buckets of chicken and sodas... That's when we were at our best... The level of spirit was good and the kids the museum's Youth Advisory Council and neighborhood were always there.[99]

Muhammad Ali, champion prize-fighter, civil rights leader.
Anacostia Community Museum Archives, Smithsonian Institution.

Kwame Toure (Stokely Carmichael), civil rights activist.
Anacostia Community Museum Archives, Smithsonian Institution.

Many Black celebrities and intellectuals visited the museum during its first five years. Some of those people were Muhammad Ali, Stokely Carmichael, Portia Washington Pittman (daughter of Booker T. Washington), Dizzy Gillespie, Shirley Horn, Georgia Jessup, Sterling Brown, Astronaut Michael Collins, Congressman Augustus Hawkins, Ambassador Moses, Jesse Owens, and Ambassador Lukumbuzya from Tanzania, to name a few. Later in November of 1967, Walter E. Washington was appointed mayor of Washington, DC by President Lyndon Johnson. He and his wife, Bennetta Bullock, were graduates of Howard University. As an employee of the Housing Authority, Washington became the executive director, holding the highest position held by an African American man in the District. Mayor Washington, in his role as mayor, was quite encouraging to the Anacostia community through the Anacostia Neighborhood Museum. On the fifth anniversary of the Anacostia Neighborhood Museum, Washington gave his warm wishes:

Dear Mr. Kinard:

It gives me pleasure to note the Fifth Anniversary of the opening of The Anacostia Neighborhood Museum. I offer my congratulations to you, to Dr. S. Dillon Ripley, your staff, and to the volunteers and contributors who have worked so hard. The Anacostia Neighborhood Museum offers a unique and relevant experience in an area long deprived of facilities for its residents to share our city's artistic and historical experiences. As Mayor of Washington, I have visited the Anacostia Neighborhood Museum and have enjoyed what I saw and experienced. The museum has provided enrichment not only for the citizens of Anacostia, but also for all Washingtonians and residents of the metropolitan area. In addition, the museum and its programs complement our other facilities in Anacostia and fit into the overall plan for the revitalization of the area so that it becomes a full and complete community for all citizens, young, old, black, white, rich and poor. I wish the Anacostia Neighborhood Museum many additional years of existence and growth and am confident it will continue to fulfill its mission.

Sincerely Yours,
Walter E. Washington,
Mayor [100]

THE MAN, THE MOVEMENT, THE MUSEUM

The Washington Riots

No strangers to change, commitment, and service, John F. Kennedy's, Malcolm X's, and Martin Luther King Jr.'s assassinations were symbols to African Americans of a public execution of declared progress. The exceptional defeats of injustices made through the efforts of these men who shaped policy and rejuvenated the nation on the road to developing unity had been killed. These men and the sacrifices of their families were so easily shattered with a bullet. A senseless deed of violence killed fathers, husbands, and men of robust power. These leaders, who saw redemption in America, represented a new thought, new generation, and a new America. The growing interest and support in these new ideals affected all generations to ultimately become a more inclusive country. Contrary to these popular new principles, values and ideas embraced by many, some found fault with this new wave of idealism. These ideals held competing interests with past segregationist thought supported by Southerners.

> In 1963, it was the assassination of John F. Kennedy, whom many blacks had come to regard as their friend. Then came the murder of Malcolm X in 1965 and the feeling, shared by many blacks, that the prosecution of his assailants was less than vigorous. In the mid 1960's there was moreover, the murder of numerous civil rights workers as well as innocent children, and for these crimes no one was convicted or even seriously prosecuted.[101]

Shock waves of anger throughout the nation, caused by hearing news of the deaths of these moral men, brewed anger and frustration. The assassinations set off dangerous levels of synchronized anger all over the nation. The pain of losing these heroes was expressed in looting and incidents of arson. In 1968, the assassination of Dr. Martin Luther King Jr. was the most heartfelt. The news of his tragic death created an eruption of anguish and anger.

> Finally on April 4, 1968, Martin Luther King Jr., was shot down in a motel in Memphis, where he had gone to give support to striking garbage workers. To many African Americans this violent act symbolized the rejection by white America

of their vigorous but peaceful pursuit of equality. In more than 100 cities several days of rioting and burning and looting ensued, a grave response by many blacks to the wanton murder of their young leader. The subsequent capture of James Earl Ray and his immediate trial, without any testimony after his plea of guilty, further embittered large numbers of blacks who suspected that such speedy "justice" was merely a cover-up for the possible conspiracy. The exhaustive inquiry into the matter by the Select Congressional Committee did not lead to a satisfactory conclusion on the conspiracy question.[102]

In many urban cities like Chicago, IL, Harlem, New York City, Trenton, NJ, Los Angeles, CA, and Washington, DC treacherous riots ensued. In Washington, DC proper, the hurt and sympathy spurred nationwide enraged youth, who used displaced anger to destroy the African American communities and popular shopping centers located downtown, which affected merchants of diverse backgrounds, but mainly white business owners. Fourteenth, Seventh, and U Streets located in Northwest, faced major destruction. Many of the merchants on these streets left the inner cities and moved their business to the suburbs. Ben's Chili Bowl is one of the only Black businesses which still exists that survived the DC riots on U St., N.W. Some businesses survived by writing "Soul Brother" on the front windows and doors of their establishments, identifying them as Black-owned.

Within a few hours of Dr. King's death on April 4, 1968, looting and burning broke out in poor black sections of Washington and in several other cities. In the capital, most of the destruction took place along three shopping streets 14th Street, N.W., 7th Street, N.W., and H Street, N.E. Stores were the major targets. Liquor stores, groceries, drug stores, and clothing stores were hard hit. Some black-owned businesses were hurt, but most of the stores destroyed were owned by white people. The disturbances lasted three days, during which the city imposed a curfew and called for assistance from army troops. In all, rioters destroyed more than 677 dwelling units. An emergency committee was formed to distribute food through churches near the riot areas. Another committee found new living quarters for many burned-out families. Black and white leaders cooperated in these emergency efforts. Despite international relief action, the riots intensified racial tensions in the city. Many small businessmen who had been burned out were bitter about the way police had handled the disturbances. Some said that policemen stood by and watched the stores being looted. Some congressmen also criticized the police for their handling of the riot. Restraint by police substantially limited bloodshed; however, of the 12 persons killed in Washington's riot, only two died by police bullets. Compared to other cities torn apart by violence, the capital's record on police-caused deaths was excellent. A larger long-range issue was how to rebuild the riot-scarred areas. The city hoped to stimulate rapid rebuilding to return services to the people who needed them. But there was much disagreement over how to rebuild and who should rebuild. Many militant black leaders said that white merchants should not return to the ghetto.[103]

All over the city, people were on edge and bothered at how some poured out decades of resentment by participating in the riots. Around the nation many activists wondered how the community could stop youth from causing this destruction. In Anacostia, there was also this thought, which was, "Would the youth riot in this community?" "Would the Anacostia Museum and other businesses be hurt or destroyed?" This Black museum, also mourning the loss of this great leader, Martin Luther King, Jr., hoped that, because of its purpose, the work and sacrifices of a community could refrain from going up in smoke. Not only did the museum go untouched, it was used as a refuge for a white man who lost his way on April 4, 1968, and found himself in the heart of the Black community during its grieving sojourn. The incident was related by Caryl Marsh:

> *I heard about this from your father, during the Martin Luther King riots. That was "68" and they came sweeping down, well it wasn't called Martin Luther King Jr. Avenue, it was Nichols Ave. They came sweeping down Nichols Avenue, and apparently your father found just out on the street a white guy, and wanted to know what he was doing in the neighborhood. And your father took him in and had him to stay there in the museum; and your father just sat and stayed in the museum the whole time when the riots were going on and nobody ever touched the museum.[104]*

The eruption of frustration all over the nation made a powerful appeal to America and, in turn, the world. They felt the hurt and effects of

the riots which caused significant economic impact on major businesses.
Between 1967 and 1969, the creation of Black Studies programs around
the country were beneficial in ending the pain felt by the loss of these great
leaders, and afforded opportunities to correct distorted images of the Black
community. As early as 1964, African American students attending HBCUs
were establishing clubs and student support groups in order to survive in
the element of the majority universities. Black students resisted creating
waves at the majority institutions, but were encouraged to organize and protest by white students like outspoken activist Mario Savio from New York.

**Professor Leonard Jeffries, Jr. delivering a lecture for a session of the
Black Museums Seminar at the Smithsonian Institution, 1976.**
Anacostia Community Museum Archives, Smithsonian Institution.

*The wave of campus confrontations that began at the Berkley campus of the
University of California in 1964 was essentially a white phenomenon, but it provided
watchful black militants with an excellent practical education in the tactics of
disruption. From such white radicals as Mario Savio, they learned that a great
university could be literally immobilized by boycotts, sit-ins, and the "liberation" of
administration buildings. They discovered the awesome secret of student power, that
the university was pathetically vulnerable to the pressures that could be brought
to bear upon it by a relatively small cadre of well organized, deeply dedicated
student revolutionaries. Blacks began to organize, and soon groups known by such*

titles as the United Black Students, the Onyx Society, the Soul Students Advisory Council, and the Black Student Union appeared on campus after campus. The names may have differed, but the common goal of these organizations was the "de-honkification" of the universities. To achieve that result, these black student unions issued a series of demands, among them the hiring of more black professors and the enrollment of more black students through recruiting, scholarships, and relaxed admissions standards. Specific demands varied greatly, including moratoriums on failing grades, blanket subsidies for minority students, and a school holiday on the birthday of Malcolm X. But one demand was virtually universal and led nearly every list of priorities. It called for the creation of programs in black studies.[105]

Later that year, the Olympic Games held in Mexico City, Mexico, created a stage for African American athletes to expose and challenge remaining forms of discrimination nationally and internationally in competitions. Tommie Smith, winning the gold, and John Carlos, winning the bronze medal in track and field, were team mates from San Jose State University and chose this event to stage a protest. As the National Anthem played in the ceremonial tradition recognizing the fitting nationality of an Olympian, the two men raised their fist in the salute of Black Power, and lowered their heads. Such controversy connected to this event led to world-wide attention on the Black Power Movement. As a result of their actions, Smith and Carlos were suspended from the USA Olympic team. Influenced by the Black Studies Movement and its formation by capable professors, one of Kinard's closest and dearest friends, Dr. Leonard Jeffries from the OCA program in the early sixties, found himself as a recruited professor to teach Black Studies coursework during this era. Jeffries also used the Anacostia Neighborhood Museum as a platform to present research connected to the success of his Black Studies programs at San Jose State University. Leonard Jeffries, then professor of Black Studies at San Jose State University, now professor of Africana Studies at the City College of New York, recalls this incident where he went to Mexico to be a steadfast and unyielding supporter of both Olympians Carlos and Smith:

In 1968 I went to the Olympics and at that point we were there to try to help out Carlos. I had gone to a conference in Los Angeles on African Studies and they said something is going on at the Olympics. We need to go down there. And we went down to the Olympics and I met John Carlos one of the men who raised his fist in defiance during that Olympics game.[106]

Dr. Jeffries, an acclaimed academic involved in shaping the Black Studies Movement, was heavily involved in local activism in his hometown of Newark, NJ. As a result of his knowledge, skill, and abilities, he was a capable choice in constructing and improving the scope of cultural foundations that developed the Black Studies period. Professor Jeffries spoke in a deep, passionate, and an ardent tone:

In the fall of 1968, somehow or another, somebody knew about my skills and knowledge of Africa. So, in 1969, they asked me to come to teach at City College. So in February of 1969, I started teaching at City College and during that time the turmoil of the cities moved into the universities and the people started taking over the universities, and so the students planned to take over the universities and open it up to our people and to put in a program of study on our communities on rural communities not just local communities. So they were demanding black studies and more black teachers. So I'm in the middle of this and in May of 1969, I'm asked to go to California for a conference on Malcolm X, and at that point people in San Jose, CA are looking for a leader of their program because they are demanding Black Studies and African Studies on the college campuses. So I get selected to go to California in May 1969. So I come back to City College and finished my work there, and in June I made the agreement to come to San Jose and it was at that point that in June of 1969 on my wife's birthday, I called her up and I told her I bought her a house, and she told me you are crazy.[107]

On many of the college campuses, there were accommodations made by the schools with the enrolled African American students to develop Black Studies programs. The need for a trained activist and philosopher, Dr. Jeffries, was valued in aiding the direction of the era. During the establishment of the Black Studies programs, neither Blacks nor whites had the slightest idea what the meaning of the Black Studies academic discipline was. This barrier in communication was indefinitely bogged down once the curriculum was identified through specially designed courses connected to the African American experience.

Another response to demands for black studies involves questioning the validity of separatist doctrines; whites question the nihilist, irritating, or anarchistic tendencies they note in separatist doctrines and, by extension, question whether the whole approach, including a trend toward black studies, is valid. Thus, black intellectual critics of the integrationist ethic students, writers, scholars, critics, historians and so on must assume an obligation to establish black studies in the curricula whose subject matter, critical thrust, and social objectives fully answer those who would question curriculum reform in the direction of black studies.[108]

Professor Armsted Robinson also added:

The students wanted me to be part of a village concept. So they said we want you as the chairman of this new black studies program, and we want you to buy a house near the college so you can be the center of the village. And we don't want you going out into the suburbs, or going up into the hills. So they said everyone in California buys a house, so they gave me four houses. All of them were near the college in walking distance to them and them to me and so I picked one of the houses and I bought it and it was one of the best financial things I've ever done for $22,000. It's worth one million dollars now. That house became the center of the village. We went to Africa first in the summer of '69 and then in September we started the Black Studies program at San Jose. The students were so well organized. We had this African experience, and we developed the strongest Black Studies Program on the west coast. And that black studies program included visiting lecturers and among the visiting lecturers was Dick Gregory, and he was so impressed by my wife and I. He said that next summer he wanted us to take his daughters Michelle and Lynn to Africa with us. And that was really a great tribute because that showed a lot of respect. Again that village thing, my children are yours, take them to Africa and give them this fantastic experience which we did. But part of the other scholars coming to the San Jose campus was Alex Haley. So in 1969-70 we met Alex and as part of our developing one of the strongest black studies programs out of San Jose and developing a community focus and village focus like your father (John Kinard) did in Anacostia.[109]

The hands-on approach to the village model was effective, and helped to create African American communities at the majority schools. These schools, which had very few African Americans, were proving to have an innovative and effective thought provoking dialogue to further act as an outlet for African American students and the Black community in the San Jose community or any other school which developed a Black Studies program. The programs helped to build a bridge of cultural understanding in a white institution much like the Anacostia Neighborhood Museum did in Washington, DC. This program Dr. Jeffries helped to build, which included Alex Haley, the author of *Roots* as an enormous tool which contributed in molding the Anacostia museum and its greater community.

In 1970 Alex came to me with a special meeting. A friend of mine arranged a dinner and he said he wanted me to help with this enormous program we had dealing with Africa and, of course, I had been dealing with Africa for ten years in a most intense way than most people could imagine and living there for a couple of years and every summer being there. So I said yes I will help you and so we began to meet and meet with others and finally he had this request from the Carnegie Corporation to submit a proposal for help with his project...and he needed somebody to help him with the project and how to handle the monies. So we helped him write the project and we submitted it to Carnegie. They rejected it at first. They gave us a $30,000.00 planning grant and then we got other people on board: Dr. Herman Blake, Dr. Laurance Reddick, and Courtney Brown. So with this team of people we knew we could develop a solid proposal and submitted it to Carnegie for $800,000.00 and they gave us, not $800,000.00 but $460,000.00. With the $460,000.00 and $30,000.00 we had a half a million dollars support from the Carnegie Corporation in order to help Alex Haley figure out his project which was the Kinte Library Project of Black Family History. And by using the Kinte project to study the archives and the library materials on Black family history, it allowed us to support Alex's writing out the book ROOTS *and his later work in pulling the TV program together. So it was through the San Jose Black Studies Program that I met Alex, cause he was based in California and living with his girlfriend Pat Alexander in San Francisco and they were trying to do the research of* ROOTS *but they didn't have resources. The monies we got from the Carnegie Corporation we used to help develop the project and also to help him further his research to produce the book* Roots *which focused on the village.*[110]

THE MAN, THE MOVEMENT, THE MUSEUM

The book *Roots* and its organic study was revolutionary. It justified the very existence of Black Studies in America. The time and effort it took to research and write was one of the greatest examples of the importance of preserving African American history, and researching African American life found in the African American community.

The educational institution has traditionally been, and is now, one of the institutions that the power structure maintains, in order to reinforce its own position. One learns to be a "better American," I assume, by going to an American university; where else could one learn to be better American than in a university? What you have to understand is that you should not fool yourselves by thinking that education is an academic thing; it is basically a political thing, and it provides identity, purpose, and direction within an American context.[111]

Kinard addressing the needs and success of the Anacostia Neighborhood Museum to an audience. Anacostia Community Museum Archives, Smithsonian Institution.

As director of the Anacostia Museum, John Kinard established a world-renowned reputation for contributing to the Black Studies era. At this museum, the visitors and the community were instructed on the meaning of Kwanza, Juneteenth celebrations, and workshops of other African diasporic traditions and achievements. The experience in OCA provided Kinard with the unique leadership style of first acknowledging the urban village found in Anacostia. The African village model which connected to Africa, illustrated a collective environment where you take care of each other. In America, this ideal was modeled on plantations during slavery, thus morphing those communities into the Black community. Although we have moved from the South to different parts of the country, the community came with us. It came to Washington, DC with Jessie Beulah Kinard, and like many families, it still exists. This urban village model and special haven for Blacks known as a place for a communal, cooperative and collective space of being without restrictions was sacred.

The Anacostia Museum is unparalleled in its ability to articulate its uniqueness, through the efforts of John Kinard, a charismatic and involved man and preacher who provided an international voice, and held a position of influence. Knowing and understanding all too well the struggle of minorities, and minority communities, the Black Studies movement further validated the work of the Anacostia Neighborhood Museum which extended the existence of this experiment into a more permanent fixture connected to the Smithsonian Institution. The noted Washington, DC scholar C. R. Gibbs thoughtfully spoke about the museum:

Other than the churches it was a primary location for the teaching of our history; we didn't have that. And the churches then as now do a haphazard kind of thing. Very few churches have a really instituted competently preformed course of study in Black History.... Before the Carver Museum (ANM) that was it for regular people. I'm not talking about college students or anything else like that; it just wasn't there... it just wasn't there... Because of your father's presence you could be assured, the institution wasn't run by some well named Negro. No this was a brother and he was in charge, and for us in those days we were very excited by the concept of black faces in high places... [112]

THE MAN, THE MOVEMENT, THE MUSEUM

Museums in Mexico, Greece, Jamaica, and all over the United States wanted to hear from the leadership of this new phenomenon. Kinard, involved in the American Association of Museums (AAM); American Association for State and Local History (AASLH); Association of African American Museums (AAAM), and International Council of Museums (ICOM) helped to be a bridge of understanding and represent African American museums. As a presenter at the ICOM conference in Paris, France, in 1971, Kinard expressed his philosophy through his thoughts and vision about proper multicultural inclusion:

> Museums can no longer serve only the intellectually elite, the art connoisseur, and the scholar. Our visitors can no longer be limited to the enlightened, and the educated and the well to do. Any institutions that call themselves museums and do not note with great care the overwhelming possibilities for service to the community should rethink their position so that there can be no undue criticism of these respected institutions and their traditions. Museums must be sensitive to the cries of modern man for a more perfect way to live and to know the truth.[113]

In addition, he said museums must also recognize:

> ...the cultural contributions of minorities. Their history must be dealt with and understood. Because some society refuses to respect the black man, the red man, and the brown man, this is no reason for museums to block them out as if they did not exist. In the USA this is an acute problem.[114]

Museums in the United States had their problem pointed out cogently:

> In the USA this problem is illustrated by the fact that you would never know from visiting the average American museum that the black man exists in America and has made significant contributions toward the development of our country. The USA would not be what it is today, economically or culturally, were it not for the black man's labor. You may search in vain in our museums to discover with what great esteem the black man is regarded, what the black man contributed to civilization, how he lived, and what he was forced to suffer. Believe me when I say the American museum has ignored the Black American, and it is only recently that a few art

museums have shown the works of black artists. In those rare instances where there is an exhibit that has to do with minorities it is designed in a fashion that represents the white man's interpretation of the particular minority. How can it be otherwise since museums have refused to hire minority people in any significant capacity? [115]

Chapter 5

NATIONAL AND INTERNATIONAL IMPACT OF JOHN KINARD

Conclusion

As a result of this period, Kinard and others contributed to a remarkable era, ingrained in redefining and embracing blackness through building a cultural institution. These institutions were found in the Black communities or urban villages and captured the explosion and rebirth of cultural definitions and new-found refinement through art, activism, and cultural reclamation. Evidence of this can be found in the Black Arts, Studies and Museums Movements.

During the 1970s, the nation was faced with continued Black liberation efforts in the form of marches, demonstrations, conventions, and press conferences. All the while, Nixon was re-elected in 1972, running against the first African American presidential candidate, Shirley Chisholm. In Washington, DC the Watergate Scandal had uncovered deceit and long-lived corruption within the Nixon administration. This same year, members of the American Indian Movement, also known as AIM, became quite vocal and militant in their demands of the federal government to honor the obligations in treaties made generations ago. Some Native Americans came from different areas of the country, and forcefully demonstrated in the office of the Bureau of Indian Affairs in Washington, DC. Prior to the resignation of Nixon, and Ford's takeover as president, women's liberation grew stronger and was greatly met with some opposition connected to the sexual revolution and the choice of pro-life or pro-choice related to the 1973 Supreme Court decision of *Roe v. Wade*. They were eager for action on women's rights and issues. The frustration and embitterment of the era brought about the unity among women of diverse cultures. Among African American women, the cause was strengthened within women's organizations to establish needed concerns and issues for understanding. Eleanor Holmes Norton and Margaret Sloan-Hunter were two of the founders of the National Black Feminist Organization of 1973. Also Shirley Chisholm, a remarkable woman who rose to prominence as a congresswoman, and in 1972 as a Democratic presidential nominee, was vocal and supportive of women's issues and concerns.

In response to the critics of the African American women's movement, Shirley Chisholm, a distinguished and articulate congresswoman who received little support from African American men in her unsuccessful campaign for the democratic presidential nomination in 1972, declared that "in many respects it was more difficult to be a woman than a black." [1]

This period proves to be strengthened entirely by the organization of political and economic power through ethnic identification during this highly charged climate among minorities. It was with this ethnic identification that spurred other ethnic concentrated studies in America. The national presence of Amiri Baraka (formerly LeRoi Jones) through his expressions of political issues elevated the significance of the Black Arts Movement. Black Arts activists set out to exorcise the demons behind what Baraka called "a John Coltrane people being ruled by Lawrence Welk." African American recording artists helped propel Black Power into American popular culture. Spoken word artists Watts Prophets, Last Poets, and Gil Scott-Heron used jazz inflected vocals, live bands, and African drums to innovate a sound that presaged aspects of rap music and hip-hop culture. Activists in urban centers such as Detroit and Chicago succeeded where Baraka had failed in Harlem, building cultural institutions to showcase the "new black poetry," thereby galvanizing the relationship between established African American writers such as Gwendolyn Brooks and young upstarts like Haki Madhubuti. These talented individuals were embraced in the cultural institutions found in the African American community demonstrating its impact and need for outlets and gatherings which ultimately became core political centers.

John Kinard was one of the founders of the Black Museums Movement and soon became one of its leaders because of his exposure and training by the most prestigious organization in the world—the Smithsonian Institution. In current circumstances he may not have been afforded this opportunity, but the chance he was given exemplified the slowly changing times America slowly made. This job was hard, demanding, challenging, and unpredictable when Kinard addressed the needs of his institution. He made the museum operate on a budget which hardly expanded, relying on grants, organizations, and affiliations to which he belonged, to partner with the museum. Kinard even found himself becoming the father of invention, and succeeded when others thought he would fail. In order to sustain and establish other Black museums to preserve their legacy, the Association of African American Museums was founded in 1978 to bring unity among these scattered cultural institutions. Rowena Stewart, well known museum director and member of the Association of African American Museums, comments on the empowering legacy Kinard left within this organization:

> If a museum cannot provide for its people a mirror of the past, then it has no relevance in the life of the African American community... That was said by John Kinard on September 1985 at the African American Museums Association Conference at the California African American Museum. I met John Kinard in Chicago in 1974 at DuSable Museum and he was coming out of a master team, in fact, he was the leader of that team. Included in that team were the founders of the movement, Dr. Margaret Burroughs, of DuSable Museum in Chicago; Dr. Charles

NATIONAL AND INTERNATIONAL IMPACT OF JOHN KINARD

*Wright of Detroit Afro-American Museum; Byron Rushing, then the Director of the
African Meeting House in Boston; and now, Representative Rushing in Boston, and
Barry Gaither, the first President of the African American Museums Association
and the current president and director of the Museum for the National Center of
Afro American Art. I was overwhelmed and certainly inspired. I thought that in the
beginning when I started in this business that I was among the few. What I realized
that in the vineyard there had already been so many people ahead of me and a way
had been made, and John, in fact, made that possible for a lot of people. There were
somethings that I need to say to you at this point and particularly at that time there
were about thirty-five of us in the field. About twenty black museums, there are now
over 400 black professionals in the field, and approximately 100 museums. John had
touched the successes of every one of these museums in some way or another. He
always let us know that he knew the business of the museum and that he was in
charge of the business. He made us love him and sometimes he made us very angry.
His love, however, for the African American Museums Association, and for the
American Museums Association was unfailing. He always wanted us to be better,
and he wanted the country's museums to be better than what they were. On hearing
the news of the shock of John's death, I was overcome with both shock and grief.
And for a moment my own personal selfishness took over, because then I suddenly
realized, he was not going to be there for me to attack, challenge. I also knew for a
moment that he was not going to be there to answer questions quickly for us, and
then something said to me, Rowena, he has empowered you and the message that
you must get over to all of us in the next few days is how we must use the legacy and
the charge that he has given all of us. That, in fact, is what I have set about to do. I
also knew that if I made the Philadelphia Afro American Museum a great museum
then part of his legacy has been fulfilled. If, in fact, Anacostia is relocated in the
place that he wanted the Anacostia Museum moved and if, in fact, the black trust
is created to collect and provide in regions a master plan for the collection and the
survival of African American culture and its preservation, then his legacy still lives.
If, in fact, Congress does pass the bill for the museum to stand and it stands on the
Mall for the contributions of African Americans to take its rightful place then, John,
in fact, his legacy has lived on. To the family I would like to thank you Margie. I
know that he knew more than anyone how much you meant to him, and I want to
thank you for sharing him with us. You did that wonderfully. To your children I wish
that you would remember that when you walk into every museum in this country,
when you walk across the door remember that your father made it better for all of
us, and that the museums are able to tell their stories better...*[2]

THE MAN, THE MOVEMENT, THE MUSEUM

Over the 22 years that Kinard was the director of the Anacostia Museum, he fought against injustice in support of cultural education, preservation, and training younger people to embrace the field of Museology. In the mid 1980s, during a time of political unrest in South Africa, many African American leaders aided the end of apartheid and supported the freedom sought by political prisoner, Nelson Mandela. Similar to American Jim Crow laws, South Africa enforced practices referred to as apartheid.

It is impossible to spend even a few days in South Africa without realizing the distinctions that are made between white and non-white. On railway stations and on trains and buses, at airports, post offices, and all public buildings, in banks, at race-courses and sports grounds, on the beaches, and in graveyards, there are separate facilities for white and non-white, and the notices "Whites Only and Non-Whites" are ubiquitous. The distinction made between white and non-white is usually referred to by the comprehensive name of the colour bar, and for purposes of closer identification an adjective is added: thus we have industrial colour bars, political colour bars, social colour bars, colour bar in sports, and so on. Much social discrimination is the result of custom rather than of legislation or regulation.[3]

Like many African Americans affected by the Civil Rights Movement, 30 years prior, many Blacks such as Kinard felt the need to get involved in political and social change. As a graduate student at Hood Theological Seminary, Kinard traveled to Africa many times as a participant in the Operation Crossroads Africa Program (OCA) where he supervised mission projects from Egypt to Zimbabwe. Widely known as the director of the Smithsonian Institution's Anacostia Neighborhood Museum, Kinard lectured around the world on the topic of cultural understanding, and in March of 1985, found himself in South Africa. Born in Washington, DC and living through the vicious system of Jim Crow, making a difference as a college student, protesting injustice and detesting the system of apartheid, Kinard was invited to come lecture for two weeks, and present to several Black and other progressive South African Organizations.

Kinard met with Mrs. Sally Motlana, President of the Black Housewives

League along with 20 other organization members. Sally outlined the social and political conditions in the country to Kinard, with special emphasis on the impact they had on Black women. She also spoke at length about the traditional practices and customs that tended to place restrictions on the role of Black women.

Kinard also addressed a group of 20 people at the South African Institute of Race Relations on the morning of March 11, 1985, where his subject was, "Evolution of Race Relations in the U.S." Kinard was well received by this audience and made a valuable contribution to inspire the people of South Africa. That evening, Kinard addressed an audience of 60 people at the Johannesburg American Cultural Center on "Community Organization and Cultural Diversity" where his own experience in the Civil Rights Movement afforded him an interesting perspective. Kinard also expressed his views on supporting the cause of the South African Black community:

> *Black Americans want to help, but do not know what to do. After Bishop Tutu's speech at Howard University, not knowing just what to do, several prominent black Americans went to the South African Embassy in Washington and sat down to be arrested. Black South Africans have to decide what they want to do, not expect everybody to do everything for them, only then will black Americans have a clear signal of the action they should take. Kinard concluded his program emphasizing that black South Africans must get over the psychological damage which Apartheid has inflicted upon them. They must strive for freedom, dignity and self reliance.* [4]

In May of 1987, John Kinard returned to South Africa to meet philosophical opposition and come face to face with the backlash of political apartheid which resonated throughout the country. Kinard traveled to South Africa, as the guest of the South African Museums Association (SAMA), to its 51st annual conference which embraced the theme: "Museums in a Changing and Divided Society," which, according to Felton and Lowe's *A Different Drummer*, convinced him to attend.

Plain spoken and fearless in speaking the truth as he viewed it, Kinard continuously challenged museums to reexamine their roles in a rapidly changing society. One of the most controversial incidents of his career occurred during his final visit in 1987. Although personally opposed to apartheid, Kinard believed more in negotiation and cultural exchange than in confrontation and crisis. He welcomed opportunities to make diplomatic and cultural inroads into difficult situations. As a result, when the Southern African Museums Association invited him to return to South Africa to address its Fifty-first Annual Meeting and Conference, May 4-8, 1987, in Pietermaritzburg (Natal), South Africa, he accepted. The invitation also called for Kinard to visit other museums before and after the conference. Together with the South Africa Tourism Board, SAMA paid for Kinard's visit.[5]

As the spokesman for a community of people who fought to change American history through the preservation of African American history, his words were heartfelt and inspirational to the conference attendees. For so long the image and contribution of African Americans had been neglected, but because of the Black Museums Movement, Kinard, representing the Smithsonian Institution as the Director of an institutional museum affiliate, gave voice to a wider audience of urbanites who aided in the development of the expansion of Black museums and cultural awareness across the nation in the Association of African American Museums.

Until John came on the scene, people didn't accept us or even think about us as serious people in the museum world. John walked among some of the great people of all kinds of all races without fear. He opened doors for us in the African American Museums Association; so that wherever we were across this country we could start to make our dreams come true... He not only inspired us to have the black museums be a very potent force in this entire country, but he encouraged us to join the American Association of Museums so we could impact the larger society and gain from them. He did this for us... He was our voice, our strong and beautiful voice.[6]

In this moment, Kinard faced a pivotal point in his life becoming a ray of hope traveling thousands of miles to be the voice of the underserved in a community much like his in America. Professor Andrew Smith, a Professor at the University of Cape Town's Department of Archaelogy and attendee at the

SAMA 51st conference, noted in his report to the Centre for African Studies his impression of Kinard:

> *These excellent presentations faded into the background with the next speaker, John Kinard, Director of the Anacostia Neighborhood Museum in Washington, DC. Kinard first pointed out that from where he came "South Africans were the most hateful people on the face of the earth" and proceeded to show how museums were guilty of high crimes and destruction of culture because South Africans knew more about the animals of Africa than they did about African people.*[7]

During this time in America, South Africa had a reputation for being a place where the most detested and socially irresponsible governments were guilty of high crimes in the destruction of culture throughout the country. In talking to South Africans, on his March 1985 trip, Kinard witnessed the fact that the South Africans knew more about the animals and natural resources than they did about the cultural traditions of the country's people. This was the high crime that the Smithsonian Institution was also guilty of until John Kinard came on the scene in 1967. As an activist of the Civil Rights Movement, he found himself in the midst of a changing society to integrate the Smithsonian Institution as the first African American director of a Smithsonian Institution Museum. This museum would later become a gathering place for the Black Power Movement and an instrument to teach multicultural awareness that plagued the nation.

Making it his life's work to preserve and protect culture for future generations, Kinard was a pioneer who took note and embraced the discouraging road Blacks faced globally. This resistance to Kinard's philosophical views was faced inherently by Kinard throughout his career and as the first African American director of a Smithsonian Museum. This bold posture Kinard took in South Africa came from having developed, not only the museum he managed, but many museums around the country.

> *Within the context of our fight for a democratic South Africa and the entrenchment of human rights can we afford exhibitions in our museums depicting any of our*

people as lesser human beings, sometimes in natural history museums usually reserved for the depiction of animals? Can we continue to tolerate our ancestors being shown as people locked in time? Such degrading forms of representation inhibit our children's appreciation of the value and strength of our democracy, of tolerance and of human rights. They demean the victims and warp the minds of the perpetrators. Through the apartheid years, people responded to the denial and distortions of their heritage with their own affirmation as indeed Afrikaners had done in an earlier period. They celebrate their heritage outside of the country's museums and monuments; in song and in ceremony; in festivals and carnivals; in the selling of their own wares and in buying items associated with their heritage; by working the history of their communities into everyday artifacts, as the women of Hlabisa weave their stories into beer baskets. With democracy we have the opportunity to ensure that our institutions reflect history in a way that respects the heritage of all our citizens.[8]

Kinard, representing the progressive militant activism produced in America, would naturally meet strong opposition, which he faced in the States, but continued to use his voice as a tool to inspire.

The deeds of a man can never fully be measured. The actions of John Kinard during his lifetime helped him to play a major role as an activist, spokesman and leader for disenfranchised communities, which gave his life meaning in the act of working with the have-nots in his quest to improve their conditions.

He could find a scarce placement in a rehabilitation center for a young addict. He could refer men and women to jobs that came to his attention. He could vouch for the character of someone about to go before the judge or a parole board. He could and did get out of his bed to go (make) somebody's bail. He could write strong letters of support for individuals and non-profit groups seeking grants and other assistance. Often a problem was solved by a strategically placed telephone call...[9]

Reflections: The John Kinard Legacy

Finally, I would like to end on a personal note. The legacy of John Kinard is alive and well. His legacy lives on through the Kinard family, the Anacostia Community Museum, the John Wesley AME Zion Church, the Livingstone

College Alumni Association, published works in the museum studies field, and through a host of extended family, friends and admirers. His daughters Sarah, Joy, and Hope are actively a part of cultural educational programs. Sarah is a graduate of Livingstone College, and Ohio State University with a Master's in Black Studies. She is an English teacher at Springbrook High School located in Silver Spring, MD. She plays an active role in the NAACP's ACT-SO program. She also has her own summer enrichment program called "Khephra" that teaches youth about African American History and Culture in the Washington, DC area. Hope is a graduate of Livingstone College, Grand Canyon University, and Walden University with a doctorate in Educational Technology. She has excelled in the STEM field and serves as a Science teacher and Educational Technology Consultant in the Washington, DC area and in Hampton, VA. Hope and her husband have five children: Christopher, Cameron, Kareem, Courtney, and Caitlyn Wilson who are brilliant and know what their grandfather accomplished. They love school and are leaders in their community. They're all being groomed for greatness. Marjorie Kinard is a retired educator. She worked in the DC Public School System, East of the River Health Center (a part of the District Government), Albright Day Care Center, and was the Dean of Enrollment Management at Livingstone College. She now enjoys retirement and consulting in the Washington, DC area as a child care professional. She enjoys sharing the role of educating her grandchildren and started the Kinard Academy—a program she started where she gets her grandchildren on holidays, and summers to teach them real life experiences and provides cultural enrichment through trips, lectures, and hands-on activities.

I (Joy, the author) have had a prosperous over twenty-year career in the National Park Service and now serve as the Superintendent of a National Park called the Charles Young Buffalo Soldiers National Monument. Growing up, my father was always gone. If he wasn't at the museum, at a community event, overseas on business lecturing, at church or visiting the sick, he wasn't home as much as I would've liked. He brought a magic to the house growing up that was sorely missed when he wasn't there. He cooked, told funny stories, bought us pets, let me practice cosmetology experiments on him, tucked us into bed, bought us books, took us to hear lectures from leading researchers in African and African American history at a young age. He also took us to museums and family functions. I witnessed him take a two-hour nap after an exhausting day at a Livingstone College homecoming and drive eight hours straight late on a Saturday night after the Livingstone College Alumni dance to preach a sermon on Sunday. I used to ask myself, why is he always gone, and where does he go? Why does he constantly do so much for others when they don't care and just use him... Why can't he be like my friend's father? He drove her to school every day, and spent time with her daily. I hated sharing my father and when he died the feeling was multiplied because so many strangers tried to comfort our family. These people were a constant reminder of why my father wasn't home often, overworked, tired, and sometimes frustrated with life. One day, I went to a book signing that the Anacostia Museum had in 2001 for DC Emancipation Day and met Dr. Elizabeth Clark-Lewis who was signing her book *First Freed*.

Elizabeth Clark-Lewis speaking at the Kinard Celebration on August 23, 2009.
Kinard Collection.

She convinced me to think about entering the Master's Program in History at Howard University and to consider doing graduate level research on John Kinard since it hadn't been done yet. I mentioned it to my mother and she was supportive but I decided not to do it, until Dr. Clark-Lewis started to politely hound me. She came to and called me on my job, she came to my church, and had other people we jointly knew ask me, "Are you going to Howard?" "Dr. Clark-Lewis thinks it's a good idea." "You should do it." I just couldn't escape her clutches if I tried. So, in the fall of 2003, I entered the Department of History at Howard University to work on my master's degree. After I finished in 2005, I re-entered Howard University to work on my doctoral degree in US history where my focused research was on John Kinard and his impact on the Black Studies Movement. It was through this experience that all the questions and perceptions I had as a young girl that I hadn't yet dealt with or processed through as an adult about my father were answered. Though expensive, it was one of the most cathartic and liberating experiences that I have ever had in my life. I was inspired by the book *A Different Drummer* that Dr. Gail Lowe and Zora Martin-Felton wrote.

Zora Martin-Felton speaking at the Kinard Celebration on August 23, 2009.
Kinard Collection.

I was equally as inspired by Jacquelin Trescott's article on John Kinard called "The Lion of Anacostia is Remembered," which was printed in the Style section of *The Washington Post*. I also couldn't have done this work without the people who were honest and forthcoming about how my father impacted them in their career or helped them in a situation. There are so many oral history interviews I conducted during this period, that I wish I could've found room to share something from everyone, especially the directors of the African American Museums he worked with on a regular basis. The archives of the Smithsonian Institution, Anacostia Community Museum, the Amistad Research Center, and the Kinard Family Collection were invaluable in telling a more rounded interpretation about my father's life and times which includes his role at the Anacostia Museum. The letters my mother kept from people who admired his work and contributions, helped me to begin to see my father as a person I never knew.

Letter from J. Clay Smith, Professor of Law, Howard University, to John Kinard, July 25, 1989. Kinard Collection.

THE FINE ARTS
MUSEUMS OF
SAN FRANCISCO
M.H. de YOUNG
MEMORIAL
MUSEUM
CALIFORNIA Lincoln Park
PALACE OF THE San Francisco, CA 94121
LEGION OF HONOR (415) 750-3661

HARRY S. PARKER III Director of Museums

Mr. John R. Kinard
Anacostia Museum
1901 Fort Place S.E.
Washington, DC 20020

Dear John:

I was sent the Washington Post article and wanted to write you.

The work you are doing and have done has made a huge difference to
the museum field and to me personally. It would be hard to
imagine American museums today without the impact of your style.
How well I recall your stirring speech at the Grenoble ICOM
meetings when you electrified that whole world. You must be
exceedingly proud of what you have achieved and be confident about
what is yet to come.

Your point has not been lost.

Yours sincerely,

Harry S. Parker III
Director of Museums

HSP:ll

26 July 1989

Letter from Harry S. Parker III, Director of Museums, The Fine Arts Museums of San Francisco, to John Kinard, July 26, 1989. Kinard Collection.

When I was a young girl, I couldn't have understood what my father was doing because as a child you are taught to speak when you are spoken to and don't ask grown folks questions. I had an idea that he was contributing to an important cause, but not at the massive level he ultimately reached as an international icon in the field of museum studies. I now know why he wasn't there and I'm proud to say I shared him with mankind to make this world better.

In 2009, I graduated from Howard University with my Ph.D. in U.S. History with minors in Public History, and Caribbean Studies. To celebrate this achievement and to recognize the twentieth anniversary of my father's death, which was August 5, 1989, after with a battle of myelofibrosis, the Washington, DC Chapter of Livingstone College created a scholarship fund to help support students from the Washington, DC area who attend Livingstone College. Now that scholarship fund bears the name of both John Kinard and Grace Littlejohn as the Kinard-Littlejohn Scholarship Fund. Grace Littlejohn was an amazing leader and community activist who mentored and supported many Livingstone College graduates like John Kinard as a young man. So many people came to John Wesley AME Zion Church to the Kinard Celebration which drew people from all over the country. This event was held on Sunday, August 23, 2009, at John Wesley AME Zion Church in Washington, DC. There were over four hundred people in attendance to honor my father's legacy and my recent accomplishment on a hot summer afternoon. So many people gave remarks like, Zora Martin-Felton, Director of Education, Emerita Smithsonian Anacostia Community Museum, Lonnie Bunch, Director of the National Museum of African American History and Culture, Camille Akeju, Immediate Past Director of the Anacostia Community Museum, Maudine R. Cooper, President and CEO of the Greater Washington Urban League, Robert G. Stanton, Assistant Secretary of the Department of the Interior, Leonard Jeffries, Retired Professor of Black Studies, The City College of New York, Dr. Elizabeth Clark-Lewis, Director of Public History, Howard University, Janette Hoston Harris, Historian for the District of Columbia, Barbara Poe, President of the DC Chapter of the Livingstone College Alumni Association, Leonard Dunston, graduate of Livingstone College and family friend, Marjorie A. Kinard, wife of John Kinard, Vernon A. Shannon, Pastor of John Wesley AME Zion Church and classmate of John Kinard, James Gray, Chairman of the Kinard Celebration Committee and member of the DC. Chapter of the Livingstone College Alumni Association, Clennie H. Murphy, Jr., Chairman of the 160th Anniversary Celebration of John Wesley AME Zion Church and high school classmate of John Kinard, Rita J. Colbert, Washington District Presiding Elder, Bishop Warren M. Brown, Presiding Prelate of the Mid

Atlantic II Episcopal District, Bishop Cecil Bishop, retired bishop of the AME Zion Church.

Hermon Felton gave remarks on behalf of Jimmy Jenkins, the President of Livingstone College, and a host of clergy that served with John Kinard, Lewis M. Anthony, Frederick B. Massey, and Heath Cheek. I spoke and Christopher Kinard Wilson, my nephew, spoke at this event.

Robert G. Stanton speaking at the Kinard Celebration on August 23, 2009. Kinard Collection.

Camille Akeju speaking at the Kinard Celebration on August 23, 2009. Kinard Collection.

Leonard Jeffries speaking at the Kinard Celebration on August 23, 2009. Kinard Collection.

Lonnie Bunch speaking at the Kinard Celebration on August 23, 2009. Kinard Collection.

Maudine Cooper speaking at the Kinard Celebration on August 23, 2009. Kinard Collection.

THE MAN, THE MOVEMENT, THE MUSEUM

It truly means the world to me to have known a man like John Kinard. For him to have been my father, and for me to have the same blood running through my veins, is the greatest honor in the world. There isn't a day that goes by that my family and I don't run into someone who was touched by his life. The biggest reward in life isn't financial gains, but to offer your whole life to serve others. His legacy was built every day he lived. Knowing his full story and sharing it through this book, I hope it becomes a tool to inspire hope in the minds of other children of great leaders to find comfort in knowing that the world their parents are trying to change and make better, is being changed for you too, to become empowered and unstoppable. You must embrace their legacy and take ownership of it and tell their story before strangers take it and misinterpret or misconstrue it.

Coda

John Kinard was an ordinary man with a big heart. This research has given credence to the Smithsonian Institution's contributions to history. He was a leader in the movement to empower the African American community to control its images of newfound "Americaness" through the founding of the Anacostia Museum. Today, the National Museum of African American History and Culture exists as a result of the planting of its firm foundation, like the "beanstalk." John Kinard's valiant dedication and determination established identities that continue, to this day, to be embedded in the traditions of African American cultural institutions. These cultural institutions originated, not with the inception of the Anacostia Neighborhood Museum, but within the confines of the African American church, as early as the nineteenth century, and other African American museums that were scattered throughout the African American communities throughout the United States. John Kinard's beliefs and ideologies of African American history were rooted in the church and served as an incubator for his visions to become manifested.

Notes

Introduction

1. Elizabeth Clark-Lewis, *Living In, Living Out: African American Domestics in Washington, DC, 1910-1940* (2010), 5.
2. Caryl Marsh, "A Neighborhood Museum That Works," *Museum News* 47 (1968): 2-3.
3. Sidney Dillon Ripley, *The Sacred Grove: Essay on Museums* (1969), 106-107.
4. Marsh, 3.
5. John Kinard, "Intermediaries Between the Museum and the Community," reprinted from *The Papers of the Ninth General Conference of the International Council of Museums*, Grenoble, France (1971), 152.
6. Jacqueline Trescott, "Museums on the Move," *American Visions* 1 (1986): 24.

Chapter 1

1. Robert Olwell, "The Long History of a Low Place: Slavery on the South Carolina Coast 1670-1870," in *Slavery and the American South* ed. Winthrop D. Jordan (2003), 118.
2. Darlene Clark Hine and Kathleen Thompson, *A Shining Thread of Hope: The History of Black Women in America* (1998), 167.
3. Clark-Lewis, 11.
4. George A. Devlin, *South Carolina and Black Migration, 1865-1940: In Search of the Promised Land* (1989), 137.
5. Ibid., 140.
6. Jessie Beulah Kinard of Washington, DC, interview by Sarah Kinard, August 13, 1992, Washington, DC, tape recording.
7. Clark-Lewis, 23.
8. Jessie Beulah Kinard of Washington, DC, interview by Sarah Kinard.
9. Ibid.
10. Carter G. Woodson, "The Negro Washerwoman, a Vanishing Figure," *The Journal of Negro History* 15 (1930): 273.
11. Mary Church Terrell, *A Colored Woman in A White World* (2005), 29.
12. Jessie Beulah Kinard of Washington, DC, interview by Sarah Kinard.
13. Audrey McCluskey and Elaine M. Smith, eds., *Mary McLeod Bethune: Building a Better World, Essays and Selected Documents* (1999), 67.
14. Jessie Beulah Kinard of Washington, DC, interview by Sarah Kinard.
15. Ibid.
16. Carter G. Woodson, *A Century of Negro Migration* (1969), 163.
17. Jessie Beulah Kinard of Washington, DC, interview by Sarah Kinard.
18. Keith E. Melder and Melinda Young Stuart, *City of Magnificent Intentions: A History of Washington, District of Columbia* (1997), 464.

19. McCluskey and Smith, *Building a Better World* (1999), 8.

20. St. Clair Drake and Horace R. Cayton, *Black Metropolis: A Study of Negro Life in a Northern City* (1962), 379.

21. William Kinard of Laurel, MD, interview by author, November 20, 2004, Laurel, MD, tape recording.

22. Melder and Stuart, 477.

23. Charles Flint Kellogg, *NAACP: A History of the National Association for the Advancement of Colored People, 1909–1920* (1967), 183–84.

24. Melder and Stuart, 547.

25. Juanita Jefferson of Washington, DC, interview by author, October 1, 2007, Washington, DC, tape recording.

26. Constance M. Green, *The Secret City: A History of Race Relations in the Nation's Capital* (1967), 288.

27. Ibid., 290.

28. Terrell, 413.

29. Charles Houston, "Our High School's Overcrowding, Hit Each Carries Over Capacity Load, Building for Whites Lack Pupils," *The Washington Afro-American* (March 26, 1949): 1.

30. Clennie Murphy Jr. of Silver Spring, MD, interview by author, July 8, 2008, Silver Spring, MD, tape recording.

31. Lawrence Otis Graham, *Our Kind of People: Inside America's Black Upper Class* (2000), 61.

32. Clennie Murphy Jr. of Silver Spring, MD, interview by author.

33. Kellogg, 61–62.

34. Marjorie Kinard of Burtonsville, MD, interview by author, November 14, 2004, Burtonsville, MD, tape recording.

35. Melder and Stuart, 550.

36. Freda Alston of Washington, DC, interview by author, November 13, 2007, Washington, DC, tape recording.

37. Marjorie Kinard of Burtonsville, MD, interview by author.

38. William H. Jones, *Recreation and Amusement Among Negroes in Washington, DC: A Sociological Analysis of the Negro in an Urban Environment* (1927), 66–67; also see Patsy Mose Fletcher, *Historically African American Leisure Destinations Around Washington, DC* (2016).

39. William Kinard of Laurel, MD, interview by author.

40. Clennie Murphy Jr. of Silver Spring, MD, interview by author.

41. Henry Louis Gates, Jr. and Evelyn Brooks Higginbotham, *African American National Biography*, Vol. 6 (2008), 434.

42. W.E.B. DuBois, "The Ruling Passion: An Estimate of Joseph C. Price," *Crisis 23* (1922): 224–25.

43. College Academic Transcript of John Kinard, Livingstone College, Salisbury, NC, July 29, 1960.

44. Vernon A. Shannon of Washington, DC, interview by author, June 23, 2008, Washington, DC, tape recording.

45. Marjorie Kinard of Burtonsville, MD, interview by author.

46. Howard Zinn, *The Southern Mystique* (1964), 217.

47. Howard Zinn, *Postwar America 1945-1971* (1973), 127.

48. Bayard Rustin, Devon W. Carbado, and Donald Weise, *Time On Two Crosses: The Collected Writings of Bayard Rustin* (2003), 9.

49. Dr. Samuel Varner of Virginia Beach, VA, interview by author, December 29, 2008, Virginia Beach, VA, tape recording.

50. Jeffery J. Crow, Paul D. Escott, and Flora J. Hatley, *A History of African Americans in North Carolina* (2002), 183.

51. Rev. Richard Stewart of Mt. Vernon, NY, interview by author, December 30, 2008, Mt. Vernon, NY, tape recording.

52. Vernon A. Shannon of Washington, DC, interview by author.

53. Ibid.

54. Crow, Escott, and Hatley, 189.

55. Raymond Arsenault, *Freedom Riders: 1961 and the Struggle for Racial Justice* (2006), 120.

56. Ibid.

57. Rev. Richard Stewart of Mt. Vernon, NY, interview by author.

58. Ibid.

59. Vernon A. Shannon of Washington, DC, interview by author.

60. Marjorie Kinard of Burtonsville, MD, interview by author.

61. Ibid.

62. Peniel E. Joseph, *Waiting 'Til The Midnight Hour: A Narrative History of Black Power in America* (2006), 51.

63. Marjorie Kinard of Burtonsville, MD, interview by author.

64. Ibid.

65. Paula J. Giddings, *When and Where I Enter: The Impact of Black Women on Race and Sex in America* (1984), 252.

66. Ibid., 250.

67. Marjorie Kinard of Burtonsville, MD, interview by author.

Chapter Two

1. Marjorie Kinard of Burtonsville, MD, interview by author.

2. Ibid.

3. Aggrey Memorial Dinner and Fellowship Program, 1963, Marjorie Kinard Collection.

4. President John F. Kennedy, Inaugural Address, Washington, DC, January 20, 1961, John F. Kennedy Presidential Library and Museum.

5. Dr. Samuel Varner of Virginia Beach, VA, interview by author.

6. Ibid.

7. Zora Martin-Felton and Gail Sylvia Lowe, *A Different Drummer: John Kinard and the Anacostia Museum, 1967-1989,* (1993) 7-8.

8. Ruth T. Plimpton, *Operation Crossroads Africa* (1962), 13.

9. Dr. Leonard Jeffries of Newark, NJ, interview by author, December 29, 2008, Newark, NJ, tape recording.

10. John Kinard of Washington, DC, interview by Anne M. Rogers, July 1987, Smithsonian Archives, Washington, DC

11. John Kinard to Marjorie Williams, July 21, 1962, Marjorie Kinard Collection.

12. John Kinard to Marjorie Williams, August 1, 1962, Marjorie Kinard Collection.

13. Kwame Nkrumah, *Africa Must Unite* (1963), 19.

14. Ibid., 52.

15. Emory J. Tolbert, *UNIA and Black Los Angeles: Ideology and Community in the American Garvey Movement* (1980), 9.

16. George Shepperson, "Notes on Negro American Influences on the Emergence of African Nationalism," *The Journal of African History* 1 (1960): 311–12.

17. David Birmingham, *Kwame Nkrumah: The Father of African Nationalism* (1998), 1.

18. Clayborne Carson, ed., *The Autobiography of Martin Luther King, Jr.* (1998), 111–12.

19. Cheikh Anta Diop, *Black Africa: The Economic and Cultural Basis for a Federated State* (1987), 7–8.

20. Dr. Leonard Jeffries of Newark, NJ, interview by author.

21. *Operation Crossroads Africa: A Decade of Achievement* (1968), Marjorie Kinard Collection.

22. Dr. Samuel Varner of Virginia Beach, VA, interview by author.

23. *Operation Crossroads Africa: A Decade of Achievement.*

24. John Kinard to Marjorie Williams, July 26, 1962, Marjorie Kinard Collection.

25. Robert Chrisman and Nathan Hare, eds., Pan-Africanism (1974), 107.

26. Ibid., 109.

27. Neal W. Sobania, *Culture and Customs of Kenya* (2003), 184.

28. Stokely Carmichael and Mumia Abu-Jamal, *Stokely Speaks: From Black Power to Pan-Africanism* (2007), 26.

29. John Kinard to Marjorie Williams, August 15, 1962, Marjorie Kinard Collection.

30. Robert G. Kaiser, "Africans Aided by Two Area Men," *Washington Post* (September 2, 1963): D14.

31. Aggrey Memorial Dinner and Fellowship Program.

32. Joyce Johnson Harrington of Buffalo, NY, interview by author, December 29, 2008, Buffalo, NY, tape recording.

33. Harold T. Pinkett, *National Church of Zion Methodism: A History of John Wesley A.M.E. Zion Church* (1989), 69.

34. John Hope Franklin and Alfred A. Moss Jr., *From Slavery to Freedom: A History of African Americans* (2006), 536–37.

35. John Kinard to Marjorie Williams, June 30, 1963, Marjorie Kinard Collection.

36. David Howard-Pitney, *Martin Luther King, Jr., Malcolm X, and the Civil Rights Struggle of the 1950s and 1960s: A Brief History with Documents* (2004), 99–101.

37. John Kinard to Marjorie Williams, July 4, 1963, Marjorie Kinard Collection.
38. John Kinard to Marjorie Williams, August 4, 1963, Marjorie Kinard Collection.
39. Memorandum, Rev. James Robinson to Mr. Springsteen, October 24, 1963, Operation Crossroads Africa Collection, Amistad Research Center, New Orleans, LA.
40. Ibid.
41. Dr. Leonard Jeffries of Newark, NJ, interview by author.
42. Ibid.
43. Operation Crossroads Africa, Inc., *Participants Handbook* (1964), 4. Operation Crossroads Africa Collection, Amistad Research Center, New Orleans, LA.
44. Ibid.
45. Carson, 267.
46. House Committee on Un-American Activities, 88th Cong. 2nd sess., 1964, 1926–1927.
47. Ibid.
48. Ibid.
49. John Kinard of Washington, DC, interview by Anne M. Rogers.
50. Ibid.
51. Memorandum, October 1963, Operation Crossroads Africa Collection, Amistad Research Center, New Orleans, LA.
52. Inter-Office Memorandum and attached Travel Schedule, April 30, 1964, Operation Crossroads Africa Collection, Amistad Research Center, New Orleans, LA.
53. Ibid.
54. Memorandum, John Kinard to Mrs. Robinson, January 15, 1964, Operation Crossroads Africa Collection, Amistad Research Center, New Orleans, LA.
55. Letter, Jessie B. Kinard to Mrs. Robinson, February 10, 1964, Operation Crossroads Africa Collection, Amistad Research Center, New Orleans, LA.
56. Letter, Jessie B. Kinard to Mrs. Robinson, February 28, 1964, Operation Crossroads Africa Collection, Amistad Research Center, New Orleans, LA.

Chapter Three

1. Zinn, *Postwar America*, 209.
2. Ibid., 207–208.
3. Ibid., 208.
4. Carmichael and Abu-Jamal, 43.
5. Ibid.
6. Ibid., 13.
7. Ibid.
8. Melder and Stuart, 44.
9. James H. Cone, *Martin and Malcolm and America: A Dream or a Nightmare* (1991), 2.
10. Franklin and Moss Jr., 625.
11. Zinn, *Postwar America*, 221.

12. John Kinard of Washington, DC, interview by Anne M. Rogers.

13. Martin-Felton and Lowe, 5.

14. Pinkett, 31, 55.

15. Ibid., 67.

16. Omar M. McRoberts, *Streets of Glory: Church and Community in a Black Urban Neighborhood* (2003), 100.

17. Ronald W. Walters and Robert C. Smith, *African American Leadership* (1999), 21.

18. Ronny E. Turner, "The Black Minister: Uncle Tom or Abolitionist?" *Phylon* 34 (1973): 87–88.

19. Pinkett, 75.

20. Ibid.

21. Barbara Murphy of Silver Spring, MD, interview by author, July 8, 2008, Silver Spring, MD, tape recording.

22. Ibid.

23. Ibid.

24. James Banks quoted on the Audio Tape from the Wake for John Kinard, August 10, 1989, John Wesley AME Zion Church, Marjorie Kinard Collection.

25. Stanice Anderson, *I Say A Prayer for Me: One Woman's Life of Faith and Triumph* (2003), 13.

26. Ibid., viii.

27. Butch Hopkins quoted on the Audio Tape from the Wake for John Kinard, August 10, 1989, John Wesley AME Zion Church, Marjorie Kinard Collection.

28. Marjorie Kinard of Burtonsville, MD, interview by author.

29. Theresa Jones of Washington, DC, interview by author, March 11, 2008, Washington, DC, tape recording.

30. Martin-Felton and Lowe, 3.

31. Jennifer Hamer, *What It Means To Be Daddy: Fatherhood for Black Men Living Away From Their Children* (2001), 25.

32. Jacqueline Trescott, "In Tribute to John Kinard: Anacostia Museum's Lion Is Remembered," *Washington Post* (September 15, 1989): C3.

33. Ibid., 26.

34. Sarah Kinard of Burtonsville, MD, interview by author, May 9, 2007, Burtonsville, MD, tape recording.

35. Hope Kinard of Washington, DC, interview by author, April 2, 2009, Washington, DC, tape recording.

36. Earl Ofari Hutchinson, *Black Fatherhood: The Guide to Male Parenting* (1992), 92.

37. Trescott, "In Tribute to John Kinard."

38. E. Franklin Frazier, *Black Bourgeoisie* (1997), 224.

39. Hope Kinard of Washington, DC, interview by author.

40. Martin-Felton and Lowe, 9.

41. Hope Kinard of Washington, DC, interview by author.

42. Linda Wheeler, "Restoration Bringing New Pride to Old Anacostia," *Washington Post,* (February 11, 1980): C1.
43. Sarah Kinard of Burtonsville, MD, interview by author.
44. Ibid.
45. Romaine B. Thomas of Washington, DC, interview by author, April 17, 2007, Washington, DC, tape recording.
46. bell hooks, *We Real Cool: Black Men and Masculinity* (2004), 103.
47. Ibid., 105.
48. Marjorie Kinard of Burtonsville, MD, interview by author.
49. Ibid.
50. Ibid.
51. Ibid.
52. Martin-Felton and Lowe, 9.
53. Marjorie A. Kinard, "Women United," Speech, Women's Day, Church Service Tape, John Wesley AME Zion Church, September 23, 1984.
54. Ibid.
55. E. Franklin Frazier, *The Negro Family in the United States* (1966), 119.
56. Dexter Scott King and Ralph Wiley, *Growing Up King: An Intimate Memoir* (2003), 89.
57. Patrice Gaines-Carter, "Anacostia Honors Memory of a Man With a Mission-1,000 Attend Funeral of Museum Director," *Washington Post* (August 12, 1989): B1.
58. Marjorie A. Kinard quoted on the Audio Tape from the Wake for John Kinard, August 10, 1989, John Wesley AME Zion Church, Marjorie Kinard Collection.
59. Ibid.

Chapter Four

1. Louise Daniel Hutchinson, *The Anacostia Story,* 1608–1930 (1977), 3.
2. Ibid., 4–5.
3. Ibid., 6–7.
4. Ibid., 14.
5. Ibid., 7.
6. Ibid.
7. Ibid.
8. Ibid., 34.
9. Ibid., 37.
10. Ibid., 34.
11. Melder and Stuart, 70.
12. Ibid., 71.
13. Hutchinson, *The Anacostia Story,* 81.
14. Ibid., 82.
15. Ibid., 82.

16. Ibid., 111.

17. Ibid., 119.

18. Stan Anderson Oral History Interview, October 2, 1989, Anacostia Historical Society, Washington, DC.

19. Andrea Hauenschild, "Claims and Reality of New Museology: Case Studies in Canada, the United States, and Mexico."(PhD diss., Hamburg University, 1988), 51.

20. Diane Dale of Lanham, MD, interview by author, February 4, 2009, Lanham, MD, tape recording.

21. John Kinard of Washington, DC, interview by Anne M. Rogers.

22. Ibid.

23. James Speight Jr. of Washington, DC, interview by author, February 21, 2005, Washington, DC, tape recording.

24. Stan Anderson Oral History Interview.

25. Martin-Felton and Lowe, 16.

26. Ibid.

27. Ibid., 16–17.

28. John Kinard of Washington, DC, interview by Anne M. Rogers.

29. James Speight Jr. of Washington, DC, interview by author.

30. Paul H. Oehser, *The Smithsonian Institution* (1970), 53–54.

31. Hutchinson, *The Anacostia Story*, 93–95.

32. Oehser, 1–10.

33. Ibid.

34. Oehser, 23.

35. Ivan Karp and Christine Kreamer, *Musems and Communities* (2013), 574–75.

36. Martin-Felton and Lowe, 17.

37. Melder and Stuart, 485.

38. Carmichael and Abu-Jamal, 160–161.

39. Ripley, 105–106.

40. Marsh, *A Neighborhood Museum That Works*, 11–16.

41. Caryl Marsh of Mitchellville, MD, interview by author, December 3, 2004, Mitchellville, MD, tape recording.

42. Ibid.

43. Ibid.

44. Ibid.

45. Caryl Marsh, *A Proposal to Establish an Experimental Neighborhood Museum* (1966), 2, March Collection.

46. Ibid.

47. Ibid.

48. Clennie Murphy Jr. of Silver Spring, MD, interview by author.

49. Diane Dale of Lanham, MD, interview by author.

50. Eric Foner, *Who Owns History? Rethinking the Past in a Changing World* (2002), 150-151.

51. Harold G. Cureau, "The Visual Arts in the Historic Black Colleges," *The Journal of Negro History* 58 (1973): 443-444.

52. Ripley, 106-107.

53. Martin-Felton and Lowe, 17-18.

54. Marsh, *A Proposal*, 4.

55. Ibid. 7.

56. Ibid., 1.

57. Ibid., 7.

58. Ibid., 7.

59. Caryl Marsh of Mitchellville, MD, interview by author.

60. Bettye Collier-Thomas, "An Historical Overview of Black Museums and Institutions with Museums Functions, 1800-1980," *Negro History Bulletin*, 44 (1981): 56-58.

61. "Colored Collectors Negro Antiquarians Interested in Historical Research. The Dorsey Collection Efforts of Robert Adger, Jr., to Assemble Memorials of the Slavery Struggle," *Philadelphia Times*, June 8, 1890. Dorsey Collection, Moorland Spingarn Research Center.

62. Cureau, 443-444.

63. Bryant F. Tolles Jr., ed., *Leadership for the Future: Changing Directorial Roles in American History Museums and Historical Societies* (1991), 169.

64. James Hope of Washington, DC, interview by author, March 23, 2007, Washington, DC, tape recording.

65. John Kinard of Washington, DC, interview by Anne M. Rogers.

66. Martin-Felton and Lowe, 15.

67. Ibid.

68. Caryl Marsh of Mitchellville, MD, interview by author.

69. Ibid.

70. Robert Stanton of Fairfax Station, VA, interview by author, December 29, 2008, Washington, DC, tape recording.

71. Ibid.

72. Ibid.

73. Ibid.

74. Karp and Kreamer, 563-64.

75. Carmichael and Abu-Jamal, 72-73.

76. Emily Dennis Harvey and Bernard Friedberg, eds., *A Museum for the People* (1969), 30.

77. Edward P. Alexander, *The Museum in America: Innovators and Pioneers* (1997), 148-149.

78. Ibid., 147.

79. Caryl Marsh of Mitchellville, MD, interview by author.

80. Ibid.

81. Zora Martin-Felton of Washington, DC, interview by author, February 1, 2005, Washington, DC, tape recording.

82. Roger Kennedy of Washington, DC, interview by author, February 24, 2009, Washington, DC, tape recording.

83. Ibid.

84. Marsh, *A Neighborhood Museum That Works*, 3.

85. Ibid.

86. Carson, 346–47.

87. Lewis L. Gould, *Lady Bird Johnson and the Environment* (1988), 115.

88. Ibid., 117.

89. Ibid.

90. Caryl Marsh of Mitchellville, MD, interview by author.

91. Nighbert, 12.

92. Ibid.

93. Ibid.

94. Ibid.

95. Caryl Marsh of Mitchellville, MD, interview by author.

96. Zora Martin-Felton of Washington, DC, interview by author.

97. Caryl Marsh of Mitchellville, MD, interview by author.

98. Kenneth Hudson, *Museums of Influence* (1987), 181.

99. Martin-Felton and Lowe, 27.

100. Nighbert, 25.

101. Franklin and Moss Jr., 549

102. Ibid., 549-550.

103. Melder and Stuart, 510.

104. Caryl Marsh of Mitchellville, MD, interview by author.

105. John W. Blassingame, ed., *New Perspectives on Black Studies* (1971), 19-20.

106. Dr. Leonard Jeffries of Newark, NJ, interview by author.

107. Ibid.

108. Ibid.

109. Armsted L. Robinson, Craig C. Foster, and Donald H. Ogilvie, eds., *Black Studies in the University A Symposium* (1969), 5.

110. Dr. Leonard Jeffries of Newark, NJ, interview by author.

111. Robinson, et.al. 37-38.

112. C.R. Gibbs of Washington, DC, interview by author, June 26, 2008, Washington, DC, tape recording.

113. International Council of Museums, eds., *The Museum in the Service of Man Today and Tomorrow: The Papers from the Ninth General Conference of International Council of Museums* (1972), 152.

114. Ibid.

115. Ibid.

Chapter Five

1. Franklin and Moss Jr., 556.

2. Rowena Stewart quoted on the Audio Tape from the Wake for John Kinard, August 10, 1989, John Wesley AME Zion Church, Marjorie Kinard Collection.

3. See also Leo Marquard, *The Peoples and Policies of South Africa* (1969), 127.

4. Memorandum by JHB, ABPAO Pugh, 1985, Kinard Papers, Smithsonian Institution, Washington, DC

5. Martin-Felton and Lowe, 12–13.

6. Amina Dickerson quoted on the Audio Tape from the Wake for John Kinard, August 10, 1989, John Wesley AME Zion Church, Marjorie Kinard Collection.

7. Report by Dr. Andrew Smith, University of Cape Town (1987), Kinard Collection Smithsonian Institution, Washington, DC. See another article on John Kinard by Michael Welzenbach, "Lion of the Anacostia Museum...," *Washington Post* (July 19, 1989): D1.

8. Kader Asmal, David Chidester, and Wilmot James, *Nelson Mandela in His Own Words* (2003), 296.

9. Martin-Felton and Lowe, 50.